MANUFACTURING 'BAD MOTHERS': A CRITICAL PERSPECTIVE ON CHILD NEGLECT

Child neglect has been characterized over the past century as a problem of deficient care of children by mothers. A complex and punitive child welfare system has emerged, based on a view that the children of these mothers require legally sanctioned rescue by those better suited to care for them. Karen Swift challenges both the accepted view of child neglect and the present official response to it.

Beginning from a critical theoretical perspective, she argues that our usual perceptions of neglect hide and distort important social realities. This distorted perception only serves to reproduce the conditions of poverty, marginalization, and violence in which these families live. The current child welfare system, far from rescuing neglected children, helps instead to ensure the continuation of their problems, and the outcome is especially dramatic and damaging in Aboriginal communities.

Swift explores the historical, organizational, and professional dimensions within which child neglect becomes a visible social reality. Also examined are relations of class, race, and gender embedded in our usual understanding of child neglect. The discussion shows how these relations are continually reproduced through ordinary, everyday work practices of social workers and others who deal with mothers accused of child neglect. The 'good parent' model, through which help and authority are apparently merged, continually indicates that the mothers are unworthy of help. Their own experience disappears as they are faced with procedures designed to examine their present suitability for the job of parenting. The same procedures produce a situation in which children are being helped through the exertion of state authority over their parents – but most of the help provided children is theoretical, and some of it is quite damaging.

Swift also looks at both current and alternative notions of helping families. Finally, she argues that each of us can help to transform oppressive social realities.

KAREN SWIFT is an assistant professor in the School of Social Work, McGill University.

KAREN J. SWIFT

Manufacturing 'Bad Mothers': A Critical Perspective on Child Neglect

UNIVERSITY OF TORONTO PRESS
Toronto Buffalo London

© University of Toronto Press Incorporated 1995
Toronto Buffalo London
Printed in Canada

ISBN 0-8020-2978-7 (cloth)
ISBN 0-8020-7435-9 (paper)

Printed on acid-free paper

Canadian Cataloguing in Publication Data

Swift, Karen
  Manufacturing 'bad mothers' : a critical perspective
  on child neglect

  Includes index.
  ISBN 0-8020-2978-7 (bound) ISBN 0-8020-7435-9

  1. Child abuse. 2. Social work with children.
  3. Social service – Methodology. I. Title.

  HV873.S85 1995   362.7'6   C94-932770-0

University of Toronto Press acknowledges the financial assistance to its
publishing program of the Canada Council and the Ontario Arts Council.

To Sheila, with thanks

Contents

Part 3
The Response System

Acknowledgments

Many people and organizations have assisted me in the preparation of this book. I would especially like to thank academic colleagues for their time, ideas, and thoughtful critiques over the years. Allan Irving, Ralph Garber, Ernie Lightman, and Gillian Walker all provided useful comments and support at various times. Dorothy Smith's theoretical guidance has been central to the direction my work has taken over the past several years, and I thank her for her patience and direction. Marge Reitsma-Street offered helpful suggestions on the original draft of this manuscript. Marge, Lyn Ferguson, and Mike Birmingham have been friends and colleagues over many years, and their ideas, beliefs, and warm support through trials and tribulations are much appreciated. I would like to offer a special word of thanks to Sheila Neysmith, to whom the book is dedicated. Her generous and thoughtful critiques of my work over many years have provided me with the help and support I needed to find my own way.

My original research was made possible through a doctoral fellowship provided by the Department of National Health and Welfare. I am especially grateful to Rob Hart, for his interest in and support of my work. Two grants from the McGill Faculty of Graduate Studies and Research, one for computer equipment and one for developmental research, were invaluable in helping me through the later stages of this work. Thanks also to colleagues at the McGill School of Social Work for their confidence and support. Julia Krane, Barbara Nichols, Maureen Baker, Tim Stainton, Eric Schragge, Peter Leonard, Jordan Kosberg, and Frank McGilly have offered assistance and support along the way.

I owe a special debt to the agency staff and especially to the social workers who participated in my 1990 study. It is courageous to submit one's work to the scrutiny of research. These workers have helped me to understand the problems and prospects of social work more clearly.

My family deserves a special thank you. My parents, Marion and Sylvia McCallum, have always encouraged and supported my academic studies. Thanks also to Peter and to my wonderful sons, Julian and Evan, for love, patience, and inspiration.

PART 1 CONSTRUCTING KNOWLEDGE

Part 1 deals with the construction of the problem of child neglect as an illustration of critical theory and research. In Chapter 1 the illustration of a well-known and highly publicized case is used to illustrate how knowledge, beliefs, and values are embedded in everyday life and in widely available information bases.

Social work issues, debates, and paradigms of knowledge and reality introduce Chapter 2, and some basic elements of critical theory, which informs the text, are elaborated. Chapter 2 shows how these elements are used to frame this book and informs the reader about critical theory and its agenda for social change. In keeping with the critical approach, Chapter 3 is designed to place the issue of neglect in its historical and social context, setting the stage for the issue-based material presented in Part 2.

1

Home Alone

This is a book about child neglect. In this book, I examine the concept as it has evolved over the past one hundred years, exploring both public and professional understandings of what child neglect is and how neglect has come to be identified and treated in the professional domain, especially in Canada. This is also a book about professional social work, its heritage and values, and the kind of knowledge and practice it has developed over the past century to deal with the serious social issues that are central to its mandate. It is a book about the complexity of work and the dilemmas faced by those who are employed to identify and act on cases of neglect – child welfare workers. And it is a book about change, about seeing, knowing, and working differently.

WHAT IS CHILD NEGLECT?

Child neglect presents itself as one of the more durable categories in professional social work, having been a central social work issue for over one hundred years in Canada. It was the impetus behind the first child welfare legislation, both in Canada and in the United States. In an important way, child neglect was at the root of professional social work as we have come to know it, for this legislation provided a definite agency structure and organization of work, a base of funding, and an issue around which social work could begin to develop in a professional direction.

Child welfare remains central to professional social work today, for it is the only arena of work primarily controlled by social workers. For this reason alone, child welfare issues require the ongoing attention of the social work profession. Child welfare also requires interest and study by social workers, because in one hundred years of effort, the problems addressed, including child neglect, have not only not been alleviated, but appear by our own reckoning to have grown substantially. Identified cases of neglect are typically characterized as demonstrating 'dramatic increases,' and are considered to be the largest category of child maltreatment (Rose and Meezan, 1993; Trocme and Tam, 1994). Whether one accepts this view or not, there can be no question that a good many children and their parents are living desperate and unhappy lives, and the efforts of child welfare institutions do not seem to be alleviating these problems. Each child welfare worker has the well-known problem of case overload, each organization is chronically underfunded, crises abound, virtually everyone involved complains of feeling ineffective, and many have come to feel that the system does not work. Yet we continue on in the familiar way. Critiques and change efforts are regularly mounted, and yet both the system and our conceptions of child neglect have remained remarkably similar to the original model.

My personal interest in child neglect derives from the experience of being a child welfare worker at a much earlier stage in my career. The character of child welfare work appeared to me from the outset highly practical – investigating complaints of inappropriate or dangerous child care, serving legal documents, arranging day care for a harried mother. I found the work peculiarly atheoretical. I recognized in it many contradictions, yet had no trouble carrying out the tasks with a minimum of soul-searching. The children involved often *were* at risk, the mothers clearly under-resourced. The job appeared to be one of providing 'carrots' to the mothers, such as homemakers and bus tickets, with the legal system as a 'big stick' in the background.

The specific issue of neglect took my attention later on as I attempted to conceptualize it for a book on child welfare practice that I was co-authoring (Falconer and Swift, 1983). The small literature available on this issue did not quite match recollections of my work experience. In fact, I could not remember ever using the term 'child neglect' in practice. Children had been left alone in risky circumstances, badly clothed, not sent to school, poorly fed, had not received appropriate medical attention, and so on. My attempts to write about it therefore involved some mental work in trying to make academic models knit together with the practice of my memories.

In its broader meaning, child neglect is not simply a child welfare concern. Rather, the concept has a complex life, constituted of official child welfare meanings, public usage, and informal understandings. At parties or social gatherings, mothers sometimes joke about being charged with neglect as they discuss their difficulties at home. Sinks full of dirty dishes, an unwashed or squalling child, or general disorder in the household can produce these remarks. I sometimes make them myself. Also, items regularly appear in the daily newspaper about families charged under the Criminal Code with 'failure to provide' or negligence. Although I work with and write about child neglect, I react just as others do to these stories of 'real neglect': How could she? How could a mother allow her child to become malnourished to the point of death? How could she allow drugs or alcohol to take priority over her children? How could she fail to know where her children were at 2 a.m.? How could she allow her child to fall from a balcony? And then there are the official but usually mundane cases of neglect that child welfare workers deal with every day, frequently as the largest part of the workload. These cases are most often undramatic, involving the minutiae of everyday child caring work, handling complaints made by angry neighbours, and writing letters of supplication on behalf of impoverished clients.

The range of issues represented in these versions of child neglect certainly intersect, but do not fully overlap. What is it, then, to neglect children *really*, and what are the boundaries between ordinary lapses of attention committed by all parents and 'actual' child neglect?

'KIDS ABANDONED AS PARENTS VACATION IN MEXICO'

In late December of 1992, North American newspaper readers devoured the details of a real 'home alone' story. The parents of two young children had gone on vacation in Acapulco, apparently leaving their two daughters, ages 9 and 4, to fend for themselves for more than a week. The situation was uncovered when a smoke alarm went off in the home, and the children went to neighbours for help. Several newspaper accounts of this story referred to the surface similarities between this event and the fictional story in the box office hit movie *Home Alone*, in which a middle class family living in the Chicago suburbs accidentally leaves a young son behind as they depart for a Christmas holiday in Europe. The new home alone family was also reported to be living in an affluent middle class Chicago neighbourhood (Halifax *Chronicle-Herald*, 2 January 1993). These surface similarities led to the dubbing of this as the real 'home alone,' and it is a story that has brought international attention and interest to the subject of child neglect.

While the hugely successful movie version drew laughs on behalf of the harried parents and admiration for the resourcefulness of the abandoned child, the media left readers in no doubt that the real life version was neither entertaining nor accidental, and neighbours and onlookers of these real life parents did not find their behaviour funny. Witnesses to their arrests at the Chicago airport heckled and 'yelled insults' at the parents. Details of the case were widely circulated, and reporters sought background information about the lives of the parents. Newspaper accounts painted the parents' behaviour as 'startling' and the case as 'bizarre' (Halifax *Chronicle-Herald*, 30 December 1992). The father was reported to have lost his pharmacy licence some years before, over alleged theft of drugs. Furthermore, the family had 'always acted strangely,' according to neighbours. Pieces of evidence gathered to support this contention were that the children were 'forbidden to play with others,' and that the father 'often threatened to call the police if anyone stepped on his lawn'. Perhaps most damning of all, the mother's own father was quoted as saying he believes 'both of the parents need psychiatric care' (Halifax *Chronicle-Herald* 2 January 1993). Although few details about the children were given in the early reports, the older one was quoted as saying, 'For a long time, I was feeling really lonely and wondering what they [the parents] were doing' (*Calgary Herald* 30 December 1992). The children were placed in a foster home overnight, then 'turned over to the grandmother the next day' by 'the authorities' (Halifax *Chronicle-Herald*, 30 December 1992).

Subsequent reportage suggested that the 'home alone' incident was just the tip of the iceberg of bad parenting by the couple. Allegations of kicking, scratching, choking, and confining the older daughter were made. A sixty-four-count indictment was eventually returned by the Grand Jury (*Toronto Star*, 10 February 1993); thirty-nine of these charges were against the mother. Charges included in the indictment ranged from cruelty and neglect to possession of marijuana (Toronto Star, 12 February 1993).

Then the story melted to a small item on the back pages. Readers learned that the couple pleaded guilty to neglect, based on the Christmas incident. They were to receive suspended sentences, and predictions were that the children would likely be back in the custody of their parents within a couple of months (*Toronto Star*, 20 April 1993). A few months later, the picture changed again. As of this writing, the reported disposition of the case is that the parents have permanently surrendered their children (*Toronto Star*, 11 July 11, 1993). Public and media interest in the story have dissipated. But the words 'home alone' have come to be inextricably connected to neglect.

'HOME ALONE' AS A STORY OF CHILD NEGLECT

What might this story have to teach us about the issue of child neglect? Certainly, we understand from widespread interest evoked by the events reported that care of children in the private domain is important to a wide audience. It also reminds us that the North American reading public knows and understands something about child neglect and has powerful opinions about certain kinds of child caring that should and must be carried out by parents, as well as harsh opinions of those who fail in this task. However, this story, and the widespread interest in it, also suggests that only some aspects of child neglect are well known and interesting to the public.

To illustrate, we can examine the treatment of abandonment in the story. Abandonment is one of several subcategories of child neglect. The 'home alone' story, and the shock expressed by witnesses to it, seems to imply that child abandonment is rare – it is headline news. On the contrary, the abandonment of children is in fact a commonplace occurrence on child welfare case-loads. Even quite small children, as any child welfare worker knows, are left unattended for hours or days. The very origins of child welfare, as Chapter 3 details, reside in the issue of child abandonment. However, the abandoned children usually seen by child welfare authorities are now – and historically have been – the children of the poor and marginalized. Their parents are not going to Mexico on vacation. The 'home alone' story becomes fascinating not because child abandonment is rare but because of the destination of the parents, and the fact that they are on vacation while their children suffer alone. The experience of the children, left behind while their parents enjoy themselves, is overlaid in the reading with the experience of exclusion: In addition to being left alone, they are excluded from the benefits enjoyed by their parents. The reader struggles to imagine how parents could be so insensitive, so selfish. The aspect of exclusion does not manifest itself in the same way, of course, when parents are poor; where they go when children are abandoned is not enviable, not something we think children should be sharing, and what is happening to parents is not usually so dramatically different from what is happening to the children. The experience of being left alone is not necessarily less frightening to poor children, but simply less interesting to the public. Abandonment of poor children is not news.

The window into the world of child welfare that the story provides for a wide audience makes visible only fragments of the issues and subsequent interventions. Although not immediately apparent to many readers, there is embedded in this story of child neglect considerable information about North American values, assumptions, beliefs, and interests. In some ways the window provided to us by the story reflects the ordinary, everyday processes of child welfare in a case identified as neglect. The affluent, suburban 'home alone' couple certainly could and did 'pass' as an ordinary, relatively successful American family. The apparent abandonment of their children at first appears incomprehensible. Then personal details about this family uncovered and reported by the media help to single out this family as at least a little out of the ordinary, as people in some way conforming to an image of 'child neglecters'.

The 'home alone' parents are not by any means unique in having been sized up and 'produced' in this way. Indeed, the procedures of information gathering seen in this story result from the same procedures of thought and reasoning that govern virtually all assessments of child neglect. A set of facts is collected and matched to an idea of neglect. Child welfare workers often refer to this procedure as 'looking for patterns.' These facts are also compared with notions of appropriate child care and with ideas of the personal characteristics of good parents. If the assembled facts seem to match an idea of neglect, or of poor care, the case can properly be categorized as one of neglect. As we will see, this procedure incorporates many assumptions that lie far beneath the surface of conscious thought. Furthermore, this procedure operates to produce important social effects.

The eventual resolution of the 'home alone' case also reflects familiar issues in cases of neglect. The children are apprehended and placed in foster care; facts are accumulated; various accusations are made; charges are reduced or dropped; somewhat inexplicably, parents are promised an early return of their children; just as inexplicably, the parents give up their children. As in the 'home alone' story, actual workers in child welfare agencies remain as disembodied authorities in these procedures. Readers of the story may well ask what has happened in the space between the sixty-four count indictment and the promised return of children, and again between the promised return and the apparent final outcome of the couple surrendering their children. Cases dealt with by child welfare workers often have this same appearance of dreadful mistreatment, followed by return of the children, sometimes followed by permanent separation.

Of course, there are differences between this story and the many thousands of neglect cases handled across North America every day. For one thing, the 'home alone' children are not in the 'hard to place' category as are many children of child welfare clients. These children are white and middle class, and will most likely find a 'good home.' They have relatives with some interest and capacity to help. The pitiful loneliness and bewilderment of these appealing children, as reported in the press, will undoubtedly have the effect of producing many volunteer foster families. This is not the fate of most children separated from their parents because of neglect. In subsequent chapters, the repeated removals of children from their parents, placement in many different foster homes, long-term foster care, and/or return to natural parents to share a poverty-ridden existence will be seen as the usual case outcomes. It is not only the notoriety of the 'home alone' case that marks it as different; it is different by virtue of class and race as well.

It is commonplace to say, with the voice of authority, that neglect is a classless phenomenon, that parents in all walks of life neglect their children. The reading public would probably like to believe that when *any* parents are guilty of lapses, as the 'home alone' couple evidently were, these lapses are routinely subject to the everyday attentions of appropriate authorities. But the international headline space captured by the 'home alone' story over several weeks belies this belief. Clearly, one reason the 'home alone' story is so startling is that somehow most of the reading public knows full well that child welfare authorities deal mostly with the poor and marginalized – those living below the poverty line, single mothers, and minority groups. This is true both historically and currently (Gordon, 1988; Callahan, 1993). The popular image of neglect is virtually synonymous with the image of poverty.

How then is the public to understand these middle class, white parents as fitting into the neglect category? This disjuncture is one reason for the attention given the story. The media and the public have conspired to produce a plausible reason. A profile of these parents has been constructed that clearly differentiates them from the rest of us. The structure of the story tells readers that this family is to be understood as different from other white, middle class families, and that the behaviour of these parents can be explained in terms of some more generalized abnormality. They have a slightly shady past; their neighbours recognize them as somewhat odd; even family members think they need help. They are not 'normal,' and witnesses, neighbours, and casual onlookers are seen as easily recognizing that this is so. This structure sets the reader up to perceive 'facts' as fitting a particular implied scheme: child neglect is abnormal parental behaviour; these children were neglected by their parents; therefore these parents are abnormal.

At another level, the story appears to corroborate the idea that such social categories as child neglect regularly include offenders from all backgrounds and walks of life. The story suggests that even middle class families deviate from accepted practice, and that when they do, they are caught and punished. I can assure readers from the outset, however, that the vast majority of middle class parents, regardless of their child-rearing practices, will not be charged with child neglect and will never come under the scrutiny of child welfare authorities. The category itself and the system developed to investigate it are designed for other purposes. Neglect, as a socially constructed category, is not and never has been intended to catch out ordinary people in parenting lapses, although it occasionally operates in this way. As Pelton (1981) noted years ago, the 'myth of classlessness' is a very effective device that hides reality from us. The myth – and it is a myth – becomes confused with another assumption, which is that there is a level playing field upon which all families carry out their child-rearing activities. All are subject to the same rules and scrutiny, and all who fail will be caught and punished by the same systems. If poor, single, and non-white parents occupy this category in disproportionate numbers, this fact can then be attributed to individual failures by these parents, caused by the same 'defects' that have placed them in the poor, single-parent category in the first place.

The 'home alone' story, in sum, captures important contradictions in our understanding of neglect. The story appears to demonstrate that child neglecters come from all walks of life, although this is not at all the case. It also appears to demonstrate that neglecting parents have defects of character that 'normal' parents do not have, suggesting that child welfare workers properly deal with deviance rather than poverty and marginalization. The story works up abandonment as a rarity, while concealing the fact that poor children are found abandoned all the time. In other words, the story reports the 'facts of the case,' while hiding and distorting facets of reality. This way of presenting reality is conceptualized in this book as *ideology*. As will be demonstrated in subsequent chapters, this ideological way of talking, thinking, and writing about neglect is common – it is in fact the usual presentation. The 'home alone' story provides a beginning example.

SOCIAL REPRODUCTION AND SOCIAL CHANGE

Social workers have traditionally dealt with society's most vulnerable groups: the poor and unemployed, immigrants, the disabled, and the elderly. As feminists have recently made explicit, many of our clients are also women and children. I have tried in this project to understand why certain social structures that do not appear to benefit these clients, that seem in some cases actively to harm them, and that come under regular and severe attack both from within the field of social work and from without, nevertheless continue on relatively unchanged over decades. Social workers share a professional commitment to work for change in the interest of social justice. Along with other human service professionals, we are positioned to witness suffering, to see how features of social structure allow injustice. Many of us work actively over years to produce change, often with disappointing results. These experiences have caused me to enquire more deeply into the apparent imperviousness to change that characterizes social structure and into our own ineffectiveness in producing changes to which we profess a commitment.

In this project, some underpinnings of social structure and its reproductive mechanisms are examined. The analysis involves discovery and examination not only of the complexities of social reproduction but also of how we ourselves participate in reproducing the very structures we would hope to change. It shows how our own practices of thought and feeling, our everyday work activities, our usual way of knowing about and acting upon social reality help to produce this result. The conclusion is that the changes we seek in social work must begin with an understanding of the dialectic between ourselves and the larger social world.

My academic examination of how we come to understand and think about child neglect has involved two alternate ways of 'knowing' (Swift, 1988). Most published studies about neglect are based on the traditional social science paradigm, often referred to as 'positivism.' Critique of this knowledge base reveals three important characteristics of this literature. First, current knowedge about neglect has been limited almost entirely to questions about the supposed causes of neglect and the effectiveness of various treatment models. It is, in other words, a highly individualistic approach, based on a view of neglect as a disease entity in need of a cure. This approach assumes the continuing need for the current array of social services and programs. That these programs have not reduced the scope of the problem over the past hundred years (Nagi, 1977; Rose and Meezan, 1993) is not addressed. Second, neglect is not explored as a social category. The category itself is treated in most research as a given, while the production of neglect cases in bureaucratic settings is, with few exceptions, ignored. Third, the predominant research and knowledge base about neglect is ideological, actually concealing important information. For instance, neglect is presented as a gender-neutral category, but even a cursory examination of the issue reveals that it is focused almost exclusively on women and mothering.

A different approach to developing knowledge about neglect begins from the standpoint of examining the processes that produce and maintain the concept of child neglect and showing how the practical accomplishment of tasks within a child welfare setting fit together with larger social processes to produce and sustain this social category. Through this approach, implicit social goals achieved by maintaining both the category and the arrangements that produce it can also be explored.

A central theme of this book is that seemingly ordinary social concepts perform functions of social reproduction, that is, reproduction of 'the structure of the power relations' among groups and classes (Bourdieu and Passeron, 1977). This occurs in the obvious way of categorizing people in and out of groups such as child neglect. That the reading public is riveted to the story of a white, middle class, two-parent family caught in an act of neglect demonstrates very well a widespread understanding that these are not the expected members of this group. Neglect is a category known to be reserved primarily for poor, marginalized, and usually mother-led families. Locating people in this category performs clear social control functions, as outlined in Chapter 8. It puts people in the position of having to accept ongoing surveillance within their own homes as well as direction from many professionals in the running of their private lives.

Categories of deviance such as neglect also work in more subtle ways. For instance, they produce a group of scapegoats, giving us somebody to blame when society is not working well. They also provide legitimation for designated authorities to enter into the private affairs of individuals and families. The designation of neglect allows authorities to enter, scrutinize, evaluate, and reorganize private family life. It even allows the permanent removal of family members. Although the rescue and saving of children is the apparent reason for allowing such intervention, other social purposes are more effectively met through this process. Chapters 5, 6, and 7 demonstrate how the slotting of poor, female, and racial minorities into the neglect group serves less visible functions such as controlling social costs and reorienting the behaviour of particular people in ways that benefit groups other than themselves.

Among their more insidious purposes, categories effectively hide the reproduction of social divisions such as racism and sexism. Apparently neutral names like neglect cover over the fact that membership is reserved almost exclusively for poor mothers, a disproportionate number of whom are non-white. Simultaneously, categorizations also serve to create divisions among natural groupings, giving the appearance of different characteristics and interests for subgroups. In hiving off some women to be grouped as child neglecters, or 'failed mothers,' for instance, the common interests and problems shared by all mothers disappear. In doing the work of categorizing poor minority women into various groups, commonalities of women's lives shared between client and worker are also lost.

Who benefits from these effects? This is a central question to be posed, for the answer helps us to understand the inner workings of categories. The answer lies in an understanding of social reproduction and its purposes. Chapters 5, 6, and 7 demonstrate that although the supposed beneficiaries of child welfare resources and efforts are children, frequently children do not benefit and in fact often suffer in spite of or directly as a result of child welfare interventions into their families. The analysis suggests a highly complex social organization through which values and social arrangements favoured by elites are perpetuated in their own interests. Scientific knowledge is an important mechanism through which this complicated structure is supported and legitimated. Examination of the creation, legitimation, maintenance, and use of child neglect as a social category shows us how this works.

Everyone involved in the planning and delivery of human services plays a role in maintaining this status quo, via such seemingly innocuous activities as file recording. The practices of child welfare workers – examined here in depth – reflect the knowledge, values, and beliefs of the larger society. In other words, child welfare workers import and apply their experiences as members of society to their everyday reasoning and decision processes. They do this in the context of organizations structured in the same way as other modern organizations, using similar kinds of work practices. A study of these processes, structures, and work practices can therefore reveal a great deal not only about child welfare and child neglect but also about the society we live in, about how specific groups of people come to be positioned within that society, and how those positions are sustained through everyday work practices.

A major objective of this book is to bring to consciousness our own participation in practices through which social reproduction is accomplished, to examine why this occurs, and to suggest how we might think and act differently in our everyday world of work. A central argument is that both social reproduction and social change are forces that lie within the realm of human endeavour and control. They are the outcomes of concerted endeavour, and each of us is an active participant in their creation. Human service workers have a responsibility to understand these processes and to take control of their own part in them.

In this broader sense, then, this book is not only about a child welfare issue, but about the way social knowledge is acquired and used. The first step in change-making processes is the development of knowledge designed to reveal the full complexity of social reality, knowledge that credits perspectives of all participants, that includes actual experience, that provides a view of our own part in social processes, and that attempts to unravel contradictions and dispel illusion. It is hoped that this work contributes to that effort and that it plays a role in encouraging the commitment of readers to social change.

2

A Critical Approach to Child Neglect

Social work, as an applied form of social science, has for most of its life as a profession 'been marked by a desire to be scientific' (Irving, 1992: 9). Science has generally been interpreted to mean that stream of research known variously as 'logical positivism,' 'logical empiricism,' 'rank empiricism,' or 'neopositivism' (Piele, 1988). This form of knowledge has been increasingly pursued in the twentieth century as the basis for the social sciences, including social work. Karger (1983) observes that 'hard' research has grown increasingly dominant in social work since the Second World War, partly as a way to legitimize the profession.

During the 1980s, some challenges to empiricism as the best or only form of knowledge for social work were mounted. The first focus of this challenge was on methodology, although larger questions about the nature of reality, truth, and knowledge were implied. The nature of the empirical model, its utility for social work, and whether it is in fact required for credibile research were hotly debated in prominent social work journals during the 1980s, represented for instance by a debate between Hudson (1983) and Heineman (1981, 1982) in the *Social Science Review* about the nature and purpose of science. Heineman, as the challenger, took issue with what she considered to be overly narrow parameters of traditional methods and noted an incompatibility of this approach with social work's value-based mission. Hudson, in contrast, took the view that scientists must be concerned with observable entities, a reflection of Durkheim's flat statement that 'social phenomena are things and ought to be treated as things' (Durkheim, 1938, trans. 1966: 27). The scientific method in social work research, Hudson maintained, involves a process of attempting to define an issue 'with sufficient precision [to] observe it.' If these steps are successful, 'it' can then be measured and then re-defined with yet greater precision: 'If you cannot measure a client's problem,' according to Hudson, 'it does not exist. If you cannot measure a client's problem you cannot treat it' (1983: 252).

Following this debate, more articles in professional journals appeared, with various intents to broaden, deepen, resolve, or alter the focus of discussion about knowledge and methods in social work. Although the debate remains unresolved, these discussions have stirred interest and opened the way for further thinking about the nature and uses of knowledge within the social sciences. Neuman (1991), Harvey (1990), Park (1993), and Thomas (1993), for instance, have worked to clarify characteristics of various knowledge paradigms. The framework developed by Neuman (1991) to describe and distinguish the three most prominent paradigms – positivism, the interpretive school, and critical social science – are briefly summarized here in order to clarify their characteristics and differences.

Positivist social science, as the social work debate made clear, is by far the most popular and familiar research paradigm in the social sciences. It is so commonly used and its premises are so widely known and subscribed to that positivism is often viewed as synonymous with science itself. Positivism assumes social reality to be a configuration of orderly, stable, pre-existing social patterns that shape individual human beings and that it is the business of science to discover. As reviewed by Neuman, positivist social science relies on logical systems of interconnected facts, concepts, and definitions. The evidence used to verify theory is, as Hudson argued, based on observation; and the conditions of fact finding are tightly controlled in an effort to ensure that the facts observed by scientists are not confounded either by external events or by the perspective of the scientist. The fundamental purpose of this kind of science is the prediction of events and the control of human behaviour in relation to those events. Values have no place in this paradigm; the goal is to discover reality, not to evaluate it.

Interpretive social science, which Neuman traces back to Weber, essentially seeks knowledge for the purpose of better understanding human beings and the nature of their social interaction. In contrast to positivism, interpretive social science sees reality as fluid, and human beings as having the capacity to make sense of and negotiate fluctuating social situations. There is no fixed boundary between everyday knowledge, or common sense, and scientific knowledge, because people regularly draw on whatever social knowledge they need to understand and manage their social context. The appropriate site of research is the social context, in all its complexity, and the purpose of knowledge building is to enhance understanding of human interaction through the provision of descriptive research. It is assumed that both researcher and subject will bring values to the research; however, no one value is given priority over another.

Critical social science, which originated with Karl Marx, shares some ideas with the interpretive school, particularly concerning social meanings and interaction, but is fundamentally concerned with changing oppressive social realities. A basic assumption of the critical school is that reality is not at all self-evident, as posed by positivism, but is complex and contradictory by nature. Reality is defined as being composed of both apparent phenomena and hidden realities, or 'essences,' which operate to shape surface appearances. Unlike positivism, which views human beings as subject to forces outside themselves, the critical approach sees social forces as created and sustained by individuals. Human beings are viewed as creative, adaptive, and able to act in the interests of changing reality. The contradictory nature of social reality means that people can be misled and oppressed by myth, illusion, and 'false consciousness,' – devices which allow those with greater power to maintain positions of control. The purpose of knowledge development is to reveal the hidden realities behind illusions and to provide people with the tools needed to change social reality in a way that reduces or eliminates oppression. Appropriate evidence for critical social science is evidence that effectively works to accomplish these purposes. Unlike positivism, this kind of science does not assume that neutrality is either possible or desirable. Rather, it insists that the goal of eliminating oppression is the proper starting point for knowledge development.

As Neuman's discussion makes clear, each of these paradigms arises from different social purposes, concerns itself with different problems, and seeks knowledge for different purposes. They also use different evidence and 'truth tests' as proof of veracity. The data, information, form, arguments, and knowledge presented in this book are informed primarily by critical social science. Some use is made of the interpretive model to investigate meanings and interactions between people, and many examples of discourse arising from the positivist school are examined. Most formal knowledge about child neglect up to now has been developed through positivist science; this knowledge, as I have argued elsewhere (Swift, 1988), has created and sustained a partial view of neglect – based almost exclusively on observable data. Primary purposes of this book are to explore hidden realities behind the apparently obvious phenomenon of child neglect, to demonstrate how ordinary practices embedded in child welfare work operate to reproduce these hidden realities, and to suggest how we might begin to alter practice in the interests of social change. The remainder of this chapter explores the roots and characteristics of critical social science in more depth and explains how I have used this theoretical approach in my examination of child neglect.

REALITY AND KNOWLEDGE: MARX AND ENGELS AND THE CRITICAL SCHOOL

A major focus of the theoretical work of Marx and Engels was the relationship between material conditions of life and human consciousness. In their early work, known as *The German Ideology* (1846, trans. 1947), they proposed that knowledge based only on appearances would be distorted, as it would omit the effects of the material conditions that create those appearances. For Marx and Engels, the nature of consciousness is at the root of debates about knowledge, because the development of ideas is seen as proceeding from human consciousness, which in turn is derived from the conditions of 'real life.' Consciousness, in other words, is thought of as a social product: 'Life is not determined by consciousness but consciousness by life' (Marx and Engels, 1846, trans. 1947: 15).

'Life' here refers to the social and material circumstances involved in the productive processes necessary to sustain human life. Marx and Engels explain the relationship this way: 'The production of ideas, of conceptions, of consciousness is at first directly interwoven with the material activity and the material intercourse of men [*sic*], the language of real life ... Men are the producers of their conceptions, ideas, etc. – real, active men, as they are conditioned by a definite development of their productive forces and of the intercourse corresponding to these' (1846, trans. 1947: 14).

Science, through which formal knowledge is produced, argued Marx and Engels, must begin in real life, rather than in 'speculation' and abstractions. In *The German Ideology*, they ridiculed those who saw science as a matter of theorizing. They were particularly scornful of certain German philosophers of the day who conceived of ideas as having independent existence detached from the material conditions of life. This view, maintained Marx and Engels, allows increasingly abstract ideas to hold sway. It is this detachment of consciousness from real, historical conditions that allows ideas reflecting the interests of the ruling class to be represented as universal and equally applicable to everyone. It follows that where conceptions are employed as descriptors of reality, those conceptions cannot be taken for granted but must be deconstructed as part of the scientific endeavour. This deconstructing process is intended to reveal the social relations and practical activities that operate to produce and legitimize the abstraction. In this book, the concept of child neglect serves as our example of abstraction.

Marx and Engels argued that human beings produce human life and that our awareness of life necessarily follows from the conditions of that life. Thus, the proper starting point for science is not conceptions but 'real life': 'Where speculation ends – in real life – there real, positive science begins: the representation of the practical activity, of the practical process of development of men' (1846, trans. 1947: 15).

Because real life occurs in a definite place and time, the field of knowledge suggested by this conceptualization is dynamic and complex. Phenomena must be seen both as interrelated and as developing within a specific historical context. Also, the different social locations of members of society must be accounted for, because the positioning of people within society inevitably produces different and conflicting forms of consciousness among them. In capitalist society, the competing interests of labour and capital necessarily produce different ways of thinking, a different consciousness for workers from that of owners of the means of production (Weedon, 1987). As we will see, the consciousness of workers and clients in the social work process also develops very differently, based upon their locations in the system and what they attempt to extract from it. Knowledge, which reflects human consciousness, cannot therefore be seen as absolute or as reflective of immutable laws of nature but must be grounded in the different historical and material conditions of actual people.

The character of the reality that Marx and Engels wanted to examine was conceptualized as having a dual nature. They saw reality as a unity of both surface appearances, which we often think of as objective reality, and of hidden realities, or essences, which represent the social relations acting to create and sustain surface appearances. Because reality is seen as grounded in real, ongoing relations among people, essences are not an absolute property of reality; in other words, there are no eternal truths for science to discover. Rather, essences are constituted of dynamic social relations among people, which exist prior to or outside of the experience of individuals but which enter into and organize individual lives, giving them a particular appearance. The 'home alone' case, cited in the previous chapter, illustrates this point. Readers of this story implicitly understand that responsibilities for child care are allocated to parents and enforced by representatives of the state; without this understanding of social relations, not explicitly present in the text, the story would not be sensational or even comprehensible.

In the approach to reality posited by Marx and Engels, the objective world is not viewed as independent and separate from the purposive activities of individuals, but rather as a set of conditions, constraints, and possibilities within which individual subjectivity becomes possible (Bologh, 1979). Similarly, the subjectivity of individuals is not seen as a private matter but rather is viewed in its relation to society. The idea of this dialectical relationship between the subject and object worlds has important implications for science. Subjectivity is not construed as a bias to be reduced or eliminated from science but must be explored as a central feature of reality; also, the object world must be examined in relation to the active, knowing subjects who create it. This conception stands in considerable contrast to that of the positivist model, which generally implies a more 'mechanical' view of human activity, governed by causal laws external to individuals (Neuman, 1991).

Marx and Engels developed the concept of 'practice' as a way of showing how the subjective and objective worlds relate to and create each other. Practice is defined as purposive labour that transforms both the material world and the individual who performs it (Larrain, 1979). Thus, practice represents both the subjective and the objective; practice performed by individuals transforms both external reality and the individuals who carry it out. Practice requires imagination, a quality which Marx said distinguishes 'the worst architect from the best of bees' (*Capital*, 1886, trans. 1906: 198). Marx recommended examination of imagination as a means to understand the dialectic between individuals and their social and material worlds, for it is through this examination that the relationship between the social structuring of material life and the consciousness of individuals can be revealed. In imagination, as Berger and Luckmann (1967: 121) wrote, we see 'the particularization in individual life of the general dialectic of society.' Through this particularization it is possible to examine aspects of the social world experienced by the individual. In this book, the practices of child welfare workers, both in thought as well as action, will illustrate these points.

Marx explored this basic notion of reality further in *Capital* using the commodity as an illustration of the relationship between appearances and hidden realities. However, other aspects of Marxist thought and its political implications on the world stage occupied scholars for a number of years, and these earlier ideas were not as actively pursued and developed as some others in the Marxist tradition. In the 1960s, Habermas and others associated with the critical school began to recover and expand upon these basic ideas of social reality. Since then, various branches and offshoots of 'critical theory' have emerged. The core of these ideas, outlined above, has been employed in an extensive critique of empiricist, or more precisely positivist, research (Morrow, 1985). However, this perception of the dual nature of reality, and the implications it has for the nature of knowledge, goes well beyond a critique of positivist research and empirical methodology. It provides the framework for a different kind of social science, one which values the actual life experience of individuals and the social context of this experience. Because of this connection, it is especially useful for social work, which focuses – at least in theory – on the relationship between individuals and their social context.

The idea of 'contradictions' is also central to critical theory. This idea is embedded in Hegel's notion of dialectical synthesis (1812–16, trans. 1966), which proposes that all phenomena contain their opposites within themselves. The idea of contradictory reality was basic to the thinking of both Marx (1886, trans. 1906) and Engels (1878, trans. 1939), about the process of change. Conflicts inherent in life itself and in social relations provide the impetus for a synthesis of opposing elements, a process that produces a constantly evolving social reality. This idea, while somewhat difficult to grasp, is important to critical social research, for it allows a 'way in' to the exploration of complex social phenomena. In child welfare, a well-known illustration is the contradiction between providing assistance to clients and exerting authority over them. Both processes are contained within the social work helping process, and various ways have been found to describe and resolve these apparently contradictory activities. Chapter 8 illustrates in more depth the idea of contradiction, exploring the issues of help and authority, and offering a critique of the usual 'synthesis' or resolution.

PHENOMENOLOGY: CONTRIBUTIONS TO METHODOLOGY

Marx's reasoning, according to Sayer (1983), is neither deductive nor inductive, for both imply governing, transhistorical laws. Marx's aim is to unearth the mechanisms that bring about certain empirical correlations and the conditions in which these mechanisms operate. Explanations then proceed from the properties of these mechanisms and conditions. In other words, Marx posits hypotheses (mechanisms and conditions) that explain the existence of phenomenal forms. The phenomenologist Edmund Husserl developed a way of thinking about reality that is in some respects similar to the thinking of Marx and Engels. Husserl proposed that 'facts' are only part of the subject of science. Meanings, or 'hidden essences' are also significant features of reality requiring scientific examination, according to Husserl (1913, trans. 1969; 1950, trans 1964). Building on this idea, phenomenologists have made a substantial contribution to the methodology of exploring hidden realities. In addition, phenomenology has contributed to the interpretive approach of understanding social meaning. Alfred Schutz (1962), for instance, explored the way individuals apprehend and give meaning to their lives. This analysis emphasizes both *attention* and *intention* as constituents in the creation of reality. Individuals, suggested Schutz, are always in the process of selecting from a wide range of information in the objective world those features that are useful for their particular purposes in 'everyday life,' which for Schutz is the primary reality. It is through this selection process, through attention to specifics, and through intentional behaviour, that an individual creates a sense of reality. Furthermore, because these features are chosen from a socially constructed world, the individual's sense of reality necessarily reflects both social purposes and structures. Subjectivity, then, is not idiosyncratic (Natanson, 1970) but reflective of the social world. Consequently, subjectivity can be seen as a proper site for the study of society, and the examination of attention and intention provide tools for this study. This idea is similar to and expands on Marx's notion of studying human imagination. Building on these insights, a number of studies based on the interpretive paradigm have been carried out that explore individuals' methods of constructing social reality in particular work settings (Cicourel, 1976; Garfinkel, 1967; Zimmerman, 1971, 1974). These studies show how people draw from 'common knowledge' and implicit assumptions about the object world to structure and give meaning to their everyday work activities. The 'home alone' story has provided an example of this use of common knowledge. Witnesses, neighbours, and the media all drew upon common knowledge of appropriate parenting practices to reach their judgments, as did the child welfare authorities. Furthermore, in order to try and make sense of their behaviour, they further drew upon common assumptions that parents who abandon children must be 'strange.' This approach to examining the construction of reality illuminates Marx's idea of practice, showing in depth and detail how people apprehend, use, and reproduce the object world.

IDEOLOGY

Phenomenology provides direction for methodologies and tools needed to apprehend and examine subjectivity. However, as Smith (1980) notes, studies based on these ideas are constrained by the requirements of observation; consequently, only surface realities are revealed. The critical paradigm employs the concept of ideology to explore more fully the connections between hidden reality and appearances. In popular usage the term 'ideology' often means a system of ideas and/or beliefs about the world, or the 'world view' held by particular individuals or groups. Ideology may also be characterized as 'a backdrop of ideas' against which an individual organizes thoughts and actions (Grayson, 1980). In Marx's work, although ideology was an important (but unevenly developed) concept, its meaning was from the outset more complex than this popular understanding. Several later theorists have made important contributions to ideas about the meaning and effects of ideology. A common theme among these theorists is that 'ideology serves as a subtle mechanism which helps win a population's consent to the ways a society is organized' (Waitzkin, 1989). Underlying this approach is the idea of different and often antagonistic social locations of the members of a society. These differences produce contradictory ways of experiencing and knowing social reality. However, the class that dominates or rules a society wants its own vision of the society to be reproduced – and ideology is central to this reproductive process.

Gramsci (1971) examined in some detail how groups in power maintain and reproduce the relations of production, positing two primary methods. One is coercion, which is achieved through legal means of violence. Wars and other military interventions are common examples. The second is hegemony, or predominance, of ideology that works to support the interests of the ruling class and that is, in the end, according to Gramsci, the more important mechanism of class reproduction.

Ideology is a 'distorted kind of consciousness,' according to Larrain (1979), 'which conceals contradictions' and thus facilitates the reproduction of existing power relations. Georg Lukacs (1971) explored mechanisms through which dominant ideologies are conveyed and how they come to shape individual consciousness. Lukacs used the term 'reification' to describe how social relations (or hidden realities) are transformed in conscious thought to 'things' that screen out the relations standing behind them. In social thought and research, for example, these 'things' are the concepts or 'entities' that we earlier noted Hudson describing as the objects of science. Child neglect is one such 'thing,' a reified concept that has been studied as though it were a given of nature. The processes of perception, decision making, recording, and so on, through which neglect becomes visible as a 'thing' generally remain invisible (Swift, 1990). As the critical theorist Habermas (1968, trans. 1971; 1970) argued, science, through its sanctioned categorizing processes, can thus be used in an ideological way to obscure rather than illuminate the essences of surface appearances. Habermas, in fact, posited science as the best example of ideology because of its claims to be objective and neutral and thus above ideology.

Louis Althusser (1971) also examined the nature of ideology. He began from a Marxist tradition of a focus on class struggle, based on necessary reproduction of both the means of production and of the relations of capitalism. Althusser posed the question how these relations are reproduced outside the workplace, an issue which Marx himself had not investigated particularly well. Wages, Althusser noted, are the material means of labour reproduction.

Wages are 'that part of the value produced by the expenditure of labour power which is indispensable for its reproduction' – that which is necessary in order for the 'worker to present himself' at the place of work each day (1971: 4–5). Wages are a primary means of reproduction dispensed within the workplace.

How then is the worker brought to accept his or her place in the ongoing processes of production outside the workplace? Like Gramsci, Althusser thought the 'reproduction of relations' is secured on the one hand by repression, meaning the legal-political systems attached to and empowered by the state. These he refers to as 'repressive State apparatuses' or RSAs. Another process of reproduction is achieved through what he calls ideological state apparatuses, or ISAs. Althusser provides a tentative list of what these might be: education, the family, religion, trade unions, culture, politics, and communication (p. 24). These ISAs he describes as 'multiple, distinct, "relatively autonomous"' in character, and as operating behind a 'shield' provided by the repressive state apparatuses. Neither is a pure form: RSAs have ideological components, while ISAs have elements of coercion. The child welfare organization, in fact, provides an excellent example of a structure within which both forms coexist. It is vested with a legal mandate to remove children from their families, and this mandate is clearly used as a form of coercion. The agency also houses ideological methods through which specific groups of people are brought to perform their roles in the reproduction of class, gender, and race relations. The ruling ideology, according to Althusser, mediates this relation between repression and ideology to ensure 'a (sometimes teeth-gritting) harmony between RSAs and ISAs' (1971: 23, 24) and between these two functions within the same institution. Connecting ideology to the reproduction of capitalist relations, then, Althusser goes on to propose that the most important of the ISAs is education, for it is here that ideology – disguised as knowledge – can be passed to the masses at large, fitting each one for the post to be assumed in the relations of production, imposing submission to the ruling ideology for some, mastery for others. Using the illustration of child neglect, we will see many examples of how knowledge operates in an ideological fashion within the context of child welfare work to promote reproductive processes.

Of importance in Althusser's work is the furthering of thought about the definition and nature of ideology. Ideology for Althusser includes 'beliefs, meanings and practices in which we think and act, for the purposes of installing people in imaginary relations' (Macdonell, 1986). What exists in ideology, then, is not the real relations of production but the imaginary relation of individuals to the real relations in which they live. Althusser critically examines the concept of ideology found in *The German Ideology* as 'pure illusion,' 'pure dream,' 'nothingness,' suggesting that Marx's own formulation is 'not Marxist' (p. 33). Althusser proposes instead that ideology must have a material existence, and he invokes the traditional structural image of a base (productive processes) supporting a superstructure (ideas, ideology). Thus, ideology is not illusion but always relates to the supporting structure of material reality. Furthermore, in Althusser's view, ideology necessarily exists and is conveyed within an apparatus and its practices (pp. 39–40).

Althusser and others have posited the idea of struggle as basic to ideology, suggesting that ideology grows out of antagonistic relations, taking shape through opposition to other ideologies, but 'pinned down where it acts as a weapon' (Macdonell, 1986: 33). That is, competing ideologies may develop through conflict, but the ideological practices of those who rule achieve effective expression through existing apparatuses. What this suggests is the importance of examining the sites of class struggle for an understanding of the dialectic between and among ideologies and of the processes through which particular ideologies prevail. Although rarely posed in the existing social work literature as 'sites of class struggle,' social welfare institutions, certainly child welfare agencies and organizations, historically and at present fit this description. Looking at child welfare from this perspective of struggle illuminates features of its operations and the behaviour of key players in a decidedly different way than traditional study and writing suggest to us.

POSTSTRUCTURALIST THEORY: LANGUAGE AND DISCOURSE

Poststructuralist theory of the 1970s and 1980s has added another important dimension to knowledge debates, that of the social construction of meaning. Both critical and interpretive social science view meaning as socially structured rather than inherent in the object world. Thus, the same object may be given different meanings by different people in different historical periods. In poststructural theory, language is the central focus for understanding the way meanings are produced. Language is seen as 'the place where actual and possible forms of social organization and their likely social and political consequences are defined and contested' (Weedon, 1987: 21). Study of the use of language and the meanings it is given by particular people in context becomes, thus, a way of understanding the power relations of a group or society. In this approach, the issue of subjectivity is once again taken up and amplified. For poststructuralists, subjectivity is a site of disunity and conflict. For the subject, meaning is not a static 'thing' expressed by language, but is constituted by and produced through language.

Furthermore language exists within and is transmitted through specific, historically located discourses. The term 'discourse' implies dialogue, a field that is not static but is continuously shaped by interaction within a particular context. Discourse also represents competing interests: 'A discourse takes effect directly or indirectly through its relation to, its address to another discourse' (Macdonell, 1986: 3). Any discourse concerns itself with certain concepts at the expense of others. 'Once language is understood in terms of competing discourses, competing ways of giving meaning to the world ... then language becomes an important site of political struggle' (Weedon, 1987: 24).

Recent work on discourse is important in relation to knowledge because it calls into question fundamental positivist precepts of knowledge created over the past two centuries: especially the idea that there is a basic human experience, a human nature, which it is the business of knowledge to reveal. Examination of human experience through the concept of discourse is a search for meaning, and often for different, competing, and changing meanings, some of which assume prominence and power and others of which remain obscure and undeveloped.

Pecheux (1975, trans. 1982) suggests that discourses do not have natural boundaries. They do not emerge 'whole' out of particular apparatuses, but rather are dynamic, representing statements and ideas drawn from different sources and emerging from sites of struggle in the social world. Dorothy Smith's definition of discourse as 'conversations mediated through texts' (1987) is useful in this regard. This idea allows us to imagine the ongoing construction of a discourse through the analogy of a conversation. The knowledge debate in social work journals cited earlier provides us with an example of discourse. This is a conversation, with statements and replies, assertions and rebuttals, and even a personal tone as the 'speakers' castigate each other's evidence and comprehension. Readers of social work journals, witnesses to this conversation, can be expected to know what is meant by the terms of the argument, for instance, by the terms 'treatment model,' 'social work values,' and so on. Because readers are likely knowledgeable about social work research and familiar with countless examples of it, it is unnecessary to explore specific research projects in depth in order for the conversation to proceed. Study of discourses reveals that meanings of words and statements may be different depending upon the context of their use, on who is using them, and on the social position of both the speaker and the reader. Thus, as Piele (1988) argues, meanings of the same words, especially the term 'logical empiricism,' compete in the social work debate. Each side struggles to have its own meanings predominate, and each draws its meanings from other, also competing discourses, about the nature of reality and of knowledge. A key issue for discourse analysis is accounting for the positions and viewpoints of speakers, just as one ordinarily does in verbal conversation.

The word 'texts,' noted by Smith, introduces the idea of social forms that produce discourse, directing attention to institutions that produce, house, and distribute speech in its written as well as verbal forms (Smith, 1987; Foucault, 1972b). In the social work knowledge debate, for example, conversation is mediated by professional social work journals, and by their attendant funding structures and professional ties and loyalties, as well as by the conventions of academic publishing. Arguments are submitted by 'qualified' individuals, usually lodged in approved academic institutions, written to conform to particular styles, with a sufficiency of references cited. These features of the conversation limit its form and distribution, and they provide readers with implicit criteria for crediting particular arguments.

Foucault's work (1972a) has extended our understanding of these processes, showing how we might expand and change the study of meaning. He examines how meanings are embodied in technical processes, institutions, patterns established for general behaviour, forms of transmission, and pedagogical styles. His work attempts study of the full range of hidden mechanisms through which a society conveys its knowledge and ensures its survival under the mask of knowledge. Although Foucault's work is different in many respects from the Marxist tradition (Beechey and Donald, 1985), his ideas are in some ways similar to Althusser's concern with reproductive mechanisms. Foucault's analysis in *Discipline and Punish* (1977), for instance, challenges in both form and substance the traditional view of history. He examines how disciplinary tactics change form but not necessarily function. His description of the architecture of the military camp, for example, could also be read as a description of the modern child welfare bureaucracy: '[The camp] was a way to render visible those who are inside it ... to transform individuals ... to act on those it shelters, to provide a hold on their conduct, to carry the effects of power right to them, to make it possible to know them, to alter them' (1977: 174).

DOCUMENTARY REALITY

In the example of child welfare, a wide variety of bureaucratic practices, carried out routinely in workers' everyday work with clients of the system, allow exactly this kind of power and discipline. Work processes through which we come to 'know' and try to change clients in the context of child welfare are explored in Section II. At the centre of these practices are documentary processes, and much of the analysis focuses upon the idea of documents, lodged in and constituting discourses, as mediators of reality. In the modern technological age, little of what we know has actually been experienced directly by us. We receive much of our information about the world 'second-hand' through books, news, articles, or in talk about information derived from these sources. Through documents, decisions about meanings and fact are conveyed to an audience not present at the actual events. These decisions then become 'known' in common with other members of that audience (Garfinkel, 1967). An analysis of this 'documentary reality' attempts to make explicit the activities involved in producing documents, demonstrating procedures involved in writing and reading accounts, and showing how the account is legitimated within itself as an actual account (Smith, 1973).

D.E. Smith, who has written extensively on textual analysis, proposes that two distinct modes of relating experience exist. One is primary narrative, a 'method of recapitulating past experience by matching a verbal sequence of clauses to the sequence of events which actually occurred' (Labov and Weletzky, 1967, quoted in Smith, 1983: 325). The second is a 'formalized impersonalized' account, in which 'the experienced becomes social'. That is, the underlying social relations that generated the text supply order and meanings not always explicit in the text. Smith describes this process as follows: '... the interpretive schemata selecting the terms and generating the grammatical, logical and causal connections of the account originate in a textual discourse (a "conversation mediated by texts") rather than being constrained by connections arising as expressions of the lived actuality. Hence, the selection of terms and connectives (of various types) is instructed by and conforms to, an ideological "grammar," a set of rules and procedures derived from the textual discourse. The interpretive schemata made use of in the reading of the text are similarly the schemata of the textual discourse and must have been learned as such if the text is to be intelligible to the reader' (1983: 325).

Smith uses the term 'ideology' here in much the same way as does Althusser, to refer to practical activities rather than belief systems. In this usage, ideological practices are seen to have the characteristics of separating the actual life activities of people and reformulating this activity into abstract language. In the course of this analysis, these kinds of procedures as they occur in the working up of child welfare cases will be examined in detail. In the process, individual actors disappear and experiences are 'nominalized'; that is, they appear independent of actual individuals. These reasoning practices produce concepts and theories that then appear in textual discourses as the explanatory connectives of people's lives and relations to one another. In the 'home alone' story, the 'strange behaviour' of the parents performs this function. This family, like any other, has a complex but largely unseen history. The 'facts' that have been collected and displayed about them are selected facts, ones that conform to a schema of child neglect and of deviance more generally. Having cited these facts, the parents can properly be placed in the neglect category; they have been made to fit. At the same time, we can notice an unseen but operative schema of neglect that provides the framework directing the selection of facts. These two operations reinforce one other: The facts that are selected are both directed by the framework and operate to substantiate, justify, and reproduce the framework. In Section II, examination in considerable detail will show how features of private family life come to be perceived, selected, and documented in conformity with a largely unseen framework that legitimizes them as cases of child neglect.

In Smith's view, the manner of our interpreting what is read constitutes the completion of the communication process. The activities of interpreting texts are not random; they are learned in a social context. Knowledge of the social nature of these processes allows us to analyse texts for meanings that readers supply through their knowledge of relevant discourses (Smith, 1977). Thus, discourse enters unseen not only into writing practices but also into the reading of texts in a manner which invokes interpretive schemata not actually present in the text. Practices of writing and of reading are frequently ideological in character, Smith argues, and their overriding purpose is to reflect the interests of the ruling class: 'Our "knowledge" is thus ideological in the sense that this social organization preserves conceptions and means of description which represent the world as it is for those who rule it, rather than as it is for those who are ruled' (1973: 267).

Because so much of what we 'know' about the world is derived through texts, the images and meanings conveyed through them have considerable power to shape consciousness and to produce particular kinds of knowledge. Examination of textual discourse provides, thus, a powerful analytical approach to the study of the processes which reproduce the world of those who rule.

FEMINISM: LIVED EXPERIENCE

Here, I return to the issue of what constitutes reality. As Smith's work suggests, the notion that observation is unimpeachable has come under severe fire as theories of ideology become more sophisticated and powerful. Another source of that critique has emerged from the women's movement over the past three decades. Feminist scholars have effectively criticized formal knowledge as 'written from the standpoint of men located in the relations of ruling our societies' (Smith, 1987). Modes of ruling, like the sciences that are used to support and reinforce them, are objectified and impersonal. In fact, as Keller notes, 'objectivity, reason and mind' have been cast as masculine, while 'subjectivity, feeling and nature' are perceived as feminine (1985: 7). Because objectivity has been promoted by empiricists as critical to the production of 'real' knowledge, many feminists contend that science as we know it not only privileges men as 'knowers' but promotes a kind of knowledge that specifically excludes the subjective experience with which women are identified.

The early wave of modern feminist scholarship took up this issue from the perspective of the way women themselves and their life experiences had been omitted from whole areas of history and social critique. Since the 1980s feminists have moved on to a consideration of the way 'feminine' and 'masculine' poles of experience have selected not only the content of scholarship but have shaped the form of science itself. It is thought proper in this mode of knowing to separate 'facts' from subjectivity, to strip away the context of their production, and to present them as a pure representation of reality. Knowledge produced through these processes, as we shall see in the case of child neglect, has separated meaning from the actual experiences of women's lives in a way that hides, glosses over, or distorts the nature of that experience. Feminists thus identify 'reality disjunctures' between what is actually experienced by women – their lived experience[1] – and that which is presented by science as factual knowledge about this reality.

One important outcome of this work is that the traditional Marxist view of social antagonisms as primarily class based has come up for review. Social location, and the life experience that ensues from it, is also determined by gender. Feminists have identified important differences between the kinds of experiences men and women have in our society. Capitalism has in fact provided the conditions for a widening gap between the experiences of men and women, as the 'extralocal, impersonal universalized forms of action [have become] the exclusive terrain of men while women [have become] correspondingly confined to a reduced local sphere of action organized by particularistic relationships' (Smith, 1987: 5). Knowledge, of course, is produced in the public domain, although it is often about private matters. Knowledge production occurs via the social relations of capitalist production and also of patriarchal relations, and it thus has allowed men to claim knowledge that is both universal and neutral (1987: 4). The feminist precept 'the personal is political' challenges the claims to truth of this knowledge. This idea exposes the division of the public and private domains and points us in the direction of examining the interests served by maintaining this conceptual separation.

In the past fifteen years, there has been a change in the degree to which women are represented in knowledge production (Weedon, 1987: 14–15). As this occurs, a challenge arises not only in relation to what should count as 'real' knowledge, but also to what constitutes *useful* knowledge from the standpoint of women. The boundaries established by the male-dominated scientific and academic institutions are questioned, as well as the forms of knowledge produced through them and previously accepted by most of us as 'good enough.' Of special interest in this research has been the issue of the caring work that women do, in both the public and private worlds. In both domains, it is usually women who do the work that allows men to function in the abstract, conceptual world. However, this caring work has remained largely invisible (Baines, Evans, and Neysmith, 1991). In our society, according to Daniels (1987), only paid activities are classified as work. While work in the public arena of the labour market has 'moral force and dignity,' unpaid work carried out in the private domain does not, and it thus remains unnoticed. Even caring work done in the public domain is devalued (Evans, 1991); it is often poorly paid work, and analysis of it has until recently remained very limited.

The low visibility of this form of labour – especially in the private, unpaid domain – helps to explain why social reproduction has been so poorly understood by Marxist theorists. The work that women do in the private sphere is central to the reproduction of the labour force. Not only wages are required in order to provide the physical sustenance necessary for 'the worker to present himself' at work. A substantial amount of labour is also required in order to feed, clothe, and clean up after those who must present themselves at a place of work or training for work. Also, as we shall explore further, considerable labour is required to inculcate and maintain the skills and attitudes needed by members of the present or future labour force. As feminists have begun to show, it is usually women who do this work, which is sometimes referred to as 'caring.' A feature of this work, one that differentiates it from many other kinds of labour, is that it is usually performed in the context of personal relationships. This is true of caring work in the public domain, such as social work, but is particularly true of caring work in the private sphere, because this work usually is done for close family members. Feminist study of caring, thus, usually notes that the concept includes both feelings, or 'caring about,' and activities, often referred to as 'caring for'

(Waerness, 1984; Dalley, 1988). These two aspects of caring seem to merge in the work of mothering, possibly because of our strongly held belief that it is natural for mothers to both love and labour for their children, an issue I take up in detail in Chapter 6. More generally, explication of the concept of caring work is an important one in beginning to understand both the experiences of mothers classified as neglecting and the work experiences of child welfare staff. Also, the social purposes served by the invisibility of this labour will be examined.

RACE AND CULTURE: CREATION OF THE 'OTHER'

A second arena in which the truth claims of science have been subject to serious challenge is that encompassed by issues of race and culture. Modern science and its conceptual categories have been characterized as containing 'a powerful ideological layer of self-interest, in-group favouritism, and ethnocentrism' (van Dijk, 1993: 160). The perspective of this challenge – that of racial and ethnic minority groups – may appear somewhat obvious and even unified at first glance, but it actually represents a rather confusing and often atheoretical field of critique and enquiry.

In keeping with Pecheaux's notion of discourse as having relatively loose boundaries, the discourse of race, culture, and minority status derives from many divergent streams, and there are considerable arguments within it. Even the central concepts that define this arena are subject to confusion and argument. Whereas the category 'women' is a relatively well-defined social and biological grouping, the category 'race' is not. Traditionally, and in everyday usage, race is understood as a biological category. Some recent writers argue that race is primarily a physiological category. Others take a 'sociohistoric' perspective, suggesting that race refers to differences in skin colour, hair, and facial features that are used as 'markers for ascribing differences in power and privilege' (Jaynes and Williams, 1989: 565). This definition verges into a definition of racism as a means of protecting privilege (Wellman, 1977). Implicit in this idea of race is that physical characteristics have come to signify and suggest the existence of other, more important differences among population groups (Davis and Proctor, 1989). Some commonly held ideas of difference are intelligence, propensity for violence, skill potential, and moral character. The existence of such differences by racial grouping is, of course, considered highly debatable, and much feeling is invested in denials and disagreements. Bolaria and Li (1988) declare that there are no scientific grounds to support the existence of such differences, and they propose that this suggestion is a thinly disguised legitimation of white supremacy. Most current writers in the social science field, in any case, do take account of both physical traits and social meanings in their attempts to define race.

Another way of defining minority groups is by cultural background. Culture has also proven problematic to define, although there is some acceptance that culture refers to the 'ways of life' of a group of people. A typical definition is provided by Devore and Schlesinger: 'Culture refers to the fact that human groups differ in the way they structure their behaviour, in their world view, in their perspectives on the rhythms and patterns of life, and in their concept of the essential nature of the human condition' (1991: 22).

An important issue in defining culture[2] is that of *process*, as Bissoondath notes in a trenchant and funny critique of multiculturalism in Canada (1993). In the attempt to 'pin down' features that distinguish one cultural group from another, the very concept of culture is simplified and made static, according to Bissoondath. Culture becomes 'theatre,' 'an object for display,' 'folklore,' and reduced to easily digested stereotypes. Perhaps most importantly, it is removed from its historical roots, from years or centuries of development. Cultural groups become 'exotics' available for display and study (1993: 373–87).

In discourse, the ideas of race and culture are not always conceptually distinguished from one another. Bolaria and Li (1988: 17) usefully define racial groups as determined by socially selected *physical* traits, while ethnic groups are distinguished by socially selected *cultural* traits . Of course, there is considerable debate as to whether race or culture is the dominant defining characteristic of minority status. When groups or individuals represent both cultural and racial minority status, however, it is racial signifiers that provide the most immediate and powerful justification for oppression: 'It is the combination of physical traits and social attributes that makes racial oppression unique,' according to Bolaria and Li (1988: 18). Eventually the stigma of oppression becomes indistinguishable from physical characteristics.

This idea of the predominance of race because of its immediate visibility is captured in Miles's discussion of 'racialization' (1989). Miles's work derives from a Marxist tradition and takes a view of race in relation to the part it has played in the development of capitalist relations of production. He defines racialization as a 'dialectical process by which meaning is attributed to particular biological features of human beings.' (1989: 76). Through racial signifiers, groups of people are characterized in such a way that their assignment to particular 'posts' in the social and economic arrangements of a society seems obvious and justified. Through racialization of a population, groups can be established as inferior in various ways – and as appropriate to exclude from decision processes. In defining the Other in particular ways, the

Self is also defined. Implied in the definition of one group as inferior is the contrasting view of the definers as superior. As this process unfolds, a world of common meaning is created in which both groups come to see themselves in this relation. While racial characteristics are the signifiers that identify a group of people, cultural characteristics become the objects of efforts at change. Those traits that do not fit with the assigned post must be transformed and/or eradicated. Often it is these 'undesirable' cultural characteristics that are castigated by the ruling group as inferior. In time, populations actually can be transformed in ways that both fit them for their assigned posts and bring them to accept the assignment. Miles's work is an important elaboration of Althusser's work, for it reveals racially based and culturally legitimated mechanisms through which people are allocated to their posts in the labour process. Both race and culture become mechanisms for this allocation process.

Some recent Canadian writing from a Marxist perspective helps to tie issues of race and culture to the context of their development, and particularly to productive processes. Bourgeault (1988, 1991), for instance, describes how the development of captalist work processes in Canada transformed the organization of the Native population from cooperative social forms, based on kinship groups that provided mechanisms both for the distribution of labour and consumption, to a marginalized and vulnerable group dependent upon the more individualized forms required by capitalist production and consumption. As Bourgeault shows, the experiences and eventual social locations of Native women and men occurred somewhat differently in this process. Not only specific cultural traits of Native women but also their sexuality were incorporated into development processes, with the result that the social location of these women, both in relation to the ruling group and in relation to Native men as well, was transformed.

This kind of analysis has considerable theoretical promise for illuminating the experiences of people created as Other in capitalist societies. The analysis is historically specific. The outcome is a view of the Other that is not homogeneous – but rather reveals the specific forms of coercion, transformation, and resistance experienced by various sub-groups. Also, this approach allows 'culture' to be seen in the process of its production. The usually accepted definition of culture as 'the ways of life' of a group implicitly poses each group as homogeneous, with all members benefiting equally from the arrangements. Groups are also posed as autonomous; as having the freedom to develop 'ways of life.' This kind of definition detaches culture from its economic roots and from relations of oppression, removing from view the social relations of production out of which specific cultural forms were born.

Thus, the surface appearance of culture does indeed become exotic and often inexplicable. As explored further in Chapter 7, this concealment has implications for social work practitioners. In the 1990s service deliverers are exhorted to become 'culturally sensitive.' Many practitioners find this advice confusing and contradictory, as indeed it is. Only some cultural characteristics and norms are selected for attention by social work, and these are usually extracted from the historical context of their development by unwary workers representing the interests of the dominant society.

A central feature of the process of transforming racial and cultural groups to conform with the requirements of ruling elites is that of the ongoing construction of these groups as the Other (van Dijk, 1993). This process occurs in all kinds of discourse, from the most academic to the most popular. Discourse, it will be recalled, includes not only actual written words but the sites and processes through which words are spoken and read. Child welfare organizations are themselves the sites of intersecting discourses as well as the producers and consumers of discourse. Chapter 7 explores specifically textual processes through which the Other is produced as a part of everyday social work practices, and examines the effects of these procedures.

FRAMEWORK: SUMMARY AND SOURCES

This book begins from an explicit agenda of identifying and struggling against oppression. In particular, the book is occupied with organized practices of ruling (Smith, 1987), including conceptual practices that perform oppressive functions. Child neglect, it is argued, is a concept through which more powerful groups maintain their dominant position over particular vulnerable and marginalized groups. The fundamental structure underlying the analysis in this book is the idea from Marx and Engels of the nature of reality as a unity of surface appearances and hidden realities. The analysis poses the surface reality of child neglect against the hidden realities that exist outside particular lives and settings, but that enter into and organize them and give them a particular appearance. Through use of the critical approach, the analysis focuses on the dialectic – or dynamic interconnectedness – between individuals and their social context and between specific forms of social organization and the social processes that create them. This view of social reality directs our attention to an examination of the otherwise hidden domain of social relations and processes that select and organize particular details from individual lives to create and reproduce an appearance that we recognize as child neglect. A substantial part of the analysis is occupied with the identification of everyday work practices through which this effect is produced, with the ultimate purpose of bringing to consciousness our own often unwilling participation in the reproduction of conditions of oppression.

Child neglect has been selected for study partly because it is an accessible issue. It is one that most social workers will have confronted at some point in their working lives. It is also accessible on a more personal level, because the arena of study involves ordinary tasks and responsibilities of caring for children. Furthermore, the location of child neglect within a state apparatus – child welfare – that has both repressive and ideological features, and also within a professional discourse, offers many opportunities for critical analysis. The analysis of child neglect may also serve as a prototype; it is one example of how critical theory can be applied to the examination of concepts created and housed in different sets of apparatuses.

To some extent, this book draws upon a research project carried out in a Canadian child welfare agency (Swift, 1990). In that study, workers were interviewed about child neglect. They were asked to discuss their work practices in relation to selected cases they viewed as 'typical' neglect, to reflect on the families and problems in the case, to discuss some of their feelings about their work and to consider how their work was related to knowledge and discourse about child neglect. File recording of selected cases was also reviewed. Because neglect cases are generally long running, these files reflected a considerable array of agency and work practices over time, as well as the file notes of several dozen workers operating in different social and legal contexts. Because families accused of neglect are frequently involved with many agencies and institutions over time, these files also revealed connections among social institutions, discourse, knowledge, and understandings. The research demonstrated, in other words, that a case file provides much more than facts about individual clients. When examined from a critical perspective, the case file provides a wide and deep view of social structure and social relations, and this view informs the analysis here. Especially in Part 2, data from this research project are drawn upon in illuminating the way surface and hidden realities are mediated by social work practices.

The analysis also draws upon extensive examination of discourse and the interaction of discourse with work practices. The intent is to 'map' the way knowledge – forms of thought, symbols, and concepts – develops and travels from one site to another, including how these travel back and forth between the sites of their production and academic discourse. Furthermore, features of critical thought explained in this chapter are applied to practical problems in social work, especially in Chapters 4–8, in order to elucidate hidden realities that create and sustain child neglect as a visible and legitimate social category.

The concept of practice is a particular focus of investigation. As used here, practice involves a broad definition of work, including those activities of practical reasoning, speech, and writing through which the tasks of child welfare are both produced and accomplished: 'those processes that both produce and are ordered by the social relations of the institutional process' (Smith, 1987: 166). This definition preserves the concept of the dialectic of Marx and Engels and expands upon it to make observable the institutionalized processes within which work practices are located. The practices most available for study, given my sources, are those of child welfare workers; some practices of mothers themselves as they interact with workers in the context of child welfare are also explored.

The concept of ideology is also central. It is seen as operating through the medium of imagination, but as grounded in real life. Ideology is more than ideas; it is also practices and organization. In later chapters of this book I show how ideology works in relation to child neglect in a way that both secures and sanctions existing arrangements of class, race, and gender. This notion of ideology builds upon and helps to explain how reality exists as both hidden and apparent phenomena and how people are brought to participate in social arrangements that are oppressive.

The term 'apparatus' refers to sets of relevant social relations, connected directly and indirectly to state power, and performing both repressive and ideological functions. Although not commonly used in social work discourse, the term is useful in its power to evoke social relations that are otherwise not named or categorized and that are normally not perceived as connected. Althusser's conceptual differentiation of the repressive and ideological functions of apparatuses will be employed in an analysis of child welfare and its institutional arrangements.

Relations of class, gender, and race are explored in several chapters. These are explored as sets of relations, based on unequal power, that are maintained and reproduced through work practices in child welfare settings. The idea of contradictory experience is reflected in these relations. The identification of contradictions and examination of their resolutions help to reveal important mechanisms of ideology and of social reproduction. In the final chapter, the conceptual framework will also be invoked to explore issues of social change through social work practice.

3

The Social Context of Neglect

Child neglect is commonly seen as a social problem manifested by particular individual parents. This is the surface reality of neglect that we saw produced in the 'home alone' case. Although neglect usually constitutes a large share of the cases in child welfare agencies, a relatively small amount of research and writing has addressed the issue in recent years. With the exception of occasional high profile stories like 'home alone,' neglect has tended to slide to the background of child welfare practice and concern over the past two or three decades. The existing literature focuses mainly on research into causes of the problem, incidence, factors associated with neglect, and with the efficacy of various treatment programs. In addition, there is a body of literature criticizing various aspects of the role of the state in addressing this issue (Swift, 1988). This discourse is primarily preoccupied with adults – the characteristics of neglecting parents, their faults, flaws, and lapses, and the potential for changing them. The needs and feelings of children generally appear as background issues rather than as the central focus of child neglect, except with respect to harm of children, an issue addressed in this chapter and in Chapter 5.[1]

Critical social science, as we saw in the last chapter, requires that the issue under examination be placed and understood in its historically specific social context. Three overlapping and interactive courses of human activity (or social processes) through which the image of neglect is structured and maintained are discussed in this chapter. These are legal processes, professional social work processes, and organizational processes, all of which reflect the development of Western economic and political life, and especially the growth and transmutations of late capitalism in North America. Also, views of 'the family' and the place of children figure in the way neglect has been conceptualized. Figure 3.1 shows the field of relations in which child neglect

Figure 3.1
Relevant Relations of Neglect

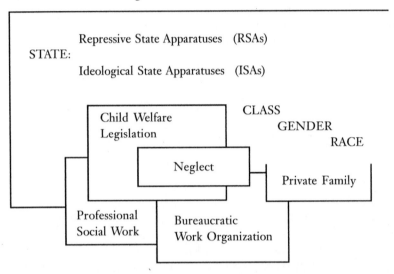

as a social category is embedded. The diagram also represents the exension of bureaucratic forms of organization into various sets of relations. The structure of the private family, as well as the relations of class, gender and race are relevant features of the larger society that also operate to shape the idea of child neglect.

LEGAL PROCESSES

Both historically and in modern everyday child welfare work, neglect is fundamentally a legal concept. That is, neglect came into being through the development of a succession of legal principles and specific legislation relating to the family and to the welfare of children within families. The family, as Eichler (1988) describes so well, is not a uniform structure in present-day Canada, although in discourse it is often treated that way. Eichler's analysis shows that the modern family represents a vast array of forms, functions, and interests. However, it is the nuclear family and its traditional functions and prerogatives that are assumed, preserved, and addressed in child welfare legislation. Definitions within this legislation assume that parents or suitable replacements are responsible for ensuring the safety and development of children and that the role of the state is not to provide but to enforce needed care by the original family or an alternative. The foundations for this approach are embedded in both English common law, which identifies parents as responsible for the maintenance, protection, and education of children (Farina, 1982), and in French civil law, which stresses parental power and authority as well as the duty of parents to protect their children.

According to Harris and Melichercik (1986: 160), the idea of children as the property of parents is fundamental to the development of child welfare as we know it. This concept provides a basic rationale for both parental responsibility and for the right of parents to raise children as they see fit. Children in both the English and French traditions were viewed as belonging to their parents, and substantial rights to discipline and control children traditionally accompanied this approach. Modern child welfare legislation reflects a belief that only in cases of actual or likely harm to the child should the state intrude upon these rights. Clauses in the legislation therefore stress injury, harm, risk, safety, security, and – more recently – development of the child; as noted, child welfare discourse also reflects this focus. As a result, discussions about neglect, from both legal and professional perspectives, have tended to focus on enforcing the minimal requirements of caring for children rather than on promoting their optimal development.

Another fundamental concept shaping the relation of the state to children is known as *parens patriae*, literally meaning 'parent of the nation.' Legislation developed in English Canada has tended to emphasize *parens patriae*, while Quebec has focused more strongly on the tradition of parental rights (Harris and Melichercik, 1986). *Parens patriae* is in fact deeply rooted in English history. Custer (1978) has traced the idea to the time of Edward I (1272–1307). The original intent was to invest sovereigns with the power to protect lunatics. An interesting feature of the early origins of this concept is that extension of this power to infants occurred as the result of a printer's error, not as a matter of policy (Farina, 1982: 66). Nevertheless, the doctrine took root and was eventually codified by Blackstone in 1765. In its transference to the United States and Canada, the power of *parens patriae* became dispersed between the central and subsidiary governments. It remains a powerful idea, one that has often taken precedence over due legal process. As Farina (1982) notes, it is a doctrine that can be used with humanitarian intentions to protect children from the excesses of their parents, but it is also a power with a strong tendency to expand. This doctrine underlies the legislation and social policy that have developed to deal with identified child welfare issues, including neglect.

Gordon (1988) describes child neglect as we now think of it as having been 'discovered' in North America at the turn of the century. The issue of neglect in Canada, however, has its roots in the poverty and abandonment of large numbers of children in the earlier years of industrialization. In Canada, the first legislation relating to the protection of children appeared during the beginning years of settlement. In those years many children were in fact an asset to their parents in the tasks of farming and settling a new land. Nevertheless, by 1799, sufficient numbers of children had been orphaned or abandoned in Upper Canada that legislation for their 'protection' was deemed necessary. Thus, the Act for the Education and Support of Orphans or Children Deserted by their Parents (1799) was passed. It provided for the binding out of children as apprentices, which was the accepted mode of 'care' for homeless children at the time. Through this legislation, public responsibility for the protection of children was established in Canada.

In urban Quebec, similar conditions of overcrowding, illness, and poverty existed for many families, accompanied by high rates of infant illness and death, and the abandonment of many children. Quebec adopted legislation directly concerned with protecting the rights of children and youth in 1869. However, the primary response to protection issues in Quebec was the development of church-sponsored institutions – orphanages and foundling homes – to provide for children when their parents could not. Temporary placement was common, suggesting that institutions were not simply an alternative to the family as caregiver but a community response designed to assist families in need (Bradbury, 1982). Perhaps because of this response, Quebec alone among Canadian provinces did not develop formal child welfare legislation until well into the twentieth century.

Although institutions to house abandoned children also existed outside Quebec, English-speaking Canada came to rely more heavily on state involvement to assist neglected and abandoned children. In the latter part of the nineteenthth century, two pieces of legislation were important in laying the groundwork for later developments with respect to neglected children. The Act Respecting Industrial Schools (1874) attempted for the first time to define a neglected child and provided that a child could be returned home if the parents were deemed reformed, orderly, and industrious (Farina, 1982: 147–9). This act did not specify, however, who would be responsible for investigating or taking action to protect children. A later piece of legislation, the Children's Protection Act of 1888, provided for the principle that the state has a right to evaluate the suitability of a child's environment and provide for the removal of a child from that environment if it is seen not to be in the child's interests.

Towards the end of the nineteenth century several sets of conditions conspired to produce organizational and legislative action for more explicit protection of children. During the latter part of the century thousands of homeless children were sent from the United Kingdom to Canada for placement. Although these children were to be apprenticed, some placements did not work out, and many children eventually made their way to urban centres (Sutherland, 1976). The 1880s and 1890s also were a period of intense industrialization in Ontario. During this time the homelessness and exploitation of many children became a visible problem, especially in cities.

Simultaneously, the growth of the economy produced a new middle class for whom standards of living were high and increasing. The social climate for this group was one of energy for social change. Out of this group grew a social reform movement that addressed itself to the issue of improving living conditions for deprived children, known at the time as 'child saving' (Jones and Rutman, 1981). Among the significant results of reformers' efforts was the organization in Toronto of the first Children's Aid Society in Canada, founded in 1891. Two years later came the passage in Ontario of legislation specifically addressed to the Prevention of Cruelty to and Better Protection of Children. This act became the basis for later legislative views of the issue of child neglect. The act defined a neglected child in these ways:

- A child who is found begging or receiving alms
- A child who is found wandering about without any home or proper guardianship
- A child who is found associating or dwelling with a thief, drunkard, or vagrant, and growing up without salutary parental control
- A child who is found in any house of ill-fame or the company of a reputed prostitute
- A child who is found destitute, being an orphan or having a surviving parent undergoing punishment for crime.

In this definition evidence of poverty and need for care of the child are addressed; also, moral issues concerning the activities of caretakers and guardians are introduced. For decades, following the mandate of this legislation, child welfare workers quite directly pursued information about the moral character of parents, especially mothers, as an integral part of their investigations (Swift, 1995a). According to Rose and Meezan (1993) this is one feature of child neglect that has become less important over time, although it is still specifically mentioned in Quebec's Youth Protection Act.

Punishment for cruelty to children was stressed in Ontario's legislation, including fines and imprisonment up to three months. The family was viewed as the appropriate source of care and nurture for children. Consequently, a foster care system, modelled on the English and American programs, was to be developed as the primary method of care, replacing both apprenticeship and the long-term institutions that had emerged in the nineteenth century. The act also authorized children's aid societies to administer the act, and the concepts of apprehension of children from their parents and of legal guardianship by the authorized agents of the state were also important features of the act. Ontario's legislation was the first of its kind in English-speaking Canada, but several other provinces soon followed suit. Eventually, all Canadian provinces (except Quebec), the Northwest Territories, and the Yukon developed legislation modeled to some extent on Ontario's, which in turn descended from English traditions. Implicit in the legislation was an assumption that 'Britain was entrusted by God with a special civilizing and evangelical mission throughout the world' (Macintyre, 1993: 40). Ontario's act was amended many times in the intervening years, and was eventually replaced altogether in 1984; other provinces have also made recent changes in their child welfare legislation, and Quebec passed protection legislation in 1977. The fundamentals of the original legislation appear in all Canadian legislation, notably the notion of state intervention to protect children under the doctrine of *parens patriae* and the focus on family as the appropriate source of care, with fostering as the primary form of substitute care. Quebec has also moved from a previous focus on institutional care to more use of the foster care model over the past several decades. Punishment remains a central feature of the Canadian approach to child welfare, although the forms have changed. In cases of serious harm to a child, parents may be charged under the Criminal Code of Canada. Otherwise, as Foucault describes so well, 'the ceremonial of punishment [has] tended to decline; it survive[s] only as a new legal or administrative practice' (1977: 8). In subsequent chapters of this book, some of the more punishing legal and administrative features of child welfare will be explored.

There are significant new issues emerging in legislation passed recently. With respect to neglect, some important features of the debate surrounding the new legislation and trends contained in it are significant. Neglect is now mentioned less prominently in legislation. It is more common to employ a phrase such as 'in need of protection,' which in turn is defined by phrases echoing themes of abandonment of and failure to provide for children found in the original legislation. In modern legislation the term 'abuse' is more likely to be mentioned and to be used in a generic sense as the main framing concept in legislation. Manitoba's 1986 Act, for instance, did not include neglect in its introductory list of definitions. Instead, the term abuse is used, defined as 'an act or omission by a parent, guardian or a person caring for a child which results in (i) physical injury to the child, (ii) emotional disability of a permanent nature in the child or is likely to result in such a disability, or (iii) sexual exploitation of the child with or without the child's consent.'

Several points can be made about this shift of definitions. Child neglect was the original concept behind child welfare legislation, and it remained the primary organizing idea in child welfare work until the 1960s. With the publication of work by Kempe et al. (1962) on 'the battered child syndrome,' neglect began to assume a lower profile as the public and social workers responded to this far more dramatic idea of maltreatment. The identification of this 'syndrome,' according to Hutchinson (1990) accounted for quick passage of extra funding and mandatory reporting requirements in the United States, with Canadian jurisdictions following suit. This narrow definition of child maltreatment was soon broadened to include aspects of neglect, which then reappeared as subcategories of abuse. Thus, neglect is implied in the definition of abuse cited above by use of the term 'omission.'

It was not necessarily the intent of legislation that neglect come to be implied as a subcategory of abuse; this understanding is created through discourse, which works to supply this meaning in the absence of more specific definitions of the term. In child welfare literature, it has become common to differentiate neglect from abuse in terms of parental action: 'The parent who abuses ... is guilty of a crime of commission; neglect is more frequently a crime of omission' (Kadushin, 1967: 210). Some current legislative wording embodies that definition. The subsuming of neglect into abuse also reflects a re-priorization of problems in the daily practice of child welfare work. This issue is pursued in Chapter 4 in relation to the way neglect comes to be made visible.

The concept of emotional maltreatment of children is relatively new. Concerns have been expressed in the literature about whether emotional harm should be specifically mentioned in legislation (Whiting, 1976) and how it is to be identified in practice (O'Hagan, 1993). The problem of specifying for legal purposes what constitutes emotional harm has proved difficult, with the result that very few children have been removed from their families on grounds of emotional abuse or neglect. Knowing this, workers may be reluctant to bring these cases before the courts. However, the phrases 'emotional harm' or 'emotional injury' now appear in some provincial legislation, for instance, in Alberta's, which specifies causes, conditions, and appropriate evidence needed to establish emotional injury. The inclusion of such definitions in legislation suggests that emotional harm is increasingly being taken up as an important child welfare issue; recent research substantiates this view (Trocme and Tam, 1994).

The issue of actual injury sustained by a child as a criterion of abuse is reflected in a political debate occurring over the past two or three decades questioning the use of discretionary power of child welfare workers under the *parens patriae* doctrine. Most child welfare legislation in the middle part of this century was based on quite vague definitions of abuse and neglect. Beginning in the 1960s, however, a critique of the discretionary power allowed to child welfare workers by these definitions ensued, a critique firmly lodged in a much wider discourse concerning individual rights vis-à-vis the powers of the state. The fundamental dispute, in an era influenced strongly by rights movements, has focused on whether the rights of 'the family' to privacy and autonomy in child-rearing practices should supersede the rights of children to protection from abuse and neglect by parents.

A vigorous debate over this issue took place in the child welfare literature. Wald (1976), for instance, voiced opposition to the idea of intervention premised primarily on parental conduct. Wald argued that demonstrable harm to the child should be the criterion, because the alternative is that social workers and courts interfere with private family life based on predicted future harm. Mnookin (1973), another influential critic, also objected to the 'wide discretion' allowed to professionals in their intervention decisions. He called into question the knowledge base of professionals who make decisions about intervention, calling it subjective knowledge, based on unproven theory. This debate, as Hutchinson (1990) notes, continues to the present time, with the family autonomy position currently prevailing. Although it appears primarily in the American literature, it has had an effect on some Canadian legislation, in the form of clauses concerning harm as a criterion for intervention (for instance, Ontario's Child and Family Services Act of 1984). Also, during the 1960s and 1970s, scrutiny of the large number of children being brought into care raised concerns about the grounds used to apprehend children in Canada. Research such as the work done by Hepworth (1980) on the large percentage of Canadian children in care and by Patrick Johnston (1983) on the overrepresentation of Native children in the child welfare system, fuelled arguments about whether the powers of agencies, workers, and the courts should be restricted and what grounds should be used to justify intervention in private family life. It has now become common in child welfare legislation to commence with a 'Declaration of Principles' in which the province's particular resolutions of such social debates are provided.

The principle that developed in many jurisdictions as a result of these debates was the 'least intrusive' principle. Agencies operating under such a directive have the obligation to perpetrate 'the least interference with [the family's] affairs to the extent compatible with the best interests of children and the responsibilities of society' (the Child and Family Services Act, Manitoba, 1986). Child welfare workers are thus instructed to intrude upon families only to the extent necessary to protect children from actual harm.

Among the key players in the debate concerning intrusiveness were ethnic and racial minority groups. In Canada, as noted, it was especially a critique of the relationship between Native[2] families and child welfare authorities that sparked concern. Although Native families complained for many years about the treatment they received from child welfare agencies and workers, it was not until the 1970s and 1980s that these complaints became political issues. Johnston (1983) documented the 'sixties scoop,' a reference to the vast numbers of Canadian Native children permanently removed from their families during the 1960s, often on charges of neglect. Hudson and McKenzie (1981) described child welfare practices towards Native people as a form of colonialism. Native people wrote articles demonstrating the cultural differences in family life and child care between Native and dominant cultures and criticized authorities for failing to realize the difficulties of caring for children under the conditions of poverty and dislocation experienced by so many Native people (Manuel and Posluns, 1974; Red Horse, 1978, 1980). As expanded upon in Chapter 7, this critique found its way into legislation in the United States and in many Canadian provinces, in the form of special attention in legislation to Native families and culture.

Another important concept, often incorporated into statements of legislative principle, is the 'best interests of the child.' The legislation in Manitoba, for instance, states as its first principle: 'The best interests of children are a fundamental responsibility of society.' The origins of this idea lie in custody disputes, rather than in child welfare law. The concept was used by judges in child welfare cases earlier in this century, but the phrase did not appear in legislation until the 1970s. Until that time, judges attempting to employ the idea had few guidelines to go by. Two books by influential authors focused attention on the 'best interests' issue during the 1970s. These were *Beyond the Best Interests of the Child* and *Before the Best Interests of the Child* (Goldstein, Freud, and Solnit, 1973, 1979). These authors address questions surrounding state intervention into family life from the perspective of effects on children. They examine the issue of separation of children from their parents, arguing that children have strong needs for continuity of care, that they have different concepts of time from those of adults, and suggesting that biological and psychological parents need not necessarily be the same. Following from these considerations they proposed that decisions about a child's future should be made much more quickly than is commonly done, and that decisions more often be permanent in order to re-establish the potential for continuity with new parents as quickly as possible.

The viewpoint taken by these authors has been controversial. Critics note that the ideas are based in psychoanalysis and ignore social and situational factors. Some critics have suggested these ideas have been applied unevenly and in ethnocentric ways (Blanchard and Barsh, 1980). Nevertheless, as Benjamin (1981) shows, this work has influenced both family court judges and legislation. Among other outcomes of this work is the concept of 'permanency planning,' referring to efforts by child welfare personnel to locate permanent placements for children rather than settling for foster care, which is temporary in principle if not always in fact. Permanency planning has now become central to the way in which child welfare workers and the courts view decisions about children, although, as Rosenbluth (1994) shows in his study of foster care in Saskatchewan, actual practice does not necessarily mirror these beliefs. Nevertheless the ideas underlying permanency planning have become an integral part of the way we think about child welfare.

The direction suggested by Goldstein, Solnit, and Freud (1973; 1979), it would seem, suggests early and relatively intrusive intervention into families where the continuity of care could be at stake. The authors had hoped their work might influence courts to move more speedily towards permanent resolutions in disputes between child welfare authorities and natural parents. While there have no doubt been good intentions in this regard, the realities of court proceedings have not changed substantially since the 1970s.[3] Furthermore, political will has not been on the side of increased state intervention. Dalley (1988) notes that the conservatism of the 1980s has actually encouraged a view of the family as a buttress against the incursions of the state into the domestic domain. As the Commons Standing Committee on Health, Welfare and Social Affairs, 1974-5-6, made clear, protection of family autonomy has always been paramount in Canada: 'By tradition and law the rights of the parent have always superseded those of the child unless or until the breakdown of the family necessitates the intervention of a public authority.'

Notwithstanding such official statements, modern ideas about child development have entered the legislation and in various ways guide decisions concerning the welfare of children. This trend stands in contradiction to the least intrusive approach in its demonstration of concern with the development of children over and above issues of basic safety. Aspects of both of these standards of care are currently embodied within child welfare legislation, with the 'least intrusive' approach predominating. Both models, embedded as they are in larger social debates concerning rights, have encouraged the 'legalization' of child welfare processes. The rights of both parents and children, often assumed to conflict, are mentioned in legislation, and the use of lawyers to protect the rights of all parties has become commonplace. The ways in which these contradictory issues of rights, intrusion, and bests interests are worked out in the everyday task of determining and acting on cases perceived as neglect are addressed more fully in Section II.

THE PROFESSIONAL MANDATE

While the legal mandate is fundamental to understanding child protection work as it relates to neglect, the professional understandings and values of social workers, who are the interpreters of legislation and the 'agents of the state' in enforcing it, are also influential. The origins and current relationship of the social work profession to child welfare work are reviewed here, emphasizing those professional ideals and principles that have particular relevance to the issue of neglect.

Professional social work is inextricably entwined with the development of social welfare in Canada. Our social welfare system has evolved over many centuries of economic development in the Western world. Principles established through a series of historical events, including various modifications of the English Poor Laws, are often identified as crucial to understanding modern social welfare. Joanne Turner (1986) identifies two such principles as 'less eligibility' and 'perceptions of need.' Less eligibility is a principle that state assistance provided for people in need should be 'less desirable, less satisfactory, less eligible, than that of the lowest paid labourer' (Report of the Royal Commission for Inquiring into the Administration and Practical Operation of the Poor Laws, 1834). Most welfare programs today, including child welfare, still base the rationing of funds on this principle.

The second principle is perception of need. One way of looking at need is that people's own personal failures cause them to be in need. This idea is closely connected, as Turner points out, with the philosophy of individualism, which promotes the pursuit of self-interest as the best means of serving the interests of the group. A corollary is that those who fail to pursue self-interest will come to be 'in need' and thus will harm the interests of the group. These are the 'unworthy poor,' and individualism provides the philosophical justification to penalize them on behalf of the group for their failures. An alternative view of need is that it occurs because of the failure of social forces and the economic system to protect individuals. The British Poor Laws in effect legitimated the view that some people are in need because of social and economic factors rather than personal deficiencies, thus allowing for the idea of the 'worthy poor' to evolve.

The Poor Laws, in designating the local authority to investigate applications for relief, also established the roots of modern social casework. The volunteer charity organizations that formed in the United States following the American Revolution extended the investigative function through their 'friendly visitors,' who had the additional function of administering advice and inspiration. The women involved in these organizations were obliged by their belief in the work ethic to operate within narrow limits, confining their efforts to relief-giving only if the father of a family was absent through death or desertion (Treudley, 1980). Thus, the very beginnings of casework were embedded in both class and gender relations through which members of the middle class rationed services and support to poor and marginalized groups; and women of the middle and upper classes assumed responsibility for providing both inspiration and limited services to mother-led households. These class and gender patterns of determining eligibility and providing relief remain in child welfare today, along with the primary functions established by tradition.

The duties of visitors were spelled out early on. They were to 'visit each applicant, to examine particularly into her moral character, her situation, her habits and modes of life, her wants and the best means of affording relief' (Treudley, 1980: 136).

The 'best means of affording relief,' of course, were not always material. Moral uplift or removal of children were sometimes the prescriptions. These friendly visitors were the ancestors of the modern social worker. Eventually, expertise was substituted for the less formal friendly visit. Through professionalizing processes, 'social workers perpetuated the charity organization ideal of personal contact and influence' but on an impersonal basis (Lubove, 1965: 23). They retain the primary functions established by tradition – investigative and surveillance functions of the early visitors and some discretion to establish the eligibility of clients. In Canada, as in the United States, friendly visitors were the first child welfare workers. They focused on both the neglecting parents, seen as members of the 'unworthy poor,' and on the protection of their children, who were perceived to be innocent and therefore among the 'worthy poor.'

Early in the twentieth century, connections between child neglect and the single-parent family were made, which allowed at least some single mothers to qualify as worthy poor (Gordon, 1988). In Canada, reformers assembled in Ottawa in 1914 for a Social Service Congress, the aims of which included the 'famous first principle' that a child should not be removed from his or her home on grounds of poverty alone (Guest, 1980: 49). Many at the conference spoke of the urgent need for a system of publicly supported 'mothers' pensions' to address this problem (Proceedings, Social Service Conference, 1914). Eventually, though hotly debated, legislation was passed in all provinces, albeit with strict requirements in keeping with the principle of less eligibility. Representatives of private charity opposed the pension approach, viewing 'family relief' as their own private territory. Charlotte Whitton, who continued to see these mothers as unworthy poor, proposed that unearned money should not be given unless accompanied by 'skilled social work investigation and supervision' (Guest, 1980: 52).

The debates about mothers' pensions represented the first reformulation of neglect following the development of the 'children's aid' approach, one accomplished through social and political processes rather than through a legal route. Although the reformulation subsequently took some account of social and economic factors as they related to child care, the principles of less eligibility and of investigating the worthiness of applicants were not only retained but institutionalized, with the fledgling profession of social work offering itself as the appropriate vehicle for enforcement of these principles.

During the early years of the twentieth century, social workers in a variety of institutional settings, including children's aid societies, were 'groping toward investigation techniques and methods of diagnosis and treatment which would result in an understanding of the unique problems of each client' (Lubove, 1965: 23). Medical social workers, situated in hospitals, were particularly influential in this endeavour, and their model for the skills and knowledge needed, according to Lubove, was the physician. The new conception of social work, which began to supplant the friendly visitor model, was one of 'skilled professional service, rooted in medical science and performed in a specific institutional setting' (Lubove, 1965: 35). The moral judgments espoused by friendly visitors came to be considered too 'subjective' and therefore out of place in the new profession, as it attempted to identify itself as a profession in its own right, one modeled on and connected to the prestigious profession of medicine.

Postindustrial theorists, as Derber (1982) comments, have claimed that scientific knowledge will be the central factor in all kinds of production in the modern era. Possessors of knowledge will have power that protects themselves and excludes others. Professionals, who are the socially accredited possessors of certain knowledges, were thus to become a new and powerful social class. In female-dominated fields such as social work, nursing, and teaching, leaders intuited early on the importance of developing a body of professional knowledge that would enable them to join this new class. According to Derber (1982), however, social workers erred in adopting psychoanalysis as the basis for their knowledge because they could not then claim a monopoly that would clearly define social work as a profession. The struggle of the social work profession to make this claim continues today, expressed through attachment to 'hard' science as the basis of its knowledge claims.

Although the medical model has remained important in professional social work and has influenced knowledge development, the knowledge base of social work as it developed through the twentieth century has become characterized by eclecticism. Wickham (1986: 19) identifies two general subgroupings of this knowledge base. The first is general knowledge from the fields of sociology, psychology, political science, economics, biology, law, medicine, and social administration. The second is specialized knowledge drawn from other disciplines but 'shaped and expanded by social welfare professionals.' The most important of these are psychoanalytic theory, social learning theory, existential theory, and social systems theory. Each of these has enjoyed a period of special influence and vogue in the profession, with psychoanalytic theory and its various permutations, and systems theory, more recently redesigned as ecological theory, emerging as most prevalent. However, one idea that has survived time and trends, and that is considered unique to social work among the service professions, is that of a dual interest in the person and the social environment: 'Character, human relationships, and community life are the fields of ... study and effort,' Ida Cannon said of social work in the early part of this century (Lubove, 1965: 33).

Over the past several decades, child welfare practitioners have drawn on knowledge germane to child development in a variety of related disciplines. The work of both Maslow (1954) and Erikson (1950) has come to be used extensively in understanding and predicting developmental needs, issues, and milestones. Bowlby's work (1969) on bonding and attachment has had a powerful influence on practice, especially as it relates to decisions concerning the removal of children from their natural parents. Ideas explored by Goldstein, Freud, and Solnit (1973, 1979) concerning children's needs for stability and continuity of care enter regularly into the daily decision-making processes of workers. However, professional discussions of neglect itself have rather ironically tended to focus on parental behaviours and deficiencies rather than on children and their needs, perhaps a commentary on social work's preoccupation with the 'unworthy' poor.

Social work, like many other service professions, is value based. The inherent worth and dignity of every person is basic to social work. Francis Turner (1986b: 10) cites the client's 'ability to choose from a variety of possibilities' out of which uniqueness and individuality grow as essential to social work practice. Respect for this characteristic in the individual has come to be a central tenet of social work, one intended to caution social workers against making decisions or acting on behalf of others, or presuming to know what is right or best for clients. Many aspiring social workers express a deep desire to 'help' those with less opportunity than themselves. A substantial portion of social work education involves the taming and disciplining of this impulse in such a way that the more powerful social worker does not impose upon or behave irresponsibly towards clients, strictures that recognize the unequal power between workers and clients.

The Canadian Association of Social Workers has developed a Code of Ethics to which individuals employed as social workers are expected to subscribe (Turner and Turner, 1986: 451). The code covers issues of philosophy, skill, and competence as well as statements of value. Examples are professional positions taken against various forms of discrimination and positions in favour of equitable distribution of societal resources. One of the problems of social work has been that its knowledge base is not synchronized with its value orientation (Heineman, 1981; Swift, 1988). This contradiction is in some ways a continuation of the original split between the friendly visitors, with their value-laden but informal and personal approach, and the caseworkers who followed them, with their reverence for the more professionalized and technical model of medical science.

To summarize, social work arose out of the relations of capitalist society. Principle concepts such as the relative worthiness of poor people and the principles of rationing resources to them were shaped in relation to these features of society. The knowledge base of modern social work, while broad, reflects a belief system that stands in contradiction to its value base. These characteristics of social work appear in the practice of child welfare and in the shaping of the category of child neglect, operating to give neglect its particular character and appearance.

THE ORGANIZATIONAL CONTEXT OF CHILD WELFARE

Francis Turner defines social services as 'the network of agencies, settings, and institutions that constitutes the service component of the social welfare structure ... the organizational arrangements through which the policies and legislation related to social welfare are implemented' (1986a: 5). It is indeed through these organizational arrangements that child welfare workers, along with other social service personnel, have always operated, for this work has developed entirely in bureaucratically constituted settings that have organized and routinized the legal and social work mandates. It is through bureaucratic settings and processes that cases of neglect are processed and thus made visible.

According to Ferguson (1984), the origins of bureaucracy can be traced to attempts of monarchs in the late feudal period to extend their power. Bureaucratic systems later provided a dual system of 'force and welfare' to establish order during the transition from feudalism to capitalism. Bureaucracy, is of course, not exclusive to capitalist systems, but nevertheless has coincided with the development of capitalism. The collective tendency of bureaucracy, however, stands in contradiction to the philosophy underlying capitalist societies, which 'urge people away from collective concerns ... while simultaneously impelling legislators toward ever greater efforts to collect and centralize information and to regulate and direct activity' (Ferguson, 1984: 31). This contradictory character is of course mirrored by widespread public ambivalence about bureaucracy.

A large discourse on the nature and properties of bureaucracies exists. The work of Weber in conceptualizing the properties and importance of modern bureaucracy has been and remains dominant in shaping contemporary understandings (Gerth and Mills, 1946). Weber (1922, trans. 1968) predicted that the bureaucratic mode would supplant other organizational patterns owing to increasing complexity and specialization in society and because of its 'technical superiority' over other forms such as communal types of organization. It was, in Weber's view, an 'ideal type,' that is, a model whose characteristics are well suited to its uses. Weber characterized bureaucracy as consistent with rationality, which, of course, is highly valued in our society. The bureaucratic organization is goal oriented; as such, it is designed both to identify goals and to eliminate conduct and activity not suited to meeting those goals. The organization is impersonal, a fact to which individuals often react negatively. However, in providing for the separation of the office from the individual, bureaucracies make possible the pursuit of goals regardless of the personal fates of particular individuals. Bureaucracy is also routinized, a design through which the relations of people to one another can be simplified and regulated. These features of bureaucratic organization, in other words, provide predictable methods of ordering and stabilizing a world that might otherwise be chaotic and unstable.

Many sociologists have viewed these characteristics as positive, describing bureaucracy, for instance, as 'that mode of organizing which is peculiarly well adapted to maintaining stability and efficiency in organizations.' (Frances and Stone, 1956). They point to the importance of predictability in planning for the future and of the need for orderly change. However, serious and penetrating critiques of bureaucracy have also emerged, taking into account issues of power, class, gender, and race. Weber himself pointed out that the objective discharge of rules, which is the prime virtue of the bureaucratic form, implies an organization 'without regard for persons.' Thus, the more perfectly a bureaucracy develops, the more 'dehumanized' it becomes (1922, trans. 1968: 975). Furthermore, bureaucracies in modern society have the means to impose what Foucault (1977) refers to as 'disciplinary power' onto individual and collective life. The structure of bureaucracy is pervasive, requiring attention to it by every individual. The character of bureaucracy in modern societies allows the inculcation of bourgeois virtues such as punctuality and rationality into vast areas of social life and organization. Provisions for entry into private life are made not only through repressive means but through discourse; together, repression and discourse provide means for the imposition of bureaucratic values not only inside organizations but in every sphere of life, including the private home (Ferguson, 1984: 33). Thus, bureaucracies have special uses and meanings in relation to poor and subjugated populations. As we shall see, the issue of child neglect has come to be organized by this administrative, rational approach that provides orderly procedures for regulating the private family lives of particular populations.

Bureaucratic methods of work organization also have a highly fragmenting effect. As Braverman (1974) convincingly shows, the introduction of 'Taylorism' into the workplace has effectively separated the conceptualization of work, carried out by the upper levels of management, from its execution by workers. As this separation occurs, efficiency of production as perceived by managers, who are attuned to processes originating outside the immediate setting, comes to order and in fact necessitates further divisions of labour, so that each worker has only a small part in creating the final product. Furthermore, because workers are separated from the conceptualization of the final product and its purposes, they are not positioned to see or evaluate the whole of the work process. Braverman's analysis was centred on factory and office work, but the social service delivery system shares some of these characteristics. Although social workers are supposed to be 'professionals' and thus to bring to their work ideas applying to specific clients, the overall goals, organization, and planning of the work are established at management levels and are coordinated to social and economic processes upon which they are dependent to some extent. Social workers, as Cohen and Wagner (1982) observe, are forced to sell their labour in agencies and institutions over which they have little or no control. Caseload size, 'production standards,' and other elements of work organization present the worker with an already fragmented and hierarchical context within which to carry out professional activity.

Social work, along with other fields of administrative practice, has 'redefined the relations of citizen to the polity' (Ferguson, 1984: 33). Additionally, social work brings together administrative technique with 'therapeutic intentions' intended to change people, and diagnostic categories such as child neglect are staple features of this bureacratic change process. For social work, the clientele available for change have usually been the poor. Categories are created and sustained as a feature of the orderly processes of bureaucracies, brought into play, as Ferguson argues, in order to 'normalize' the poor, with an intended result of ordering social life in a way that addresses identified problems. Through the techniques of bureaucratization, which provide for 'problem identification' and for the creation of categories ordering their solutions, service to individuals can be provided without disrupting existing class relations.

These purposes are captured in an apparatus referred to by some feminists (Fraser, 1989) as the 'juridical-administrative-therapeutic state apparatus' (JAT). This concept both captures and updates Althusser's conception of the state[4], pointing as it does to modern legal and medical methods for conveying ideology and repressing particular populations. Fraser describes this apparatus as the linking together of a 'web' of institutions and practices that translate political issues concerning the interpretation of people's needs into legal administrative and/or therapeutic matters. Through this apparatus, the compliance of clients is ensured. The concept of the 'client' is important in identifying the underlying purposes of the JAT. Clients, according to Ferguson, are 'those who must interact actively with bureaucracies upon which they are dependent but over which they exercise little or no control' (1984: 123). This definition is quite different from either the 'consumer' or the 'helpee' ideas so often presented in social work discourse, different because Ferguson refers so explicitly to relations of power and control between individuals and organizations. Through the relations of the JAT and its clients, 'rational bureaucratic control can be and has been extended into the private family, operating to order and control work processes and to rationalize production' (Ferguson, 1984: 48).

THE CHILD WELFARE BUREAUCRACY

The child welfare setting displays all of the major features of bureaucratic organization. This fact in itself creates a profound contradiction, for it is within this most rational and objective of organizational forms that some of the most sensitive and emotional issues of family life are judged and determined. In the context of the bureaucratization that has occurred over the past few decades, child welfare work has become a highly fragmented process, with each worker performing only a small piece of the work involved in 'processing' any one case or client. Child welfare also presents itself as one component in a web of organizations characterized by Fraser as the JAT, that is, it is linked through its practices to other institutions and organizations that share juridical, administrative, and therapeutic purposes.

The beginnings of hierarchical arrangements in child welfare were structured into the first legislation (Jones and Rutman, 1981; Farina, 1982). J.J. Kelso was a crusading journalist who became the most prominent leader of the child-saving movement in Canada in the latter decades of the nineteenth century and who later became the first child welfare administrator in Canada. At the beginning of his life as the 'Superintendent of Neglected Children,' he had little budget and no staff to administer. In fact, he personally conducted investigations of individuals and families in Toronto, especially at the beginning of his tenure as superintendent. Later, he recruited volunteer friendly visitors, whose work he supervised, and the beginnings of a child welfare bureaucracy were established. By 1901 there were thirty children's aid societies in Ontario alone, for which Kelso was administratively responsible. Manitoba passed legislation modelled on Ontario's in 1898, followed by British Columbia in 1901. Eventually, as other provinces as well as the territories developed similar legislation, provisions were made for child welfare departments or societies based on hierarchical arrangements (Sutherland, 1976; Farina, 1982).

During the early part of this century, most social welfare investigations were carried out by friendly visitors. By the 1920s, however, the beginnings of professional casework were developing. As in other professions, on-the-job supervision of the efforts of these workers was seen as an integral feature of appropriate professional development, with the result that another level of management was added to the casework process. By the 1950s, when bureaucratic life in North America had become an unquestioned fixture, the larger child welfare departments and agencies had begun to create more complex hierarchical arrangements. These arrangements reflected gendered divisions of work, with men assuming the majority of management positions, while women continued to monopolize the 'front line' of personal service delivery (Swift, 1995b). Horizontal specialization also occurred as agencies expanded in size and scope. Task differentiation involved the addition of experts in child abuse, adoption, case intake, and service to special age groupings such as adolescents.

In addition to these hierarchical and specialized work arrangements, child welfare organizations have become part of a larger service structure. They do not operate as separate social entities, but are tied to an 'interlocking organizational network' (Ferguson, 1984: 132), which as Piven and Cloward (1982) note is lodged in all levels of government and outside government as well. This network, or JAT to use Fraser's idea, includes the educational system, health facilities, welfare and housing authorities, and courts and law enforcement agencies. A major task of child welfare workers is to help coordinate relations among these various institutions, using individual clients as the focus of organization.

'The management of the modern office,' Weber (1922, trans. 1968: 957) observed, 'is based upon written documents (the 'files').' The functioning of all bureaucracies indeed relies upon documents, which serve to order work internally and to connect the parts of the organizational web with each other. In documents 'facts' are worked up and conveyed from one member or one setting to another. However, 'facts,' as Dorothy Smith (1973) says, are not what actually happened. Rather, an actuality is worked up to conform to and represent requirements of the setting. The primary documentary practices of child welfare appear as records and files about specific clients. The original case records involved in child welfare work were 'complaint books,' ledgers upon which were recorded incoming complaints about particular families and, in a few words, the outcomes of the ensuing investigations (Metropolitan Toronto Archives). During the 1920s, as social work professionalized itself, record-keeping became substantially more sophisticated, and process recording came into use. Process recordings were a means through which observations of workers were recorded, often by hand, into the files of particular clients. Workers recorded, by date of contact, detailed descriptions of the clients and their homes, the workers own impressions, and their recommendations on an ongoing basis. Often these records ran into the hundreds of pages, and they provided a glimpse into very intimate aspects of private family life (Swift, 1995a). Because they are chronologically ordered and so detailed, these accounts give the appearance of presenting 'the truth' about families. Later, as the 'social work assessment' was developed, many agencies turned to a more analytical type of recording, simply dating and numbering client contacts and recording an analysis of the client's situation and prospects. This approach is now generally seen as more professional. Social work agencies, like all modern organizations, have computerized their systems of documentation (Thomas et al., 1974; Richey, 1977; Gandy and Teperman, 1990). Attempts are made not only to organize and retrieve material more efficiently but to employ computers in decision-making processes. Any approach to recording requires that conceptual procedures be used to create 'factual' accounts. When these procedures distort reality, they are ideological in the sense described in Chapter 2. Many social work accounts fit this description, as Chapters 4 and 5 show.

One powerful tie between child welfare organizations and the social processes of the larger society is the funding process, through which social priorities are made concrete. From its inception as an organized and legislated arena of social welfare, child welfare work has been allotted a very slender portion of social resources (Jones and Rutman, 1981). Child welfare services are currently funded by provincial governments, with additional Canada Assistance Plan (CAP) funding from federal sources. Relationships between the provinces and the agencies within their jurisdictions vary, as do the funding formulas used. One generalization that can be made, however, is that there is never enough. Insufficient funds are the cry of every agency, and calls for substantial increases during every budget process are inevitable. A central and ongoing issue is the question of funding for 'prevention' programs. As in other social services, a child welfare lobby exists to promote the idea of preventive approaches to child welfare issues. As Cohen and Wagner (1982) note, the workers themselves, who usually have little effective input into funding decisions, are often significant members of such lobbies. The so-called band-aid approach, which addresses presumably preventable crises, is decried by lobbies, and regular efforts are made at all levels for a redistribution of funds, plus additional funds, for the purpose of providing needed resources to families before problems reach desperate proportions. With few exceptions, however, this is not done, for agency administrators invariably find existing budgets can barely stretch to cover the services needed to handle the already existing caseload, and politicians rarely see child welfare as a priority.

Ferguson (1984) explains this outcome, which is in fact common to social services generally, as the result of organizational relationships. In service organizations, she suggests, actual delivery of service to clients is a secondary matter in funding accountability. Of more importance is evidence that the behaviour of clients is controlled and that secure links to other related organizations are maintained. Administrators are conscious of their need to serve as resources to other institutions and of the reciprocal nature of this service. In child welfare, managers play a role in the smooth functioning of the organizational web, regularly mediating disputes or differences between front-line workers representing different organizations and attending quickly to complaints about service from outside the agency. Workers are thus presented with a contradictory reality. They operate primarily from the perspective of their own organizational mandate, but invariably find the resources inadequate to the task. Operating as they do from the perspective of a caseload, their view of the overall 'web' of organizational relations is obscured.

CHILD WELFARE WORK

The characteristics of modern bureaucracies and of social service bureaucracies, outlined above, are common to child welfare agencies across North

Figure 3.2
Organizational Production of Cases

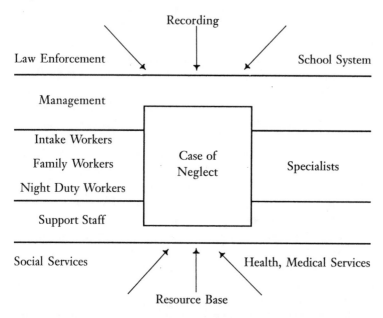

America, and they result in work settings that are easily recognizable to anyone who has been employed in the field of child welfare. Figure 3.2 shows the complexity of organization required to produce an authorized case of child abuse or neglect. From the organization's point of view, these processes are more or less orderly; from the perspective of the worker, activities on individual cases are subject to the fragmented and segmented processes characteristic of modern organizational life. Sequences are easily broken, effects separated from efforts. A brief review of work organization, with its hierarchies, specializations, and complicated sequences, shows how this fragmentation occurs.

Virtually all child welfare agencies and departments are organized on a hierarchical basis. Typically, the 'front-line' workers who deal directly with families and children in care are organized into teams of six or seven workers, assigned to handle cases in a specific geographical area. Teams have a manager, team leader, or supervisor who may also carry cases but whose main functions are managerial. Leaders assign cases, supervise the workers' activities and recording vis-à-vis these cases, and ensure that in-house policies are carried out, including both personnel issues (such as overtime hours) and procedural issues (such as intake and case closing). They also provide an information conduit between workers and upper level management, and they may have some hiring and firing authority. In larger organizations, other tiers of management may exist to develop organizational plans, ensure effective linkages with other institutions, and supervise the activities of the first-level supervisors. Every organization has a director, and many have boards of directors to whom the top manager answers and who have final authority for decision making.

In addition to this hierarchical structure, there is usually some specialization among workers. In some organizations, workers are divided into 'family workers' who work with families in their own homes, and 'children's workers' who work with foster families and the children placed with them. Often, intake is a specialized job. Intake is the gatekeeping function, the point at which it is determined whether a family will become an open case, will be referred on to another service, or will be closed. In larger child welfare organizations there will also be staff who specialize in various tasks such as adoptions or abuse investigations. Sometimes agency experts on abuse may occupy positions such as 'coordinator,' and they may have special authority to supervise and make decisions when cases are seen to fit into their mandate. In addition, there may be child care workers, homemakers, and other non-social work support staff who are available for assignment with particular families. Complaints received after regular office hours are handled by night duty workers. Serious complaints, such as abandonment, are investigated immediately, often in company of the police, and children may be apprehended and taken into care as a result. The night duty workers pass a report on to the family's regular worker, or to an intake worker if the case is new, the following morning.

Front-line social workers are assigned cases by their supervisors in accordance with such criteria as their existing workload, experience levels, and special interests. Agencies usually have norms or rules for the number of cases workers are expected to carry. Frequently, the number is high, perhaps between thirty-five and fifty, and worker complaints about overwork and overtime are a staple feature of child welfare work. Issues such as overload can and do lead to transfer of cases between workers and/or closing of cases. Although individual workers may try to keep the needs and interests of a particular client in mind in making these decisions, such practices must in the final analysis conform to organizational requirements of efficiency in workload distribution, and they lead to additional fragmentation in the life of particular cases. Generally, there are systems, implicit and/or explicit, by which workers prioritize their caseloads and determine when, how much, and what kind of attention to give a family. Explicit systems include such devices as 'high risk' criteria, which may be used to justify the allocation of more than ordinary amounts of worker time and organizational resources. Since abuse, and especially sexual abuse, have become so prominent, these types of cases are often much more likely than neglect to be seen as high risk. Implicit systems for making such judgments involve discretionary but often widely shared criteria, such as the degree of threat that appears to exist for the child and the amenability of the parent to the help offered. However, all such systems give way when a case 'blows up.' This is a common term used to describe a situation that forces the worker, by virtue of the protection mandate, to drop other tasks and attend to the issues of a particular family. Thus, within the life of a worker's activity on a single case, the worker's attention to it will be unevenly applied and distributed in accordance with competing workplace demands. Frequent opening and closing of a particular case produces further fragmentation.

Workers also must keep track of work with and services offered to client families. Streat (1987) estimates that at least 25 per cent of worker time and agency dollars are spent on the requirements of recording. Most organizations have a great many different forms available to accomplish this tracking responsibility. A number of these deal with intake and transfer or closing of cases. Other forms deal with in-house matters including information on foster and adopting families, medical care of children in care, reports of apprehensions and of night duty activity, and requests for special resources and funding. There are also consent forms, which reference aspects of the legal and accountability systems to which workers are subject in their dealings with clients. Other forms deal with inter-agency matters, for instance, communications with relevant Native affairs staff and departments. A common complaint of front-line staff is the amount of 'paperwork' that must be done.

In addition to fragmented work practices within the organization, many jurisdictional divisions exist between it and the organizational context in which it operates. At each point of intersection, boundary issues exist. For instance, several child welfare agencies may exist in a given community. In some places, different agencies exist to deal with families of different religions or cultural groups. Furthermore, both boundaries and mandates are continually in flux, and workers must attend to these changes in the organizational environment. The recent trend towards developing Native-run child welfare agencies is an example. Where more than one agency exists in a community, strict protocols are usually developed concerning information sharing, jurisdiction, and rules for the transfer of cases between agencies. As noted earlier, child welfare organizations also relate directly to many other service and treatment organizations in their communities. Workers customarily cooperate with personnel of local schools, hospitals, public health, welfare, and housing authorities, and police. When a case is opened to a child welfare agency, staff of other institutions who are already involved with the client or who are thought to be needed by the client may work together with the assigned child welfare worker, and may in fact form a 'team,' sometimes involving the client, that meets together regularly to discuss goals for and progress of the client and to distribute tasks among the involved staff. Downey (1986) discusses organizational change as a further feature complicating social work agency life. Changes occurring as the result of factors such as government review, shifting funding priorities, and demographic trends all complicate the work process and contribute to fragmentation of work efforts.

Individual files are kept on all families about whom a complaint is received and investigated and for whom any service is provided, a universal practice in child welfare as well as in most other social services. The case opening is designated as 'intake.' Frequently, as examples in Chapter 4 show (Figures 4.1 and 4.2), cases are closed at intake, following relatively brief investigations to determine whether mandated action is required. In cases that remain open beyond intake, files typically contain information such as (1) intake forms and recording; (2) 'black book' notes and other recording prepared by assigned workers; (3) legal documentation; (4) correspondence and reports from other services; (5) forms tracking movement of children in and out of care and other resources provided. As files get used, documents may be reshuffled. It is not uncommon for files to be neither complete nor in perfect chronological order, making it sometimes difficult to locate information, especially in long-running cases.

When a case is closed, the worker is generally required to summarize the initial grounds for opening the case, the services provided, the client's progress, and the grounds or reasons for closing. These closing summaries are often the main early reading material of a worker who is new to a case. To get a sense of the case, workers often read back over all the closing summaries they can readily locate, because case closing is one of the few points at which workers are required to summarize the main issues and events of a case and its current status. Contested court summaries are another.

In general, workers have recently become more aware of the possibility of their files being closely scrutinized. Files may be used in court, 'verbatim': 'It's day by day by day and every bit of contact is spelled out,' as one worker said. In court, the file is on the witness stand and available for opposing counsel to see. Police may come into the agency to subpoena files for legal purposes, and workers are aware of this possibility. Furthermore, lawsuits before the courts have encouraged workers to feel they could get into trouble or even be sued as a result of particular kinds of recording practices. These issues cause workers to be careful in their recording practices.

'Black-book' recording is common throughout North America, a trend that has accompanied the increased legalization of child welfare. Black books are notebooks that workers carry at all times, as police officers do, in order to record details of family situations on the spot or soon after. These notes have considerable weight in court because of their immediacy. Workers feel they are operating under fairly explicit instructions concerning their black-book recording. They understand they are to focus on 'fact as opposed to conjecture.' 'Dates and times of contacts,' is the understanding of one worker, while another cites 'important stuff that you might have to repeat in court later ... something special ... something major that happened,' as the instructions for notetaking. These statements reflect the court process to which workers are carefully attuned. As they record, they also have in mind future workers on the case, as well as other personnel, such as supervisors, who will be reading their files. Because many people potentially have access to files, workers have legitimate concerns about appearing judgmental or leaving the wrong impression of a family as a guide to future work.

Neglect arises and becomes visible through the processes of a specific context, the child welfare agency or department. This organization carries with it historical meanings drawn from both legal and professional discourses and is organized around bureaucratic principles. The organization of child welfare not only express these generalizing processes but must continually be geared to them, for example, through funding mechanisms. Child neglect as an abstract concept is one that implies legal, professional, and organizational mandates. That is, invocation of the term through mandated sources provides the grounds for substantial and ongoing courses of action to occur. However, the legal and professional mandates frequently prescribe somewhat different courses of action and therefore produce contradictions for workers, an issue addressed in Chapter 8. The bureaucratic features of the setting provide for the production and administration of social categories such as neglect to become visible.

There are a great many functions and work sequences carried out within any one agency or department concerned with child welfare, and between child welfare and other organizations. Most of these functions are driven by organizational requirements rather than by the needs or problems of specific parents and children. To the extent that these functions are allocated to different staff, there will be fragmentation in the work process; furthermore, the number of personnel with whom the family has to deal may be quite significant – sometimes dozens of different staff from the child welfare organization itself and from related services have contact with a single family. The child welfare worker's time and energy are applied unevenly, and are often crisis driven.

Although there are specific and local differences of law, precedent, and organizational size and structure that lead to some variation in emphasis and procedure, the work processes through which cases of child neglect (and other kinds of cases as well) must pass are attuned to larger social processes. Consequently, the working up of a case as child neglect in any location resembles features of child welfare practice generally. This resemblance enables child welfare workers, and indeed most social workers, in North America to speak easily and knowledgeably about neglect (or abuse) cases and the handling of these cases with minor rather than major diversions to explain local issues and organizational forms. In the following chapter, the specifics of producing particular situations as cases of neglect in the organizational context will be examined.

PART 2 CHILD WELFARE WORK PROCESSES

Today's child welfare workers, mostly women, tend to be young, white, and middle class. More of them than in the past are well educated, with special training in social work and often specific training in child welfare, although a significant minority continue to work with little training or education.

The work itself is daunting. In relation to some other kinds of social work, a feeling of 'real life' pervades child welfare work. Workers do deal with life and death issues and with constant crisis. Child welfare workers must become quick-change artists, as plans are always going awry, witnesses disappearing, parents changing their minds. They must be flexible and unshockable as they try to assist people who are in emotionally charged and sometimes violent frames of mind. Reasonably enough, child welfare workers are often rather cynical about the 'system,' and whether 'it' really cares about children or families, given the low level of resources allocated to this work.

The circumstances of the work thwart efforts at reflection and careful planning. Workers come to be sceptical about theories, models, planning interventions, and treatment approaches, because the scene so often changes before plans can be thought through and applied in an orderly way. They typically operate out of noisy and active offices that afford little privacy. It is expected that workers will be constantly on the phone or going out on calls, with recording squeezed in between. Meetings, supervision, workshops, and nosy researchers round out the day. Overtime is a staple, and workers typically accumulate countless hours of compensatory time, which they are always planning to take 'someday.'

Naturally enough, workers are often anxious about their decisions – they know they are affecting people's lives. They worry about being really wrong, about being 'responsible' for an injury to or death of a child, and they dread seeing their own names in the newspaper in connection with some horrible mistake. Child welfare workers exhibit strong and genuine feelings for the children they try to help and for the parents of these children. They take the worry home, and try over and again to give parents another chance.

It is these overly busy, sometimes unprepared, youthful, and caring people who have generally been blamed for mistakes of the system. A substantial proportion of the rights debates occurring over the past two decades has revolved around issues of worker subjectivity, discretion, bias, and mistakes as the cause of problems in child welfare. No doubt more training, clearer guidelines, and more manageable workloads would improve performance. However, as the following chapters delineate, these workers operate in an arena fraught with contradiction, a milieu in which 'right answers' seldom exist.

The following section provides something of a guided tour of the conceptual and organizational terrain in which these workers operate. Reported are some of the ideas, instructions, contradictions, problems, decisions, demands, rules, feelings, and accountability structures facing social workers as they confront the question of neglect in the organizational milieu of child welfare. Attention is paid to the activities and reasoning procedures workers employ in order to manage their jobs. In contrast to much that has been written about child welfare workers, such procedures are not construed as right or wrong. Rather, this section seeks to examine underlying social processes which orient workers toward particular ideas, activities and decisions, and which in turn help to reproduce existing power relations of the society.

4

Chronic Dirt and Disorder: Producing a Case of Child Neglect

Recent research confirms that neglect cases remain the largest single category of cases processed in Canadian child welfare offices (Trocme and Tam, 1994; Federal–Provincial Working Group, 1994). For workers, this means that identifying and managing cases of neglect are important and time-consuming tasks, especially in the context of crisis-ridden offices previously described. Within a legal, professional, and bureaucratic context, workers try to apply their understanding of neglect in such a way that cases of 'actual neglect' are identified and treated, and that ordinary parental slips, aberrations of care, and problems that can be corrected are not 'mislabeled' as neglect. How do workers know who should be in and who should be out of the neglect category?

Social categories frequently appear in discourse as the 'formalized impersonal' accounts described by Dorothy Smith. In this kind of account, actual experience is selected and ordered in accordance with the 'grammatical, logical and causal connections' supplied by the discourse rather than being constrained by the connections of lived experience (Smith, 1983: 325). Categories thus contain within themselves implicit social 'instructions' for their understanding, instructions that allow specific instances and experiences to be appropriately matched to them or discarded. Through these processes a wide variety of human experience can be ordered and displayed in terms that are socially understandable and acceptable. The underlying social relations that generate and sustain a category are not always explicit, and they may become completely detached from the category as it appears to us, so that the character of the surface appearance is far different from these relations.

Much of child welfare work is organized around the problems of identifying and categorizing the experience of clients to determine its 'fit' with specific social categories. Through these 'cutting out' procedures families become identified as neglecting or abusive parents. Workers use various kinds of discourse in the process of clarifying the boundaries of relevant categories.

DISCOURSE: THE INSTRUCTIONS OF NEGLECT

One source of instructions for the categorization of cases is professional discourse. Discourse specific to child neglect is not extensive. In a 1975 review of the social work literature, Polansky found published work on the topic of neglect to be sparse, fragmented, and largely in the nature of 'think pieces.' As Hutchinson (1990) notes, discussion originates from several different professional sources, including the medical, legal, and social work professions. The main body of discourse is located in journals sponsored and read by members of these professions. Although emphasis differs, there is considerable overlap among the ideas conveyed by different professions, so that readers familiar with the issue can easily understand work originating from any of these sources. This body of work – including social work literature – is often drawn from the study of individual cases as they appear in child welfare and other social service agencies, in legal contexts, and in health settings. Descriptions that appear in this literature are usually based on the appearance of particular children and on the behaviours, attitudes, and lifestyles of particular parents (Hutchinson, 1990).

Formal definitions of social categories are a primary route through which 'instructions' for their understanding are conveyed in discourse. It is common for definitional debates to emerge about the meanings of categories, debates that represent a struggle for competing meanings to prevail. Neglect is no exception. An ongoing issue in discourse concerns the problem of defining neglect, and what Hutchinson (1990) refers to as 'significant disagreements' continue to exist. Probably the most important debate about child neglect over the past two decades is whether neglect should be defined broadly, so as to allow wide discretion in protecting children; or whether the definition should be narrow in order to protect parents and children from undue intrusion into their lives by authorities. As Hutchinson (1990) points out, professional discourse provides an arena for debate between legal scholars, who argue for narrowing the definition of neglect and thus the area of discretion available to social workers, and 'family law scholars,' who argue for a broad definition to account for local community standards and the effects of social structures in creating problems. A third group consists of advocates for children, who also encourage definitions sufficiently broad to justify a range of supportive activities on behalf of children.[1] Gil, for instance, proposed a definition that brings abuse and neglect together in a broad framework calling society as well as parents to account for both good and poor care of children: 'Abuse of children is human-originated acts of commission or omission and human-created or tolerated conditions that inhibit or preclude unfolding and development of inherent potential of children' (Gil, 1981: 295).

A closely related definitional issue is the question of whether definitions should specify good care or simply a minimum acceptable standard of care. Polansky, Bergman, and De Saiy (1972) and Polansky, Chalmers, Buttenweiser, and Williams (1981) opted for the former, on the basis that existing definitions were too dichotomized and too focused on determinations of poor care. Their Childhood Level of Living scale (CLL) was based on the idea of 'adequacy of caring.' It was designed to examine specific elements of care along a continuum from poor to excellent, in the arenas of physical, emotional, and cognitive care. This measure, which remains probably the most comprehensive available, allows for deficits in one area to be compensated for by strengths in another and for patterns of good as well as poor care to be identified. The impulse to explore elements of adequate care was initially seen as an important advance in the field. However, Polansky et al.'s measures have been criticized for class, cultural, and gender biases inherent in items included in the scale (Gordon, 1988; Swift, 1990). Also, the scale came to be seen as impractical for busy workers untrained in its use.

In keeping with the 'least intrusive' approach described in Chapter 3, the trend more recently has been towards definitions that identify a minimal standard of care. Craft and Staudt (1991) take the position that neglect should represent the minimum standard acceptable, not what is desirable. Hutchinson also opts for a narrower definition, arguing that definitions of maltreatment should be used to enforce social sanctions, 'not to enforce ideal standards of caregiving' (1990: 75).

Another related issue is whether the definition of neglect should be standardized or whether it should be flexible enough to allow for different community and cultural standards. Craft and Staudt (1991) favour standardizing the definition of neglect. Their study suggests that it is not primarily values or subjective factors that create differences in assessment standards, but exigencies of the work setting, such as available resources, caseload size, and the expectations of related institutions. A standard definition, they argue, would assist workers to make appropriate judgments even when it might be inconvenient from an organizational point of view. A different view is that the definition of neglect cannot be standardized because it does vary according to community norms. This 'community' may be a neighbourhood or a class or cultural group. Wolock's study (1982) demonstrates that such a variable definition is applied in actual practice. Her study shows that whether a particular type of care is seen as neglect depends on the kinds of cases and community characteristics represented on the worker's caseload. Taking the flexible view, Garbarino (1978) proposed that maltreatment of children be explicitly defined as the violation of community or scientific standards of healthy development of children.

Yet another arena of debate is whether determinations of neglect should focus on parents or on children. Historically, in both legislation and in practice, the primary focus of child welfare attention was on determining the appropriateness of parental behaviour (Swift, 1995a). In more modern versions of this approach, both actual and predicted parental behaviours may become crucial to definitions of neglect (Hutchinson, 1990). An alternate approach is to define neglect in terms of actual or potential harm to the child. Giovannoni and Becerra (1979) examined the views of both professionals and laypeople in response to vignettes of parental care. They found that the main criterion used in defining whether abuse or neglect existed was the seriousness of impact upon the child, and that this criterion was fairly consistent across groups. Trocme and Tam's research (1994: 16) supports this view, showing increased likelihood that a case will be substantiated if 'the presence of any form of harm or risk of harm' to a child is shown.

While these various approaches and opinions differ in important respects, all consult professionals for their opinions of what constitutes neglect. Consequently, in spite of debates in discourse, we may expect substantial overlap between the understandings of professionals working in the field and formal definitions found in the research literature.

Another source of instructions concerning neglect is based on published evaluation and program research, often written by professionals working in the field (Swift, 1988). Each project requires that an operational definition of neglect be developed, a procedure generally resulting in a range of variations on the traditional theme of 'omission.' Some of these definitions, like the research they are part of, are relatively informal, often involving reference to both adult behaviour and child well-being. Such a definition of neglect is provided, for instance, by Hall et al. (1982): 'There are parents who continually fail to provide for their children's needs, and usually in many ways. These failures eventually affect the child's health and/or development adversely. Characteristically, these parents do not feel guilty over their omissions, and often simply fail to recognize the harmful consequences of the chronic neglected state of their children' (p. 6).

This definition, written in lay terms, captures ordinary child welfare understandings about neglect. The notions of chronicity, of repeated failures by parents to provide, and of eventual detrimental effects upon children are central to this common conception of neglect. Stokes (1985: 53) emphasizes these features of neglect in a discussion of legal definitions: 'Neglect is really a pattern of unacceptable child-rearing practices which have a subtle but devastating effect on the child's physical growth and development.' In these two definitions, an important feature of everyday understandings of neglect can be seen in the causal connection established between 'chronicity' of parental behaviours and the eventual effects of these patterns on children, an understanding different from the rather dichotomized approach often taken in academic discourse.

Generally agreed to in discourse is the difficulty of defining a category that in effect names the absence of something, or many things, considered important. This problem is commonly approached by creating subcategories of various types of neglect. Based on her study of child welfare records in Boston in the first half of this century, Linda Gordon (1988) suggests that in practice, neglect has been divided into two categories, physical and moral. Physical neglect includes lack of supervision, dirtiness, lack of proper food and clothing, and lack of attention to needed medical care. The early reformers focused attention on the first three items, and especially the supervision issue, which were visible and easily documented. By the 1920s medical neglect had become a prominent reason for child welfare intervention, according to Gordon (p. 121), whose American-based study is among the very few historical examinations of the issue. Moral neglect involved deviation from sexual norms; deviation from norms of proper family life such as frequent alcohol abuse; and the promotion of 'unchildlike' activities.

Rose and Meezan (1993) track nine specific subcategories of neglect. These are inadequate food, clothing, and shelter; inadequate supervision or outright abandonment; inadequate medical care; inadequate education; moral fitness of the parent; the condition of the home; mental or physical capacity of the parent; inadequate emotional care; and exploitation. Of these, according to Rose and Meezan, moral fitness is declining in importance, while emotional care is escalating as an issue noticed and commented upon by staff. They argue that among major academic contributors to the literature of neglect only Young (1964) focuses on the condition of the home as a type of neglect; however, Polansky et al.'s CLL scale suggests otherwise, emphasizing as it does many specific aspects of care of the home. Somewhat contradictorily, Rose and Meezan themselves see the subcategory of physical care – food, clothing, shelter – as producing the greatest consensus among researchers as an item of importance in defining neglect. This, they say, is because of the 'almost universal agreement that physical care is the responsibility of parents and that the absence of such care has consequences for the child' (1993: 281–2).

Writers dealing with the contemporary scene, including Rose and Meezan, generally offer subcategories consistent with items mentioned in legislation, a practice that reminds us of the overlap among professional sources of discourse. Falconer and Swift (1983) suggest these subcategories to Canadian workers: physical, medical, educational, supervision and guidance, and abandonment. These are issues that often appear explicitly in provincial legislation. In a rather more colourful version of these same items, a standard American text by Kadushin describes neglect in these terms: 'a child living in filth, malnourished, without proper clothing, unattended, and unsupervised' (1967: 210). The criteria for neglect provided by the American Humane Association (1966) are described by Polansky et al. as the 'collective wisdom of fellow professionals' (1972: 34). Heading this list of criteria is 'a child that is malnourished, ill clad, dirty, without proper shelter and sleeping arrangements.' This description of physical neglect is followed by lack of supervision, lack of medical care, denial of love, failure to attend school, exploitation, emotional disturbance, and exposure to unwholesome circumstances – again, issues commonly mentioned in both American and Canadian legislation.

Common to these subcategories of neglect, as Rose and Meezan note, is a focus on aspects of physical neglect as a first concern. This concern is mirrored in practice; as we will see, it is usually the traditional physical signs of neglect that predominate in both case records and in workers' talk about neglect. However, emotional issues have begun to take the stage in recent years. The most dramatic of these is 'failure to thrive,' usually described as an unexplained growth deficit in young children. Discourse in the medically oriented journals is centrally preoccupied with this issue, one which blends physical problems and emotional harms (Ohlson, 1979; Weston and Collaton, 1993). Another concern in the literature is emotional neglect (Whiting, 1976; O'Hagan, 1993). This type of neglect is an extension or replacement of moral neglect, according to Gordon, but a more 'psychological and scientific' category than moral neglect. The term 'emotional neglect' has been in use by social workers since the 1950s, was codified by 1960, but has eluded the specificity required for wide legal usage (Gordon, 1988: 162). Polansky et al. brought emotional neglect to the forefront as a child welfare issue in their CLL scale; 36 per cent of the items in this measure concern emotional or cognitive care of children (Gordon, 1988: 163).

Other sources of information in discourse are the 'instructions' provided by case examples. In discourse, neglect is characterized by contradictory and sometimes competing presentations of reality. Attempts to define and or argue for particular definitions of neglect are usually written in formal, scholarly language. However, it is not at all unusual that scholarly articles include descriptive passages that not only describe and dramatize issues but also reflect the disorderly way that subcategories of neglect present themselves in everyday situations. The focus and force of such descriptions provide clues not only to content but to the standard of care we are intended to notice and recognize as a real and valid instance of the category. Polansky et al., for instance, illustrate neglect through provision of a case example involving two babies, six and eighteen months old, found alone in an unheated shack, with 'their soiled diapers literally frozen to their skins' (1972: 29). Young (1964) provides this illustration of neglect: 'the baby whose hands were so crusted with dirt that he could not move his fingers.' Kadushin's illustration involves three young children left alone in a parked car for several hours, '... dirty and unkempt, cold and hungry, poorly clothed and in need of medical care' (1967: 212).

Another example in the same book demonstrates how subcategories defined as discrete items in discourse might appear in an actual case situation: 'Responded to a domestic disturbance where drinking parents had been fighting. Children were frightened and appeared to be abused by parents. The home was in disorder' (p. 212).

For workers, such a description captures the ambiguities that formal definitions seek to elude. Seldom does a single subtype of neglect present itself so persuasively that 'neglect' can be declared on the spot. Both descriptive and definitional material legitimate complexity of the category and provide images suggesting that several basic necessities must be withheld for the category to be properly invoked.

Descriptive material provides another instruction in its focus on chronicity. Malnutrition, poor housing, and crusted dirt do not materialize in a day or a week, but rather are conditions of a child's ongoing circumstances of living. Polansky and many others specifically characterize neglectful mothering as a chronic condition. Polansky et al. refer to neglecting mothers as having a 'syndrome' of 'apathy-futility' (1972). Young refers to these mothers as being in a state of 'confused inertia' characterized by 'inner disorganization' (1964: 38). These characteristics suggest chronicity, a way of life, a recognizable pattern. These descriptions provide instructions for recognizing neglect as involving physical signs, often dramatic in character, chronic patterns of disorder, and often a mixture of subtypes, all of which implicate parents. Of course, the social contract between parents and the state provides for and in fact instructs us

to make this connection. It is 'parents' after all who are charged with the re
sponsibility to provide basic necessities, including 'proper food, suitable
clothing, a sanitary place of shelter, general care and supervision and reasonable protection from harm' (Stokes, 1985).

NEGLECT IN EVERYDAY CHILD WELFARE WORK

How do workers make sense and make use of these debates, arguments,
research findings, and professional viewpoints in their everyday work? This
section explores clues to the ideas, understanding, and directives workers
absorb and employ in their daily work. In everyday practice, the tasks of
child welfare workers are to find order in the disorderly lives of real people
and to determine whether the order they find provides a sufficient fit with
categories mandated through child welfare legislation. Workers base their
investigations on the assumption of parental responsibility. Knowing, however, that lapses may occur in any and every family, the task is to determine
how many and how serious are the lapses that justify categorizing the case as
one of neglect. This is accomplished through the selection and ordering of
'facts' about particular families, procedures informed but certainly not controlled by the discourse.

Dirt and Disorder

In both speaking and recording, issues of dirt and disorder are often in the
forefront of the way workers think about child neglect (Swift, 1990). Although Rose and Meezan (1993) state that the condition of the house is un-
important in formal definitions of neglect, workers quite commonly notice
and record details of dirt and disorder in the house, details mirrored in discourse, and they associate these details with neglect: 'The case was typical
neglect. You know, the picture [in the literature] of how the house looked, it
was this one ... The carpeting had been totally destroyed because of all the food
that had been dropped on it, walked over, vomiting, all that sort of stuff.'
    Lack of cleanliness in the household is noted explicitly and often in files,
frequently in the notes of night duty workers who see the families only
briefly and who consider it part of their job to document those items that
may provide later evidence in a case of neglect. Details noted range from the
untidy to the unhealthful:

Clothes strewn about, onion peels, stale bread, and assorted garbage on the floor,
dirty dishes on kitchen counter and sink and spilled foods on the stove.

Kitchen dirty, bathroom smelled of urine, toilet plugged, very unsanitary. Remainder tidy but needs a good cleaning.

In keeping with instructions from discourse and legislation, workers also often note and record the physical condition of children:

Kids appeared neglected. Baby soaked, not changed for some time, reeks of stale urine. No diapers.'

[The children were] absolutely filthy. There were sores on the younger child and his underwear had fallen down ...Borderline physical neglect as evidenced by improper clothing, minor medical neglect and children not kept clean.

In the scrum of everyday activity, workers' descriptions of neglectful conditions often present a mix of subcategories in the same way that case examples in discourse do: 'Baby's diaper is dirty, needs bath. Mattresses on floor, dirty sheets. Parents admit drinking today, several empty beer bottles around. Mom looks like she has been beaten up.'

In this typical example of recording, the dirt and disorder characteristic of physical neglect appear, as well as evidence suggestive of lack of supervision and exposure of children to 'unwholesome' circumstances. Because readers of these files are closely acquainted with legislation and at least indirectly knowledgeable about the discourse of neglect, they are easily able to understand these 'facts' as representing subtypes of the category. However, it is not uncommon that such descriptions begin with references to physical characteristics of the house and children, regardless of the many other and serious problems that may be identified. It is also typical that other social categories are not invoked in an attempt to explain the physical evidence. In the example above, domestic violence, depression, alcoholism, and chronic poverty are problem categories that could provide additional or competing explanations for the visible conditions described. The worker's mandate, however, is to determine the existence of neglect, and the recorded details are intended to provide evidence of its existence.

Concern for effects of dirty living environments on these children comes through in workers' talk about them: 'You wouldn't be inspired to do any homework if you were Jim ... you wouldn't be inspired to take care of yourself or your home.' Paradoxically, however, the issues of cleanliness that may appear paramount in files are often not pursued by workers as central issues in the case, even when descriptions might indicate potential health threats. Realistically, little can be done to enforce an improved standard of cleanliness on an ongoing basis, and many workers are reluctant to impose what they consider to be their own standards of cleanliness on clients. Why, then, do these observations remain so prominent in child welfare work? From the organizational perspective, documented instances of dirt and disorder serve an important purpose, which is that of warranting the course of action taken by the agency. Complaints of unclean home conditions, as Figure 4.2 demonstrates, can be used to help justify intake investigations, an activity representing an 'intrusion' into private family life. In addition, documenting clean conditions of home and children can provide some of the grounds for case closing, as in this example of a closing summary: 'Homemaker put in, situation seen as stable. Mom is on the list for housing, children appear very well cared for. Home well kept. Day care in place.'

It is in fact quite common that evidence about order and cleanliness is used in combination with other evidence to justify decisions. It would not be correct to say that dirt and disorder are always necessary to warrant agency activity on grounds of neglect, for in some cases these are not issues. However, in many cases categorized as neglect, references to dirt and disorder are used to justify activity. Should the agency's activity with relation to specific families ever come into public question, such evidence can be brought forward from the files as justification for the chosen course of action. Meanwhile, case examples found in discourse serve as continuing confirmation that physical conditions of the house and children are important signs of neglect. Simultaneously, this image in discourse is continually reconfirmed by the repetition of descriptions in case files characterizing neglectful homes and families as disordered and dirty.

A second reason for noticing and documenting details of dirt and disorder is that concrete evidence over the long term is necessary to establish a case of neglect in court. Chronically dirty conditions of the household, parents, and children are seen as visible signs of undesirable parental behaviour. If a neglect case comes to court, these 'facts' will be used as one piece of evidence of the parent's neglect: 'In a neglect case ... the basis of your case is really visits over an extended period of time ... [so] you ought to have that fairly well documented. You know, there was garbage on the floor, there was broken beer bottles, there was dog poop on the floor that wasn't picked up for a long time.'

The ever present possibility that a case of neglect will eventually arrive in the courtroom means the worker's attention must regularly be directed to any observable evidence. As experienced workers know, 'soft' evidence such as 'child seemed unhappy' does not help to establish a case in court – on the contrary, such evidence may bring the competence of the worker into question. Although a child's need for nurturance, support, supervision, and guidance may be at the heart of the worker's concern, it is dirt and disorder that provide the physical, observable evidence that a problem exists. Thus, the underlying legal requirements for proper documentation of evidence ensure that cleanliness issues will continue to appear frequently in child welfare files. The repetitive nature of this documentation also continuously reconfirms the connective found in discourse between parent responsibility and the conditions of the home and children. Each documented instance connects these conditions, at least implicitly, to the character of the person responsible for meeting basic needs.

Neglect Incidents

Typically, neglect cases are perceived as non-emergencies. The very nature of the typical case is its chronicity, a characteristic that may render it low on the worker's list of priorities, given the crisis-ridden nature of the work. However, sometimes neglect cases 'blow up,' necessitating the worker's immediate response. Here is one worker's definition of a blow-up and its consequences: 'It means you have to act, and right away ... it also means the case changes direction, you are going to do something different at this point.'

Cases blowing up, in other words, provide the circumstances for immediate and substantial action in any open or potential case. Sometimes this occurs in cases perceived as neglect, as when children are left unsupervised or parents are temporarily unable to care. Among the most common of neglect issues is lack of supervision. Young children found alone, children left with 'inappropriate babysitters,' and instances of inadequate supervision because of alcohol or drug abuse by parents are staples of child welfare activity. These 'neglect incidents' frequently result in the apprehension and placement of children in foster or other alternate care, at least until parents return and/or recover sobriety.

However, in the absence of such an emergency, neglect often takes a second seat to cases of abuse. Wolock and Horowitz (1984), in their phrase 'the neglect of neglect' describe very well the phenomenon through which abuse has become a high priority on child welfare caseloads, while neglect has slipped to the bottom of child welfare priorities. In recent years sexual abuse in particular has become a high priority issue in child welfare, as evidenced by the explosion of research dollars for this topic. In the organizational setting, protocols are in place to ensure that this high priority item will be acted on by agency staff. These procedures are triggered by the word 'disclosure,' referring to a child's statement that he or she has been sexually assaulted. Disclosures are likely to produce immediate and lengthy investigations, including interview of the child and parents, possible placement of the child, and often considerable counselling within the family.

No comparable triggering phrases can propel workers into a complex sequence of bureaucratized activities when the case is classified as neglect – a child does not 'disclose' that the house is dirty or that parents have been drunk or rejecting. Provincial protocols developed to deal with child welfare issues focus primarily on abuse, and often on sexual abuse, while cases of neglect remain a background issue (Federal–Provincial Working Group, 1994). In fact, 'neglect incidents' may provide workers with their only chance to act decisively in neglect cases. Otherwise, the legal requirement of establishing evidence of chronicity ensures that the case, as well as the unhealthy conditions of the home, will have a long life. Given the busy and crisis-ridden character of the work, even neglect incidents may not be sufficient to keep a case open. Furthermore, such incidents will not necessarily warrant the worker's close attention if the case does remain open, especially if children are older. If such incidents recur many times in the same family without serious injury to the children, this recurrence may even come to be seen as an expected characteristic of the family. Indeed, because neglect is usually characterized as being of long duration, such a case may easily slip to the bottom of a worker's list of action priorities until a child is clearly put at risk.

Counting Pennies

In fact, the general direction of a neglect case is one of collecting evidence over time to establish that parents are unfit to care for children. One worker described the use of this evidence in preparing for a court case: 'So you have preparation of a number of witnesses, all the night duty people who have gone to the home, who will be subpoenaed, all the former workers will be subpoenaed ... you basically put all your pennies on the table and let the judge count them to see if you have enough.'

This 'counting' process helps us to understand workers' focus both in files and interviews on documenting discrete evidence, often physical in nature, that can be taken as symptomatic of neglect. It is important to notice that the documentary processes involved in file production do not explicitly mention work exigencies that affect the trajectory of the case. A worker's inattention to the case because of other priorities, for instance, either remains unseen or is shown as appropriately connected to case decisions. Case overload may show up as 'family stable, case closed.' The influence of a worker's high caseload or impending holiday on case decisions is virtually never disclosed. Files are 'about' families, not organizations. Such documentary practices detach the recorded activities of the family from the organizational context. The resulting descriptions produce an appearance that conforms to the in-

Figure 4.1
Progression: One Case

Intake	Referral Source	Identified Problem	Action Taken	Result
Initial December	Unknown. Emergency	Concerns re diet and family violence	Parents amenable to counselling	No neglect or abuse. Closed at intake
#2 Next August	Police	Older sibling in fight	No contact	Closed at intake
#3 October, 3 years later	Night Duty	Diet; unhealthy environment; drinking		No protection concerns. Closed at intake
#4 October, 4 years later	School	Concerns re adequate care	Child moved to aunt's	No problems. Closed at intake
#5 May, next year	Child to be admitted to care.	Child unwanted by any relations		Worker seeking admission to care

structions of discourse concerning the visible appearances of neglect and its ongoing nature, one suggesting that all problems originate within the family itself.

THE PRODUCTION OF CHRONIC CASES

While the surface appearance of neglect is one of chronicity, certain processes occurring in the child welfare agency underlie and contribute to this appearance. Intake, closing, and frequent case transfers are among these processes. Typical cases presented to me by workers show numerous examples of such processes occurring within the life of a single case. Figures 4.1 and 4.2 illustrate two slightly different examples of case progression. The figures show information drawn from files to help explain the sequence of events and, where available, reasons given by workers for particular decisions. However, as the case records demonstrate, reasons for particular decisions are not always perfectly clear.

Figure 4.1 illustrates a case involving one child. This case appeared at intake on five separate occasions, over a span of nine years. On none of the first four occasions had the case moved beyond intake to be assumed by an ongoing worker, while the fifth intake worker was planning to admit the child to care. This step would, of course, produce the need for an ongoing worker. In this latest instance, occurring when the child was thirteen, the case finally moved past intake because of the family's insistence that the child be taken into care. This case, in the words of the latest worker, typifies the 'natural progression of case files' in instances of neglect: 'There's a natural progression in files, in that we often will work with families, the case will be closed ... that same family will resurface again ... We do patchwork and then we close it and wait until it resurfaces ... That's what happens in child welfare, because we're overloaded.'

Here, the worker explicitly refers to an organizationally created effect of chronicity, achieved through repeated openings and closings of cases. Case opening suggests service needs, but the continual and speedy closings inform us that little service has been provided. Knowing this, the worker expects a later reopening. Underfunding of child welfare service is the most common explanation of ineffective child welfare service. A related explanation attends to a funding structure that favours payments for children in care but not for children living in their own homes. Linda Gordon (1988) entitles her chapter on neglect 'So much for the children after, so little before,' a reference to this funding pattern.

There is no doubt that funding arrangements are among the hidden realities underlying a case of neglect, a reality of which the worker is clearly aware but one which would not appear in any written record of the case. Instead the file records simply the events of the case, as they relate to relevant legal and bureaucratic purposes. However, as we will see in subsequent chapters, although funding issues do shape particular outcomes, neither underfunding nor the current structure of crisis funding provide adequate explanations for or solutions to the problems that exist in child welfare service delivery.

Another process underlying the appearance of chronicity is the fragmented nature of the work. Figure 4.2 illustrates a somewhat different kind of case, one involving substantial action over six or seven years. In addition to nine intakes, the progression of events shows a number of case transfer points and illustrates how a large number of different workers may become involved in a single case. In this instance, it is often the mother's change of address that occasions this number of juncture points in the case. Each new worker must become familiar with the case, get to know the family, and determine how to

Figure 4.2
Progression: Another Case

Intake	Referral Source	Identified Problem	Action Taken	Result
Initial	Unknown		No action	Closed on intake
#2 1 month later	Police	Child found abandoned		Mom returned to reserve; case closed
#3 3 months later	Self-referral	New baby – layette required		Closed on intake
#4 6 months later	Unknown	Possible failure to thrive		Mom returned to reserve; case closed
#5 18 months later	Police			Mom returned to reserve; case closed
#6 1 month later	Police	Child found abandoned	Child apprehended	
			Application for 6-month wardship	Application failed; case closed
#7 12 months later	Police	Violent destruction of property		Minimal care being given; case closed
#8 2 year later	Self-referral	Requesting relinquishment of new baby		Closed on intake
#9 1 year later	Night Duty	Mother drinking – children abandoned	Children apprehended	Returned after 2 weeks
			Children re-apprehended	6-month order of wardship
				Children returned
			Children re-apprehended	Application for permanent wardship sought

proceed. Workers are often reluctant to proceed immediately to court with a brand new case, preferring to use the skills they have been taught as social workers in the service of the client: 'Workers really feel we're in the helping professions, and by not offering any service, you don't feel like you're helping.' In addition, brand new workers sometimes feel they can correct the wrongs incurred by previous workers: 'I was fresh out of school. I'm not sure my co-workers agreed with the way I handled the case, but I had a lot of theories in mind I thought I could use.'

The professional ideals of workers, based on a helping impulse, can thus interact with the fragmented nature of agency service, to help produce a documentary effect of chronicity.

Figure 4.2 also illustrates the discontinuities for children apprehended by the agency. In this case, the children were apprehended on four occasions within a fifteen-month period and were placed in eight different foster homes during this same period. Judging from my own difficulty in documenting these moves from the file material, it would have been problematic for a new and busy worker to determine this case progression: 'Even under your very eyes [a case] that is seemingly just a difficult situation is turning into a chronic one ... There's three or four months in between where the worker's doing so many other kinds of things, then you go 'wait a minute, though. In the last year these kids have been apprehended five or six times' ... It's a cycle presenting.'

In this passage the worker describes how organizational workings of the agency operate beneath the surface of cases to help produce the effect of chronicity. The 'least intrusive' principle helps to generate this process, for it justifies repeated returns of children to their parents, based on the idea that agency intrusion should be limited to the minimum time required for protection. Long-term temporary orders of wardship and permanent orders are avoided for as long as possible, because they are the most intrusive procedures. As Figure 4.2 shows, return of children often leads also to periods of quiescence in the case, described in files as 'minimal care being given.' Common reasons why care improves are that the mother has had a rest and that she has been frightened by the apprehension and wishes to 'look good' to the authorities. In any event, improved care frequently leads to a further case closing, on grounds that the legal mandate for child welfare intrusion has ceased to apply. As most neglect cases illustrate, however, case closing does not mean the end of problems, but is rather the organization's mandated response to a period of minimal care. As one worker wrote in the file, 'case closed, pending more problems.'

In addition to case procedures, internal divisions of responsibility can affect case progressions. For instance, the perspectives of night duty workers and ongoing workers may differ substantially: 'Night duty service people would probably apprehend and go for permanent orders a lot sooner than we do ... They go out to the sniffing party ... and this lady was falling down drunk, where the kids were hiding behind a mattress in the corner of the room, where the man had passed out and the home was almost burned down ... Whereas you come in on Monday ... Mum is "oh, I'm sorry," and you're looking at another human being with problems. Your job is to help this human being, appreciate some of the things that're going on for her.'

Differences of perspective and responsibility, as this passage illustrates, help not only to prolong cases but to ensure that repeated instances of poor care will occur and eventually appear in files. The ongoing worker feels obliged to try again with the parent, knowing that alcohol and drug issues almost invariably reappear. The processes noted in this discussion are both hidden in written accounts of the case and are discontinuous, qualities that allow nobody to own the problems faced by these families. Indeed, geographical fragmentation can produce 'real estate' jokes among staff; by finding a troublesome family a 'nice home' in another district, the case can be closed by one worker, the responsibility passed on to another.

A further issue of service discontinuity is the attribution of its effects to the client. The sheer number of personnel involved in a case frequently comes to be presented as the failure of the client to benefit from service. One case summary, for example, shows children apprehended six times; three homemakers assigned to the case at various times; a variety of support services introduced; three intake workers, five different family service workers, and seven night duty workers at various times. This record was assembled and summarized as 'many services provided over a period of two to three years.' The service summary was then used to illustrate 'Mom's inability to stabilize' and offered as part of the evidence in support of an application for permanent wardship on the children. The main purposes of the record, after all, are to build a convincing case for wardship in court and to demonstrate that the agency has provided proper service. Evaluation of the actual value of services to the client is rarely done, and the effects of service overload and fragmentation are seldom documented.

NEGLECT FOR ALL PRACTICAL PURPOSES

In practice, the term 'neglect' cannot be captured, as the academic discourse attempts to do, in sets of abstract and unambiguous definitions. Rather, neglect is spoken about and thought about differently depending on the organizational and legal circumstances of the case. Although North Americans may well agree on what constitutes reportable neglect, exigencies of the work setting, as Craft and Staudt (1991) observe, result in differing decision criteria at different points in the process. The most common idea of neglect in practice is that of poor parenting behaviour over long periods of time, as signified by various commonly recognized circumstances. Physical neglect, signified by dirt and disorder, predominates in discussions and recordings because it provides concrete and visible evidence and because it can warrant entry, case opening, and ongoing activity. In practice, physical evidence of neglect is frequently merged with other subtypes via lists of possible evidence: 'House filthy, baby not changed, mom admits drinking.' Harm to children through neglect is difficult to establish in legal terms, because it is incremental, often invisible, and not directly observable as an outcome of parental behaviour. Harm in neglect cases has therefore come to be established largely through evidence of chronicity, a requirement virtually ensuring that cases – and suffering – will endure.

Another way workers think about neglect is the 'neglect incident.' In this situation, supervision rises to the top of the list as the item warranting entry, immediate action, and possibly a change in direction of the work. In these instances, children are often apprehended, although they may soon be returned. Even in such an instance, however, descriptions in files will usually include documentation of a physical nature to show effects of the problem and to provide evidence later in court. In order to warrant apprehension of children for a longer term, workers pursue evidence of recurring episodes of abandonment until they believe they have enough to make a case in court for a temporary wardship order, a process meaning that children may be abandoned many times before more intrusive action is taken.

Neglect is defined differently for purposes of case activity than for purposes of 'going for' an order of permanent wardship, a difference that represents a peculiar contradiction. If case activity indicates the substantiation of neglect, then the frequent openings and closings imply that neglect is something that comes and goes. However, for the courts, these very recurrences provide evidence of the existence of neglect. Workers are attentive to this criterion for establishing a legal case of neglect at every stage of a case. Workers know that judges will usually require a number of incidents and a certain amount of concrete evidence before making this determination. It is apparent that certain features of an agency's procedures and functioning underlie the appearance of neglect as a long-term phenomenon. The expected progression of cases, with many openings and re-openings; continual transfers; the specialized nature of the work; the organization of files so that information is geared to legal and organizational requirements; the professional inclination workers have to try again with each new client; and the anticipated requirements of family court judges all operate to ensure that cases of neglect will be long-running cases. However, this appearance of cases as ongoing comes to be attributed to the families themselves. The case record is designed, as Chapter 5 shows, to be about clients and their behaviour. The organizational underpinnings that allow and even make inevitable neglect as a long-term phenomenon become invisible in the process of case recording. Rather, these families come to be viewed as families with 'chronic and severe multiple problems' (Hall et al., 1982).

NEGLECT AND SOCIAL CLASS

Rather than taking for granted 'typical features' of social categories, the analysis directs us to examine underlying social relations that produce the appearance of these features. The chronic dirt and disorder that appear as symptomatic of neglect provide our example. It is important to remember that the category of neglect owes its existence to a set of class relations that allowed middle class reformers in the earlier stages of industrial capitalist development to apply legal sanctions to particular parents who occupied marginal positions vis-à-vis the larger economy. Reformers viewed these marginalized families, which were often headed by women, as unproductive, and they saw in them two potential threats, about which they were explicit. One was fear of the 'contamination' of their own children via exposure to the children of these families in the school system. The second was concern about the potential long-term expense to society of citizens poorly fitted out for productive membership in the labour force. Child welfare legislation provided the grounds for intervention into and rearrangement of these families, while simultaneously preserving the ideal of the private home and family for those who conformed to their own beliefs and standards.

The social relations represented by modern child welfare practices proceed from this history, which long ago validated chronic dirt and disorder in the household as the fault of individual parents and as grounds warranting entry into private homes. We see from the analysis how fragmented institutional processes continue to mediate and reproduce this class relation. If we examine for a moment the nature of these 'symptoms' of neglect, we see they are, generally speaking, characteristics of resource deprivation. The more or less continuous maintenance and supervision of clean and orderly homes and children requires labour, resources, and ongoing attention. Most of us slip up at times, but this does not constitute neglect, because neglect has been defined as multiproblematic and chronic. All but the most marginalized have access to some resources allowing eventual recovery – babysitters, relatives, bank loans, jobs, washing machines, a car, decent clothes, a cleaning person, occasional holidays, counselling, and therapy provide routes to at least minimal recovery. As we will see in later chapters, most families who become categorized as neglecting have virtually no access to these resources but must rely instead on agencies such as child welfare. However, work processes and procedures in child welfare, and no doubt other related agencies, operate to create repeated denials of outlay of resources. Case opening cannot be warranted simply by the need for resources but only by some demonstrated fit with ideas of what constitutes a mandated child welfare problem. Thus, cases are repeatedly opened and closed, and resources repeatedly given or denied, based on a determination of whether this fit currently exists. In the final analysis, ongoing outlay of resources relies on establishing chronicity, as evidenced by these repeated openings and closings.

Keeping in mind that the category of neglect is closely tied to ideas of family responsibility, we can see some important effects of this process. First, these processes of defining and fitting people to the category operate to select certain families for the category, while screening out most other families most of the time. Any single and discrete item associated with neglect could at some time be applied to virtually all families – whose child has not been filthy, hungry, or ignored at some time? Mothers with mental or physical health problems may sometimes have disorganized households. However, the category instructs us that single incidents, problems that can be solved with resources brought to bear by the family itself, serious but temporary problems in family functioning, and problems of working or middle class families that are treated through other institutions and thus have other labels attached to them, are all instances that are screened out by the instructions of the category of neglect. Screened in are problems of household and child care that appear in combination, that are generally characterized by dirt and/ or disorder, and that chronically reappear over time. These instructions work to ensure that the 'target group' of the category will continue, with a few exceptions, to be the most poor and desperate of families, and the evidence collected against them ensures that they will be seen as members of the unworthy poor. These processes help to render the 'home alone' family, seen in Chapter 1, an anomaly. Most occasional offenders either do not get caught or are able to make reparations. It is because of their inability to escape the authorities that we find them strange.

Second, institutional processes operate to reify this idea of neglect as a state of chronic dirt and disorder. The category is not static, as we shall see in subsequent chapters. New ideas of parenting enter the discourse and require that we continually readjust and add instructions to the category. However, certain basic instructions continue to apply, producing a category that appears reliable in locating and identifying particular kinds of problem parents.

Finally, in spite of the recent trend towards focusing on harm to the child as a criterion of neglect, the more usual focus of child welfare personnel is, by legal necessity, on the culpability of the parent. One reason neglect files are so distressing to read is that we see in them the dreadful conditions children endure during the lengthy period the state requires to establish evidence against their parents. Children are condemned to live like this not only because their parents are unable or unwilling to do better, but also because the only helping tool society has provided itself is to find parents guilty. While scholars debate the desirable definitional breadth of neglect, the actual standard of care enforced through the present system is desperately low – surely well below any minimum standard scholars would care to commit to paper.

5

Personality or Poverty? – Contradictory Views of Neglect

... The kind of definition a problem is given, and by whom, will in large measure determine the resulting actions taken to solve it. (Wolock and Horowitz, 1984: 531)

Poverty has always been a strong and recognized theme associated with cases of neglect. Nevertheless, the issue of neglect invariably resolves itself into one of personal problems. As Wolock and Horowitz point out, definition of problems is crucially connected to solutions. Identified social problems such as neglect must have credible definitions produced by credible people in order to justify outlays of public money for their solution or containment. As we saw in Chapter 3, there are two historic formulations of neglect. One, upon which legislation was originally based, posits parents as members of the unworthy poor. The second is a social formulation posing parents as confronting structural problems beyond their control. These remain the basic explanations of neglect in contemporary discourse. As Giovannoni (1982: 26) has posed the basic problem, 'Is "it" poverty or is "it" psychopathology?'

POVERTY AND DISCOURSE

From its inception, social work has been concerned not only with the poor but with the socialization of the poor. In its theoretical base, the profession has always linked explanations of poverty to ideas of 'a weakness of will and poverty of the spirit' (Loch, 1906, quoted in Jones, 1979: 74). Social work later drew on Freudian theory, which, as Jones notes, at least held out the hope of treating the apparent deficiences of the poor, whereas the moral legacy of the undeserving poor did not offer this route to improvement. Since the 1970s Polansky has been the foremost scholar studying neglect.

He approaches his topic from a psychoanalytic frame of reference, attempting to distinguish, within a low-income population, those characteristics that lead to adequate or inadequate care of children by their mothers. His 1972 study was undertaken in rural Appalachia. An attempt to replicate the findings in a low-income urban setting is reported in the 1981 study *Damaged Parents*. Both studies conclude that although poverty and social deprivation are important factors in neglect, the personality features of mothers are primary causal factors. This view is highly influential, and Polansky's findings have now entered the discourse as 'fact'; that is, his findings are taken for granted as true, and often reported without reference to their source.[1]

In fact, mother as the 'crucial variable' is the main theme in most writing about neglect. Role rejection (Kadushin, 1967), lack of nurturing knowledge (Jones and McNeely, 1980), immaturity of the mother (Young, 1964; Katz, 1971), and the poor nurturing of the mother herself (Hall et al., 1982) all appear as variations on this theme. While many researchers are concerned with establishing the main causal variables of neglect, they also contribute to the definition of the problem by framing it in personal and intrafamilial terms.

However, it is also well established in discourse that neglect is a phenomenon of poor populations. Pelton (1981), for instance, has convincingly argued against the idea that maltreatment of children is a 'classless' phenomenon. Horowitz and Wolock (1981), like Polansky, studied low-income populations to discover why some poor people are better parents than others. Unlike Polansky they find that poverty is the primary causal factor. Neglecting parents, they say, are the 'poorest of the poor,' and their 1980 study confirms these findings. Hutchinson (1990) confirms that the argument continues on into the 1990s. One of its permutations is the interactionist approach, which suggests that maltreatment of children is an outcome of the interaction between personal and situational factors, including poverty (Garbarino, 1978). Cohen (1992: 217) reminds us again of the confusion workers face in distinguishing between poverty and neglect: 'Many believe that children are permanently damaged at least to some degree by the *mere fact* of growing up in a home of abject poverty' (italics mine). Whatever the approach, virtually all authors concur that poverty is a factor almost invariably associated with child neglect.

Most research carried out on the issues of definition relies on a strategy of consulting professionals, or records produced by professionals, for their definitions. Furthermore, as noted in Chapter 3, the general direction of the discourse on neglect parallels and in fact has more recently been subsumed by the discourse on child abuse, in which the psychoanalytic and personal approach to definition and to the discovery of causal factors are emphasized (Breines and Gordon, 1983).

In summary, poverty is a strong theme common to all attempts to define neglect (Pelton, 1981). In spite of the pervasiveness of this relationship, poverty remains mysteriously in the background of most research efforts dealing with neglect, which are often preoccupied instead with the question of why some poor women neglect while others do not. Posing the research question in this way both excludes the non-poor from study and invariably reveals various personal problems of the neglecting mothers that are then posed as generalizable explanations. Attention is directed away from economic and social issues, as well as from the kinds of care children are subject to; instead we are led to consider how different poor women react to poverty. Personal change strategies become the obvious solution, and while most researchers also recommend that poverty be alleviated, these recommendations lack the supportive data required to force serious consideration.[2] The discourse, which draws heavily on professionals for its data, is strongly oriented towards the identification and treatment of personal problems. Some processes through which this effect is promoted in the everyday world of child welfare are considered in the following discussion.

A CASE STUDY

A child welfare agency studied for my research (Swift, 1990) serves as a case example to illustrate the disappearance of poverty and social problems in social work practice with neglecting families. The catchment area of this agency is characterized by poverty, social dislocation, and crime, and was seen by evaluators contracted to study the area to be socially and economically stressed in comparison with other areas of the city.[3] In that study, families in the area were found to be 50 per cent more likely to be poor than families elsewhere in the city. They were also 30 per cent more likely to live in poor housing, and 25 per cent more likely to be single-parent families headed by women. Data showed a fourfold increase in welfare applications by residents in the first half of the 1980s, going from 16 per 1,000 families to 61 per 1,000, a substantially greater increase than elsewhere in the city. By 1985 the incidence of welfare was 85 per cent higher in this area than in the remainder of the city. Provincial welfare, primarily serving the unemployable and single mothers, increased about 13 per cent in this area between 1982 and 1986. Housing also rated poorly, with 6.5 per cent of houses in the area requiring major repairs compared with 4.9 per cent for the city. This information suggests high levels of poverty for children as well as for

parents in this area. The area was in fact considered by evaluators to constitute a substantial part of the city's core of poverty.

Examination of the social and economic characteristics of the agency's client group showed that many of the most seriously vulnerable and disadvan-
taged families had become child welfare clients. Of the client families, 50 per
cent were Native people, although Native people were only 4 per cent of the
total population. Fifty-eight per cent were single-parent families, and of
these families 60 per cent had no working parent, and 68 per cent were
headed by a parent on welfare. At the time of the study, the population served
by this agency indeed represented 'the poorest of the poor' in the city.

In spite of the harsh material realities represented by these figures, virtually no 'social facts' appeared in the recorded file material examined for the
research study. Furthermore, virtually no connections were made in written
case material between the social and economic situation of clients and their
child welfare problems. Clients appeared in these files very much as they do
in case examples presented in the child welfare literature – as troubled, often
deficient individuals who have failed to care properly for children.

This agency is not at all unique in its recording practices. In most child
welfare agencies, 'facts' about clients are family and personal facts, not social
facts. The selection of information to be recorded in files screens out almost
all of the context of clients' lives, focusing on clients as individuals with intra-
psychic problems leading to neglectful care of children. In this sense, the
work practices of social workers are ideological in nature and outcome.

CASE FILES AS A SITE OF SOCIAL REPRODUCTION

Ideological practices, it will be recalled, have the character of reformulating
actual activities into abstractions, causing individual actors, their experiences, and their perspectives to disappear. Practices producing this effect
are not an idiosyncratic feature of this particular setting or of specific workers within it. Any child welfare setting is part of an apparatus or 'web' of
organizations, which requires particular kinds of information and work practices for its coordination. The practices of individuals in child welfare generally are both formed by and geared to this larger picture. Features of bureaucracy, as we have seen, shape this dialectic. For instance, bureaucracies
are based on rules, claimed as neutral and objective, while clients are seen as
subjective and biased. This dichotomized view, which assumes the objective
as superior, works to authorize as true what is said in files about clients.
Managers in the apparatus are the 'recognized experts of the poor,' entitled
to 'make serious speech acts,' which clients are not (Ferguson, 1984). In

fact, the point of view of the client is seldom recorded. Consequently, we take files not only to be 'true,' but also to contain all that it is necessary to know about clients (Zimmerman, 1969). This is a generalized effect that operates in any bureaucratic system.

The ideological effect of modern child welfare files is enhanced by the 'black-book' style of recording, discussed in Chapter 3, which is now a staple feature of child welfare work. Recording includes 'everything that happens,' 'dates, times and places,' what was 'said and done' – details that will be needed should the case come to court. Because this form of recording has been promoted as inclusive and objective, workers come to feel confident they are recording the salient facts of the case, that they are omitting bias and subjectivity, and that the record produced will tell the story in chronological order. Indeed, the vivid details captured in files convey a sense of immediacy and undeniable reality – actual people behaving in actual settings.

Although generally not perceived as such by the recorders of information, these recording procedures are quite selective. As Smith (1983: 260) notes, most texts are not truly detachable from the context of their production. Both readers and writers of files bring to their work an implicit, if usually unacknowledged, understanding of the organizational processes that create them; they both produce and consume information based on these understandings. The case-oriented organization of the workplace instructs us not to notice some features of reality, to attend only to certain specific features. It further requires the 'shaping up' of information in accordance with organizational purposes. Workers have expertise in these matters, although they may not always be aware of it. Both the details workers notice and the way these details are worked up and organized in files are guided by work processes and purposes. Explanatory connectives, drawn from theories easily located in the child welfare literature, are regularly supplied by workers. Together, these processes work to produce images of clients that continually reconfirm the need for the existing set of bureaucratized, individualized services to intervene in and reorganize private family life.

Meanings, as Foucault reminds us, are embodied not only in verbal expressions but in technical processes, in institutions, in patterns for general behaviour, in forms of transmission, and in pedogy (Macdonell, 1986). The technical processes of file construction, storage, and use within the institutions of child welfare convey meanings. In spite of the social problems faced by these clients, it is not surprising to find that social and economic issues do not appear in case files, which are so clearly intended to be about individual families. Child welfare and social work itself are deeply rooted in notions of the private family and the socially established obligations of parents to provide for children within the family structure. Child welfare grew out of the observation that many children were not afforded the protection and care that it was believed the family should supply. Methods developed to assist children are intended to reinforce and/or substitute for the family model. Thus, it is entirely consistent that individualized case records would be an organizing feature of child welfare work and bureaucracy.

The very forms workers are asked to complete are organized around 'the family' and its relationship to the state and its representatives. Identifying and personal information about family members is recorded. The problems identified and described must justify the agency's course of action in relation to the family, and must provide justification for resource distribution. As we have seen, a major object of recording in a neglect file is the collection of evidence over a long period of time, with emphasis on such visible issues as housekeeping and personal appearance. These are indeed the issues that often appear in files. Also appearing in files is correspondence between agency personnel and collateral organizations such as welfare departments, day care centres and health institutions. When read from the perspective of organizational purposes and linkages, these documents provide an important guide to the structure of the larger apparatus. They also allow us a small glimpse into the client's life. However, not even a knowledgeable reader can see through such file information to the everyday context with which the client must grapple. Readers could not be expected to see in files how social and economic forces impinge upon clients, although workers undoubtedly know a great deal about this. Nor are connections among the circumstances of agency clients made explicit. Each family appears as unique and individual; each could be read as the only one experiencing problems of housing, resource deprivation, and unemployment. Given the social and economic circumstances described in the previous section, the absence of social and contextual information in files, although not surprising, is very striking and certainly meaningful.

As is often the case in professional accounts, the mode of presenting clients in contact recording is one of assertion by an authorized speaker: 'This happened.' Descriptions of drinking parties, disorganized houses, and dirty children are presented as 'the facts of the case.' The immediacy of recording required by the black-book approach enhances this effect. The assertive mode does not raise questions or point to gaps in note-taking, but presents material both as 'all there was to know' and as valid beyond a reasonable doubt. It is this feature of black-book recording that allows these notes to carry weight in court. A recent trend away from judgmental statements in recording and towards precision and 'neutrality' in describing clients' behaviour also enhances the effect that a neutral and objective stance has been taken.

Human service professionals are authorized in our society to enter into the personal lives of certain others and to record and interpret information about certain events in their lives. Professionals are provided with credentials by authorized social institutions to do this and, as Garfinkel notes (1967: 77), have 'enforceable rights' to manage and communicate action and decisions. It is this process of accepted validation through orderly procedures that often works against clients, especially in court. The client stands alone in her account of what happened and what is true. She presents herself from a stance of subjectivity, and she has no 'orderly processes' standing behind and authorizing her account. However, there are understood limits on the kinds of information particular professionals are authorized to convey. In a case-oriented agency, for instance, workers are not fully authorized to comment on social context. Furthermore, social facts do not lend themselves as readily to validation through the worker's own experience. One worker I spoke to asserted knowledge about a 'reserve childhood lifestyle with a lot of running around and lack of nurturing.' Asked to expand, the worker said 'I don't know personally about it. I've never worked on a reserve.' She moved then to authenticate her assertion via 'experience with colleagues, Natives from reserves,' but finally conceded, 'that's just my opinion, I've no statistics to back it up.' This sequence suggests the importance in a casework setting of personal experience in validating accounts as factual. It also alerts us to the implicitly understood personal definition of the setting: The worker recognizes that in commenting on contextual features of clients' lives she has stepped outside the boundaries of her authorization to speak. Outside the personal arena, as she notes, statistical measures, produced through other authorized procedures, are seen as necessary for validation.

A few facts reflective of social issues do appear on forms of most child welfare agencies – for example, the parents' source of support. Such information could theoretically be used in the aggregate to demonstrate, for instance, the level of poverty among the agency's clientele. However, in their hurry to complete investigations, workers often leave out or gloss over sections not immediately relevant to their purposes. Consequently, even this minimal social information would be inaccurate and incomplete if aggregated. In fact, workers generally do not perceive files as a source of aggregate information that might be useful to them, perhaps because aggregate data are seldom collected and used in this way. Rather, files are alternately viewed as serving immediate case needs and as a time-consuming and often useless task required by the organization. A recent exception is a study carried out at the

Metropolitan Toronto Children's Aid Society, in connection with the University of Toronto School of Social Work (Cohen-Schlanger et al., 1993). This study demonstrated connections between poor housing conditions of clients and apprehension of children on the basis of 'neglect.' Such research provides an important model of the way aggregate information could be used to challenge the prevailing picture of neglect as an exclusive problem of individuals.

Case files, however, generally focus on the personal, and this approach is sustained and legitimated by organizational purposes. The character of information recorded is personal, because the mandated task at hand is to investigate and if necessary reorganize personal aspects of private family life. The file format is organized to capture identifying information about nuclear families, the broad outlines of the relations of family members to one another, and relations of the family to relevant social institutions. These are the facts needed by workers to manage cases in accordance with their legal and social work mandates and to negotiate their relations with other institutions in the apparatus. Thus, the organization of records provides a format for noticing and collecting information that simultaneously reflects and supports the personalized stream of discourse about neglect, and not the discourse concerned with poverty. Traces of organizational purposes – or hidden realities – are present within these records. However, most readers accept and use records as personal accounts of individual behaviour within the private family.

THE SCHEMA OF NEGLECT

The task of unmasking ideological meanings requires stepping back from details and procedures to reflect upon generalized effects. As case files of neglect are constructed, they produce the appearance of a reality which must be taken as authentic by interested parties, an effect achieved through the confluence of processes entering into and organizing the production of written material about clients. The cumulative effect of reading neglect files is to conclude that mothers are primarily responsible for virtually all problems described. Underlying the production of this effect is what might be termed a 'schema' of neglect; that is, a set of instructions, endorsed by theory, providing explanatory connectives between personal details in files and the category child neglect. The 'cycle' idea provides an important part of that schema.

As Jones (1979) points out, the 'cycle' explanation of inappropriate socialization of children within families can be traced to Freudian theory and its adoption by the helping professions. The cycle theory is 'softer' and less punishing than the moral approbation applied by friendly visitors. However, it has been effective in laying the groundwork for increased state intrusion into poor families, providing as it does the prospect of a solution to inappropriate socialization through interruption of the cycle and treatment of the perpetrators. Breines and Gordon's excellent review (1983) of child abuse literature over the past three decades expands on this theme. Their article is useful in helping us to understand the schema currently operating to organize information in child welfare files. This review article does not directly discuss neglect. However, the recent subsuming of neglect by abuse makes it important and even necessary to examine ideas in the literature of child abuse in order to understand the connectives workers supply in their thinking about neglect. Such an examination also shows how ideas generated through one discourse can enter into and become staple features of another, gaining force and primacy through this occurrence. The 'cycle of abuse' illustrates these points.

The explosion of child abuse literature dating from the early 1960s leans heavily towards psychological explanations of abuse, as Breines and Gordon demonstrate. Abusers are often seen as immature individuals who are excessively demanding of their children. Furthermore, 'the great majority of child abuse experts believes that there is a "cycle of abuse" – the repetition of a distorted relationship that deprives children of the consistent nurturing needed for their full development.' The implication of this belief is that 'barring intervention, the abusive cycle will continue unbroken' (1983: 494), a belief that serves to justify coercive child welfare interventions.

Closely related to the 'intergenerational continuity of abuse' are theories of maternal bonding and child development. Bonding theory postulates a critical period when mother and infant must interact in particular ways to establish a psychological bond. This bonding process is seen as essential to the development of maternal attachment that will provide the mother motivation to care for her child in the future. Defective bonding, sometimes called maternal deprivation, is postulated as a primary cause of abuse. Understandings about behaviours believed indicative of poor bonding have come to be widely shared. Most social workers, for instance, would have no trouble understanding this observation by nursing staff of a young mother in hospital shortly after giving birth: 'Mom observed to be highly emotional, tense and often weepy.' In this context, such a statement signals potential problems based on failure to bond properly. Although important theorists such as Bowlby (1969) do not insist that a child's principal attachment figure must be the natural mother, it is proposed that for biological reasons it may be 'easiest' (Bowlby, 1969: 306) for the natural mother rather than other caretakers to achieve the result of a strong attachment. In this way, as Breines and Gordon note, these theories have been used in such a way as to 'make an issue' of the mother's care of children and not the father's. These theories are also closely related to theories of child development. In both popular and professional understanding, the mother's quality of attachment and by implication her quality of care are connected to her child's development all through life. Erikson's theory of personality development (1950), often taught at schools of social work, postulates trust, established in infancy through having basic needs met, as an essential ingredient of future development. Maslow's 'hierarchy' of needs is also widely known to social workers. Maslow (1954) postulated that basic needs must be met before 'higher order' needs for self-actualization could be addressed. Bonding theories establish the mother as the primary person available to meet both basic material and trust needs, and mothers are therefore easily seen as responsible when childhood development is delayed or when a child does not develop to full potential. But as Breines and Gordon note, an exclusively psychological understanding of abuse and neglect reveals little about the 'kind of society and culture parents and children live in. The context is missing' (1983: 499).

In both files and talk about clients, the theoretical explanations suggested by child abuse literature are commonly used to explain poor parenting behaviour. In files, the incident style of recording facilitates this process by removing descriptions of both clients and their behaviours from their social contexts. This removal leaves large spaces available to be filled by causal connectives. Personal and intrafamilial explanations of problems, encouraged in the discourse, implicitly underlie workers' efforts to understand poor child care: 'Mom came from a very deprived, neglectful background. She was passed around and had no stable parent role model. Mom admits she has no way of knowing if kids are sick except their crying.'

In this file entry, the worker has begun with the idea of deprivation. Although this idea might direct readers to consider issues of class and poverty, these thoughts are quickly closed off to the reader by connecting deprivation with neglect, which implicitly signals the family as the site of deprivation. The field of concern is further narrowed in the next sentence which poses the relevant issues in terms of poor parenting. The worker never mentions the cycle idea, nor does she specifically say that poor parenting by this mother is caused by deficiencies in her own family background. Rather, the writer implies this connection and readers bring this understanding to the text through familiarity with the cycle theory.

Maslow's hierarchy of needs underlies another typical file entry. In this example, we see how the worker implicitly poses this theoretical formulation

as unassailable in explaining mother: 'Mom has experienced severe deprivation in her own childhood. As a result of this she is very much a child herself.'

Again, the word deprivation might refer readers to consider poverty as an
issue for this client. However, the second sentence closes off this thought,
pointing readers in the direction of developmental theory in understanding
this mother. Although the hierarchy of needs idea is implicit, the causal connective is made clear by the phrase 'as a result.' This phrasing shows how psychological theory is used in connection with the cycle idea 'on the ground.' As
knowledgeable readers, we understand not only that the client has unmet
basic needs from her childhood but that her children's unmet needs can be
understood to result from this background. Unspoken but understood is that
neglect breeds neglect, contained not just within the family but within the
mother–child dyad, a theme that will be explored more fully in Chapter 6.
Meanwhile attention to the material circumstances of the family remains
outside the realm of consideration.

Other workers make their use of the cycle idea completely explicit: 'We
need to stop that cycle in time. I think Mrs. G. is trying to get out of that
cycle. She might be able to break that cycle.'

These examples show some typical ways the cycle idea is brought in as an
explanatory connective in cases of neglect, and how this idea works to close
off consideration of explanatory connectives related to the social contexts of
clients' lives. Certainly there are no organizational requirements that workers
establish causal links between clients' caregiving problems and larger social
and economic processes, a fact that reinforces the use of the cycle idea to explain problems. Furthermore, it is not only child welfare workers who are
attuned to and who reproduce this schema in file recording, but other professionals, also case-oriented, who represent organizations requiring similar
accountability. In order for various workers to act cooperatively, a 'norm' or
field of mutually understandable theory about clients emerges to which
collaterals are implicitly asked to subscribe (Mouzakitis and Goldstein,
1985). This process helps to ensure that certain theoretical approaches
achieve predominance, while others sink to the background or become completely unacceptable.

IDEOLOGICAL EFFECTS OF THE PERSONAL APPROACH

To summarize, case files do not just record 'facts' but also leave spaces
available to be filled by explanatory connectives drawn from discourse. The
causal variables expressed in files and talk about neglect are generally those
that tie problems to personal characteristics of parents but not to social

factors. Underlying the selection and ordering of 'facts' about clients is a schema that validates the need for the individualized services that already exist. In short, child welfare work processes continuously operate to justify the current array of services, which are directed at changing people rather than addressing social ills.

A discourse concerns itself with certain concepts at the expense of others (Macdonell, 1986). This chapter has explored some of the mechanics through which personal and psychological issues come to be seen as the explanations for poor child care, while explanations related to poverty are continually removed to the far background. Although people accused of neglect are nearly always poor, sometimes crushingly so, both the formal discourse and the everyday reflections of workers explain the problems of these parents as personal, private, and disconnected from even the most immediate context. The argument presented here is not intended to discredit psychological theories, but rather to demonstrate their ideological use in explaining child neglect. The ideological character of the cycle idea depends on making connections between psychological theories and particular cases in a way that suggests that mothers are unable to provide care primarily because they did not receive adequate care from *their* mothers. As these connectives supply us with a satisfactory explanation for poor care, our attention is simultaneously drawn away from the social and economic context in which all these mothers have been doing their work. The cycle idea, in other words, when used to explain neglect, has the effect of reducing social reproduction to a question of psychological problems confined within a large but limited pool of poor families, who are appropriately the focus of the child welfare mandate.

This approach is appealing. It has a common sense aspect, one which fits with our own experience as family members. After all, we *do* learn something about parenting from our own parents. Dysfunctional interpersonal styles undoubtedly are passed from one generation to another, and children suffer as a result. The North American middle class is itself preoccupied with these problems, as a survey of the health shelf of any bookstore will reveal. And some poor parents undoubtedly suffer from psychological problems that both result from and create caregiving problems. It certainly makes sense that workers try to understand their clients in these terms. The organizational context, in any case, discourages efforts to do otherwise. The network of personal services within which child welfare is enmeshed constricts the range of theoretical choices that will carry currency. The crisis-ridden atmosphere of the work discourages genuine examination of the viability of selected theoretical explanations, while severe resource limitations render expensive explanations such as poverty nonviable. It is intrafamily explanations that have addressed these limitations best. They support the need for personal and often coercive interventions designed to stop the cycle. They fit with the mandate of child welfare, and suggest perhaps the least expensive alternative consistent with this mandate. They allow for hope: Even though the current generation of parents might not be amenable to change, perhaps intervention will improve chances for the next – the original child-saving impulse, reproduced in modern, scientific terms.

The overall effect is the ongoing representation of the clientele as the problem – again, the unworthy poor, those who have failed to break the cycle. The information collected in most child welfare agencies could not be organized in any case to support an argument that problems in caregiving are associated with class position. The very format of information gathering and storage could not easily provide data to keep track of welfare rates, housing conditions, common problems shared by the clientele, or other aggregate data. The information *is* organized in such a way that it is easy to confirm and build on developmental theories as the main or only explanations for neglect. The net result of these procedures is a vast and very personalized bank of records documenting 'it' as the psychopathology of particular poor people, accompanied by a vast silence on the subject of social context in the discourse of child neglect.

And as long as 'it' is psychopathology, attention of social workers to the 'weakness of will and poverty of the spirit' of individual clients will be seen as the most relevant form of child protection, while attention to the deprived material and social conditions with which clients struggle will be seen as putting children at risk. Through ordinary work procedures, neglect is produced and reproduced as a personal problem.

6

Neglect as Failed Motherhood[1]

While the category neglect appears on the surface to be gender free, implicating 'parents' as responsible for the care of children, virtually all people actually accused of neglecting their children, both historically and at present, are mothers (Gordon, 1988; Polansky and Polansky, 1975; Gil, 1970). The discourse of neglect has long since established mothers as the 'crucial variable' in neglect (Polansky et al., 1972), and this belief is echoed explicitly or implicitly by almost everyone writing about child neglect. The study of child neglect is in effect the study of mothers who 'fail.' In this chapter, I will explore how data produced through the processes of child welfare operate to reinforce the appearance of child neglect as the outcome of poor mothering. Also examined are features of the contradictory world of mothering that lie beneath this surface appearance.

For this discussion, an exploration of the relation of mothers to the state is undertaken. This relation is embedded in the nuclear family arrangements so familiar to us in contemporary capitalism. This family form has developed along with processes of urbanization and industrialization which fragmented the extended family and produced a growing separation between the private and public domains. As we have seen in earlier chapters, responsibility for the care of children on a day-to-day basis has been relegated almost exclusively to this 'nuclear family.'

The notion of parents as the exclusive and usually only caregivers for their children is closely wedded to the individualistic philosophy that is so basic to our social and economic life. Individualism provides the logic and moral force supporting the delegation of caring responsibilities to individual parents, regardless of the resources needed to carry them out. The ethic of individualism, as Dalley notes, poses self-reliance as the 'dominating virtue,' one which 'justifies the shutting of doors firmly in the faces of those unable to be self-reliant' (1988: 118).

Traditionally, although we speak of 'the family' as responsible for children, the actual work of caring for children has been allocated to women, who are seen as naturally suited to provide nurturing behaviour, and, by extension, as suited to provide the work involved. It is important to notice that implicitly included in assumptions about mothers' natural suitability to provide care is also the obverse. Fathers (and more generally, men) are not thought to be naturally suited to caring tasks, and are therefore socially exonerated from these responsibilities. The role of men, traditionally, has been the more removed and distant one of breadwinning. The concept of the 'nuclear family' thus implies not only the idea of two parents living in a private dwelling with their children, but it also contains within it this gender-based division of labour.

As Barrett and McIntosh (1982) have persuasively argued, the nuclear family has become an all-encompassing ideal of adult life and child-rearing. This family form is continually depicted in and romanticized by the media and is structured into all forms of social organization. Fraser (1989) argues that the welfare state itself and its social programs presuppose this division of labour. She suggests that these programs, which are officially gender neutral, are in fact organized by a gender subtext. One set of programs is oriented to individuals and is 'tied to participation in the paid workforce.' This set includes, for example, unemployment insurance and social security, and a majority of recipients, as Fraser shows, are males. A second set of programs, generally thought of as 'welfare,' is oriented to households; these programs are designed to 'compensate for what are considered to be family failures,' and its clients are primarily women. Both sets of programs are sustained, according to Fraser, by assumptions concerning the sexual division of labour. Society, including its social programs, is thus divided into two separate but related spheres of home and outside work, sometimes referred to as the private and public spheres, and these are women's and men's respectively.

The idea of the nuclear family serves the ideological function of concealing important features of everyday reality. The nuclear family ideal does not take account of class, race, ethnicity, or gender, nor does it address the issues faced by growing numbers of single mothers. It operates as an underlying schema, producing the vision of an ideal lifestyle to which all of us are expected to aspire. It not only dictates the division of labour in the family, but also provides implicit instructions to mothers about proper ways of caring for their children. As Gordon (1988) suggests, it also provides the organizing framework for understanding our gendered conceptions of child neglect. 'The very concept of child neglect,' Gordon comments, 'arose from the establishment of this norm of male breadwinning and female domesticity.' (1988: 166).

CARING

'Motherhood' invokes another, related ideal. Usually we think of mothering as an intimate relationship involving care for children (Griffith and Smith, 1987). Ideas of mothering in this light have taken on the contours of mythology. The idealization of mothers, of course, is ancient, but it has intensified within the past century. At a time when everyone's life was being affected by the 'frenzied growth of developing industrial capitalism,' mothers were seen as having total control and unlimited power over the development of their children. Freudian and post-Freudian psychology have produced and elaborated the centrality of the mother–infant relationship to future development to such an extent that it has dominated virtually all developmental research over the past thirty-five years (Chodorow and Contratto, 1982). Even feminist scholars, these authors note, depict mothers as all-powerful: 'If only the mother wouldn't do what she is doing, she would be perfect.'

A less familiar way of thinking about mothering is to examine it from the perspective of the work involved in caring. The concept of caring has recently begun to be explicated by feminist scholars. These writers usually begin with the idea that caring involves both feelings and activities (Waerness, 1984) or 'caring about' and 'caring for' (Dalley, 1988). In modern motherhood, according to Dalley, these two aspects of caring have been merged. They are thought of as inseparable, probably because of the underlying and long-standing belief that it is perfectly natural for mothers to both love and labour for their children (Graham, 1983). As a result of this merging, we may overlook the actual work that is done. We may also infer a deficiency in the quality of a mother's love when evidence appears to suggest that caring work has not been done, and we may further view mothers who attempt to separate these aspects of caring as deviant.

Furthermore, because we do not examine caring work closely, we fail to separate tasks of child care from tasks of homemaking. As Dalley notes, 'cleaning the lavatory and washing the kitchen floor are invested with as much significance as is reading a bedtime story' (1988: 8). Examples of child welfare workers' notes show that we do ordinarily regard these two types of tasks as synonymous. Two contrasting images from case files make the point:

Apartment reeked of stale urine; dirty diaper lying around.

Mom lives with kids in a tiny apartment which she keeps clean.

Neither of these examples relates directly to the mother's care of children, yet we can easily infer the quality of the mother's care from comments about household cleanliness. Mothers themselves recognize this to be the case, and often make efforts to clean up the house in anticipation of visits from workers.

Explication of the work involved in mothering has not emerged as part of child welfare work, a fact that seems ironic in light of the almost exclusive attention paid to mothers in the literature of neglect. In files, it is ordinarily gaps and failures in the work of caring that are documented. The actual organization of the mother's day, her attentiveness to the minutiae of children's needs and demands, and the resources required to accomplish this work are not recorded. Daniels suggests that the activities of caring for children are invisible because in our society only paid activities are classified as 'work' (1987: 407). Work in the labour market has 'moral force and dignity,' while unpaid work does not, and thus remains unnoticed. Feminists are now exploring the work of caring in both public and private spheres and identifying its complexities (Baines, Evans, and Neysmith, 1991). Caring by mothers involves both the obvious physical activities such as feeding and diapering babies, but also the minutiae of care such as finding lost mittens, fetching drinks of water, and bandaging up wounds. Caring also involves the considerable 'emotional work' of attempting to meet the needs of others. Daniels (1987) suggests some of the components of emotional work include tailoring tasks to meet special circumstances; meeting other's deadlines; and lobbying on behalf of family members. These tasks are carried out in a social and emotional context. For some women that context may promote the successful completion of these tasks. The context within which mothers accused of neglect operate is much more likely to hinder task accomplishment. However, in examining cases of neglect, circumstances must usually be inferred; as noted in Chapter 5, written records do not generally include contextual factors.

It is important to notice that fathers are not negatively assessed in terms of household cleanliness or poor child care. On the contrary, virtually any child care they provide produces a positive view of them: 'Dad bakes bread, makes pickles, and spends time with children.'

This statement predisposes us to think favourably of this father, because we know that he does not really have to do this work. It is not men's work, and the fact that he does this – even once – suggests he is helpful, cooperative, and willing to do more than his share. The very fact that he is shown to be doing this work in a case marked as child neglect also reflects badly on the mother, because he appears to be doing *her* work. However, failure to provide care and in fact the complete abandonment of children by their fathers generally produces no comment at all in these files. In cases of neglect, fathers are usually not mentioned if they are not living in the home. If they are living at home, files seldom comment on the quality, quantity, or frequency of their financial input. Clearly, these files are not about fathers, but about mothers and the responsibilities they are supposed to carry out.

Neither the disappearance of the father from the household, nor his apparent failure to 'bring home the bacon' absolves the mother of any responsibility. How she achieves this dual role of provider and caretaker is not explored in detail as a regular feature of child welfare work. Failures and lapses, for instance, in housekeeping, are noted. However, 'the prevailing ethos of family-based care suggests that normal tasks are being performed, that the roles enacted are straightforward, expected and unproblematic' (Dalley, 1988: 10). Thus the everyday caring work that mothers do disappears, while failures and problems are documented.

PARENTING

While the actual work of caring has remained largely invisible until recently, the idea of 'parenting' is well known. The importance of providing high quality care for children is not new. The original Canadian child-savers were themselves highly influenced by the Victorian notion of the home as central to the moulding of children, and in fact as a moral cornerstone of civilization, as this sample from the Victorian 'literature of moral improvement' demonstrates: 'Estimate the healing, comforting, purifying, everlasting influence which is ever flowing from this fountain, and you will understand the sacred ministry of the home to the higher culture of mankind (Brown, 1898, quoted in Behlmer, 1982: 46).

Frederich Froebel popularized for early Canadians the idea of children as seeds to be nurtured, an image still popular in the modern discourse on parenting. Parents were instructed in 'Froebelian Societies' which formed in the late nineteenth century to shape their interactions with their children (Sutherland, 1976).

The concept of parenting, now familiar to most North Americans, refers us to complex images of caring for children in modern society: providing consistency, teaching the child to behave appropriately, coordinating the child's relationship with schools and day care, supervising diet and television viewing, providing careful discipline, and so on. In this construction, the affective component of the relationship is valued and expressed largely through carrying out these tasks. Thus, a worker is able to say of a loving but inconsistent mother, 'She can't parent her children.' Carried into the processes of legal adjudication, this way of thinking about care has important implications, for it means that the evidence collected by workers focuses on completion of parenting tasks, which can be observed and measured. The resulting evaluation can then be seen as a reflection of the quality of affection a mother feels for her child. In 'parenting,' love and care are again merged.

The discourse of parenting enters every home through the media – newspapers, magazines, talk shows on television – and through ordinary events of everyday life – casual conversations, parent–teacher meetings, notices home from school. Discourse concerning parenting performs ideological functions. It invokes the standard of the two-parent family, suggesting caring work is gender neutral, performed competently and equally by both parents. In so doing, the idea of parenting directs our attention away from the well-known fact that most child care is done by mothers. Also, the discourse of parenting invokes a classless, homogeneous society, proposing kinds of activities evocative of white, middle class culture. In a recent issue of *Parents* magazine, for instance, feature articles concerned 'help in establishing rules of decorum' for children, advice from mothers who have 'opted out of the 9-to-5 life,' suggestions for dealing with 'parent burnout,' and an article on the joys of being a grandparent. Further articles provide make-up and diet 'tips' for mothers, and columns answer questions about how to entertain and educate children on holiday trips, how to put a reluctant child to bed, and whether year-round schooling is a good idea. Numerous glossy advertisements picture young, slender white women cuddling healthy, well-dressed youngsters. Few pictures of males beyond the age of four appear. Nearly all advice presupposes a two-parent, two-child family, with mother either at home full-time or organizing her paid work around what seemed to me an overwhelming number of child care concerns. One article does deal with divorce, suggesting that to avoid stress for children, they be allowed 'to continue to live in the same house and attend the same school' as before. These images and the advice proffered to parents propose expenditures of time, money, and energy commanded only theoretically even by those who fit the norm. Deeply embedded in these images are also images of 'ideal mothers.' Models who represent mothers in ads are usually white, young, well cared for, alert, attentive, attractive women. Often, nowadays, they are also portrayed as professional women, juggling office responsibilities with homemaking and child care. Of course, these 'mothers' represent not only ethnocentric ideals of motherhood, but ideals of womanhood as well.

The presentation of these images as 'normal' screens out the requirements of producing a youthful, attractive physical image for women. As black people have successfully argued, these images are virtually always white to begin with. As the Jane Fonda notion of physical fitness suggests, the slim and athletic ideal currently popular requires significant work and time. Childbirth usually results in weight gain, various health problems, and often in dental problems as well; scrupulous attention to diet and exercise are often required to maintain a slender appearance and healthy teeth. A youthful look requires money and time for cosmetics, healthy food, rest, holidays, dental care, and so on. These, in short, are features of class, well beyond the reach of the poverty-stricken women who are accused of neglecting their children.

As Griffith and Smith (1987) note, and as this discourse makes clear, a dominant characteristic of modern parenting (actually mothering) work is that it must be linked to the 'social and institutional fabric' of the society. Mothers may do much of their caring work in the private domain, in isolation from other adults, but they are not at all free to establish what those tasks should be, to organize their own working day as they see fit, nor to decide completely unfettered what standards of child care are the most important or what level of care is 'good enough.' The work of mothering is linked to and organized by institutions outside the private home, especially schools. The study carried out by Griffith and Smith (1987) demonstrates, for instance, how mothers try to organize their time at home with children in accordance with the expectations of the school. Ferguson suggests that these linkages produce an 'increasing incursion of administrative rationality' into daily life (1984: 47). The discourse of parenting provides the standards against which mothers' performances (and appearances) can be evaluated. Many mothers pursue these standards voluntarily; we purchase copies of *Parents* magazine, attempt to show our cooperation with the goals of the teacher, make efforts to look neat and healthy, and in various other ways show our conformity with the ideas if not the actual standards of parenting presented in the discourse.

Mothers who have been accused of neglect present a different picture. As shown in the previous chapter, these women are generally 'the poorest of the poor.' Through the kinds of incidents and conditions described in Chapter 4, entry by the state into these under-resourced homes has been warranted. Once entry is achieved, the problem for workers is whether grounds for re-entry exist. This does not mean that workers are eager to do this. However, if evidence of 'poor parenting' suggests it, then intrusion must be ongoing. In this eventuality, the relation of the state to the family is to ensure that parents, clearly mothers, either change in ways that produce the necessary care, or that the children be removed from their care. The tasks of workers, then, are to determine whether and how this mother needs to be changed and to supervise those changes. These tasks are performed through the bureaucratic apparatus that Fraser describes as a juridical–administrative–thera-

peutic state apparatus, or JAT (1989: 154), introduced in Chapter 3. In relation to this apparatus, according to Fraser, women are positioned princi-
pally as dependent clients, whose proper sphere is the family. The very fact
that they have come within the purview of the state suggests failure in this
regard and a need for personal change designed to enhance their chances for
more successful family lives. The changes sought do not flow from the lived
experiences of the women themselves, however, but from predetermined
categories that are not only administrable but which conform to political
goals and objectives. It is through this apparatus, Fraser argues, that the
experienced needs of individual subjects are translated into legal, administrative, and/or therapeutic matters that conform to political goals and objectives
regarding 'the family' and women's roles within it. Foucault's image of the
military camp, mentioned in Chapter 2, shows us a physical structure
through which inmates could be known and changed. In the modern era, it
is through the JAT, of which child welfare is a part, that we are able 'to know'
and 'to change' people.

MOTHERS IN THE CASE FILES OF NEGLECT

The following descriptions of mothers are taken directly from neglect
files.

Mom is slow, overweight, has dirty hair. She was wearing a tight T-shirt, obviously
braless which was totally inappropriate for her large bosomed frame.

Mom is Native, overweight, has skin problems, especially when drinking. Is less personable than her husband. Is unkempt, has scars.

Mom is obese, not wearing dentures, hair cut in a bowl shape, often dirty, Gives the
impression of being lazy and sloppy.

Mom has dirty blonde hair and protruding front teeth. She is tense, weepy, possibly
having a low IQ.

Several recurring images of mothers emerge from this descriptive material.
First, these mothers clearly depart from the physical ideals of womanhood
established in the media. The descriptive phrases used call to mind Kadushin's
description of neglecting mothers: 'Slovenly, they make it difficult for workers to like them' (Kadushin, 1967; Kadushin and Martin, 1988). Through
these descriptions, mothers are established as conforming to the picture of a
'neglecting mother' presented in discourse; their physical presentation of

self suggests neglect. Fathers, in contrast, are often not described physically at all either in files or in the discourse of neglect. Occasionally in files the father appears as a contrast to the mother's 'slovenly' appearance – Dad is 'lean and frail with dark hair.' Occasionally this contrast is made explicit, as in the comparison above of the father's more 'personable' presentation.

The current trend in recording is to focus on behaviours and events and to avoid physical descriptions. As explored more fully in Chapter 7, references especially to a 'Native' appearance could cast a racist light on workers. The focus of criticism has generally been on the attitudes of workers, because it is they who create images by writing these descriptions down. The antidote has been to limit the presence of description in the written record. However, as we inspect the instructions provided to workers in discourse, we see that such descriptions are not simply worker 'bias.' The discourse explicitly provides instructions for noticing the physical appearances of mothers. In Kadushin's statement, instructions for understanding our own reactions are also provided. We can expect that workers will continue to notice and react whether they record or not.

A second theme in files, one reiterated in workers' talk about mothers, relates to informal assessments of intelligence. Mothers are often described as having a 'low IQ,' 'dull,' 'not a really bright person,' or 'limited.' Often these statements appear as connected to the physical description: 'Mom is slow, overweight,' implying also the obverse, that thin mothers are brighter. Frequently contentions of low intelligence are unsupported by evidence, although occasionally workers do request formal intelligence testing of clients. More often, these appear as brief but authoritative assessments; they work to complete the 'slovenly' images of mothers as they are described in discourse. As readers we are set up to expect little of this mother.

Such presentations of mothers are hardly a recent phenomenon in child welfare files. During the 1930s, at a time when public fear of the 'feebleminded' population rose to considerable heights, mothers in child welfare files were very frequently described as 'subnormal' (Swift, 1995a). Kadushin (1967: 225) observes that 1950s and 1960s research on neglect frequently employed physical descriptions of mothers, such as drooping posture and dragging feet, as evidence of subnormal intelligence. Suggestions of low intelligence help to confirm for readers that such a mother is 'different,' that she can appropriately be categorized as deviant. The description of the mother and the poor care that is also documented then appear as logically connected.

Additional or alternate problems that the file examples above might indicate include depression, poverty, ill health, and alcohol addiction. While the worker may in fact attend to some of these experienced problems, connections between descriptive material and these 'unmandated' problems are not necessarily made in files. Because the worker's mandate is to locate evidence suggesting child welfare problems, descriptive material is generally connected directly to assessments of neglect or abuse. When files are constructed in this way, the cumulative effect of descriptions of mothers is one of inadequacy in many arenas of life. This effect reflects Polansky et al.'s (1972) view that neglect is not just a matter of low intelligence or slovenliness but the result of 'pervasive characterological defects' in the mother that enter all aspects of her life. This schema, which dominates the discourse, directs us to see all aspects of the mother's life as relevant to an assessment of neglect. It directs us to see poor care as closely connected to 'defects' in the mother, and simultaneously directs attention away from the experienced problems of the mother.

It is important to note that not all file images of mothers are negative. Some women are described in very positive terms by workers: 'Mom is pleasant, polite, nice. She is quite articulate.'

These capacities are not generally 'actionable' for the women, however, because their lives are narrowly confined. As the mothers of many children, they are often isolated from other adults. Their social skills may be employed primarily in their relationships with their caseworkers, as demonstrated by one mother who used her verbal skills to direct and manage team meetings organized to discuss her own deficiencies as a mother. She receives high praise from workers for her skills, but these are not actionable for her in the public arena because of her many child-caring responsibilities. Intelligence and verbal skills are likely to be seen exclusively in relation to housework and child care, as illustrated in one case of a young mother of two who 'dreams of going to university,' but is offered programs to upgrade her 'homemaking and parenting skills.' Another worker is upset with a mother who has the 'capability,' who could achieve 'just about anything she wants.' But the task at hand is to care for children, and the worker's thoughts return immediately to this arena as the one in which she must do her achieving. Consequently, even when mothers are clearly recognized as bright, capable, and skilled, they continue to appear in case material as deficient. It is parenting that counts, and within that sphere, it is gaps, lapses, and problems that appear as relevant.

NEEDY MOTHERS

Without question, the strongest descriptive theme concerning mothers, both in the workplace and in discourse, is that of 'neediness.' In discourse concerned with child neglect, mothers are very frequently described as 'needy,' 'immature,' 'emotionally immature,' and 'dependent.' In both discourse and in case material, this theme is nearly always connected to the mother's care of children. Hall et al. (1982), for instance, describe the mothers in their project as 'scared, frustrated, needy and dependent.' Workers also frequently connect the mother's 'neediness' with her caring capacities: 'She can't put her needs or wants aside long enough to meet the needs of the kids.'

Standards of maturity for mothers are implied in this construction: Meeting the needs of children is the mark of a mature woman. The abandonment of children by most of the fathers in neglect cases does not ordinarily call forth comments about their maturity levels. Since fathers are not expected to 'put their needs and wants aside' in order to meet children's needs, they are seldom appraised in these terms. Mothers are required to orient themselves to their children's needs regardless of their social circumstances. Contrast structures introduced spontaneously by workers convey this expectation. In the following passage, the worker compares a mother in her mid-twenties with a much younger mother: 'I have another 15 year old mum who is doing excellent with her little guy, just excellent. And I guess [the other mother] is just immature. I think of this other one, and wow – she's really mature to be 15.'

In another sequence, the contrast structure shows the upper reaches of maturity for mothers. This mother has complained to the worker about frequent physical abuse visited upon her by her ex-husband, suggesting that the abuse accounts for some of her problems in providing care. The worker reflects on an appropriate response: 'How many thousands of women get beat up every week? Don't give me that, that you were beaten up, that has nothing to do with it ... Some women get beat up quite severely, some are put in the hospital, with broken bones, lots of times. Those kids are loved, those kids are nurtured and cared for.'

These comparisons are not idiosyncratic; they reflect expectations easily uncovered in discourse concerned with mothering, expectations which, as Chodorow and Contratto (1982) note, reflect profound social beliefs that mothers are all-powerful and can, if they desire, be perfect. This ideal of the self-sacrificing mother makes clear that the job of mothering must be first in a woman's life, regardless of her circumstances (Leonard, 1984: 166). In child welfare, this image provides the justification for the provision of in-home services to mothers accused of neglect. It is assumed that mothers will and should do the work of child caring. The mother is expected to try, and the agency will offer, up to a point, support in this effort. A mother's efforts to escape her duty, to take a vacation from it, or to get help with the workload at 'peak' times are not justifiable in these terms, as the following sequence illustrates:

Worker: It's kind of obvious she's having problems. It's almost as though she sets it up. Sets up situations such as the weekend. Her kids were apprehended, and it's almost like, I guess she's setting it up. She needs some help or whatever.

Interviewer: But she couldn't come and say, 'I want my kids out of the house for a while'?

Worker: No, no, no.

NEEDINESS AS IDEOLOGY

In what circumstances, then, can mothers accused of neglect receive assistance? Parents are to be solely responsible for child care in our society; in a case of neglect, there is a mother somehow shirking this duty. In times past, a highly punitive stance was taken towards these mothers, and children were frequently apprehended as a result. As Hepworth shows (1980), this high number of apprehensions in turn became a problem, as many of these children remained in foster care for years. Punitive measures proved to be expensive, both in terms of agencies' annual budgets and in emotional costs for families, workers, and for the children themselves.

In recent decades the trend has been to reduce these problems by providing more in-home supports, with the goal of preventing apprehension and placement of children. This trend coincides with an emphasis on the 'cycle of neglect' as an explanatory factor in understanding the issue. As seen in the previous chapter, the cycle explanation is closely related to the notion of neediness. Social work literature instructs us in understanding this connection: 'Erikson's and Maslow's conceptions of basic human needs as a hierarchy of successive prerequisites instruct us that provisions have to be made for survival and trust before people can be expected to reach out for creativity, altruism, and self-realization; that what Maslow called "deficit needs" have to be met so that higher-order "growth needs" can be met' (Siporin, 1975: 198).

This idea , as seen in Chapter 5, provides the logic for the 'cycle' theory of neglect. In the terms of this theory, poor mothering in one generation produces a needy daughter who is then responsible for poor mothering in the next (Breines and Gordon, 1983). Asked for her theoretical understanding of a case, one worker explained the idea this way: 'I think it's pretty basic what happened to this family. I mean it's a generational and a historical thing, like I said, going back to Mrs F. and her husband ... The information we have is that she was sleeping with all kinds of men, and was a drinker and was taking pills. I mean it makes me wonder what her upbringing was like, whether she was physically or sexually abused ... I think in those kinds of terms ... how they were raised, what happened to them ... I think it's intergenerational.'

This construction, as we have seen, screens out factors other than 'upbringing' that might help explain the mother's behaviour. The social conditions of her childhood, and of the context in which *her* mother was enmeshed, including conditions of poverty, abuse by a partner, and so on, move to the background. Also, the behaviour and backgrounds of fathers, as seen in the above illustration, begin to disappear as the analysis progresses. The cycle idea moves our thinking to the directives of the mothering discourse, which instruct us to see mothers as centrally implicated in all future development of their children, and as able, if willing, to overcome any circumstance to provide the necessary nurturing. The cycle idea works to render the social and economic context not only invisible but irrelevant.

Alternate views of the problem also appear to be beside the point. One worker, asked about the theory she applies to child welfare problems, attempted to bring feminist theory into the equation: 'I explain [Mom] by looking at how women are socialized ... and viewed in our society. They have babies because they feel this is what is expected ... and then find out they're really unhappy with that.'

This line of thought produces considerable sympathy for the situation of the mother, but does not produce for the worker a viable course of action to take. The children are already there, needing care and attention on a daily basis. When the worker reverts to the cycle theory, her attention returns to this problem, and she sees the appropriate interventions as those that appear to ensure the provision of care and thus break the cycle. Even when the background information necessary to document a cycle of neglect is not available to workers, they can readily supply the missing links to produce a coherent cycle: 'She's needy, she's an adolescent ... *I think* it's because of her lack of nurturing, she hasn't had a lot of her needs met.' (italics mine).

It is important to notice that while the children's needs warrant our entry into the private home, it is the needs of the mother rather than the children that become the focus of intervention. The role of the state is to produce and enforce care for children *through* the family, which usually means through the mother. It is the need for a change in mother that provides the justification for intervention, and it further explains the kinds of interventions that child welfare systems typically offer. Mothers are presented as having deficit needs; they have not themselves been nurtured adequately. This explanation is what Fraser describes as 'needs interpretation,' a function through which personnel 'translate [clients'] experienced situations and life-problems into administrable needs' (1989: 154). In this process, other possible needs are closed off not only as legitimate but even as specifiable.

Neediness also provides connectives to two related concepts, immaturity and dependency, which are important to the process of resource allocation. As workers talk about neediness, a connection is often made to immaturity: 'She's needy, she's an adolescent ...' The idea of mother as an adolescent justifies the helping relationship as one of 're-parenting' the client, described further in Chapter 8. Intersecting at this point with the cycle idea is the parenting discourse, called up in this circumstance to provide instructions for our own intervention. As a result of poor parenting in the past, these mothers do not have 'nurturing knowledge.' The discourse instructs workers to supply this instruction, to offer help in skill development, and to provide authoritative supervision in order to break this aspect of the cycle: 'Inadequacies in nurturing knowledge may be consistent with the view of neglect as a cyclical phenomenon, a generation-to-generation life style ... The importance of breaking such a cycle is irrefutable' (Jones and McNeely, 1980).

The resources we provide in cases of neglect are in fact largely geared to this goal. Teaching homemakers, parenting courses, and monitoring and supervision of the home are the staples of our resource provision. The mother is trained for her job; she is changed in such a way that she can provide children with what they need, thereby breaking the cycle.

Neediness is also closely connected to dependency. Those who are immature are potential dependents. Evidence in files and in workers' talk refer both implicitly and explicitly to the goal of independence for these mothers: She needs to 'move out on her own'; 'she must learn to do it for herself.' Fraser's idea of the household as the unit for resource distribution helps us to understand these directives. Programs aimed primarily at women, she notes, are designed to supplement and compensate for 'family failures' (1989). The notion of what constitutes failure is, of course, closely related to social views of the responsibilities of families to provide for themselves within the confines of the household. Stack's study of welfare recipients (1974) revealed that recipients had devised a complex network of resource pooling and exchange among household units, thus transcending 'the principal administrative category' organizing relief programs. The identities of study subjects were closely guarded because of the threat that this transgression would cost them their benefits.

Similarly, child welfare service presupposes the household as the unit of service, and independence is assessed according to the extent to which mothers can fulfil their responsibilities in these terms. One mother is adept at getting outpatient clinic staff to make her sandwiches for lunch: 'She hangs around the kitchen, around the person who makes the sandwiches. This person would feel really sorry for [Mom] and would make her lunches everyday ... so she didn't have to make her own at home ... Other people took on the problem, and she didn't have to make any decisions for herself.'

Evidence suggesting that this mother is getting resources outside the legitimate channels causes her to be seen as dependent, as one who does not make her own decisions. Such evidence puts her at risk, potentially justifying more and closer supervision by authorities and simultaneously providing justification for resource cutbacks to encourage independence. In social work literature, the goal in this kind of helping relationship is expressed this way: 'To increase the ability of people to choose for themselves and to control their own lives' (Compton and Galaway, 1984: 247).

We may notice at this juncture that resources provided through child welfare are limited to addressing the mother's needs in ways intended to produce better care of her children. This approach does not necessarily de-legitimize mother as a person with needs, but interprets these needs to accord with the administrative machinery and resources of child welfare. Supervision and training of mother is logically warranted; her needs are the problem but are not the ultimate purpose of intervention. She must be supervised until she is less needy; when she is less needy she will provide better care for her children. She will be 'policed to care,' to use Reitsma-Street's phrase (1991: 106). Basic supplies, such as food, are not warranted and not provided.

A CASE EXAMPLE

In this case example, we see a mother's attempt to 'resign' from her caring work. This mother is responsible for two children, following a long involvement with child welfare. The children are in care, and a series of planned visits have been arranged at home, with a teaching homemaker involved to provide this mother with skills and guidance, pending return of the children. The mother has cooperated for a few weeks, but has now disappeared. She has called the worker, asking if there is 'something I can just sign so I don't have to take care of' the children. She has requested that they be cared for by a former foster mother whom she feels can do a good job. She outlines to the worker her reasons for wanting to be free of this responsibility, saying:

- I can't go out with whoever I want.
- If I want to go out I have to get a babysitter, or I have to bring them with me.

- I can't have men over when I want them.
- I gotta get up in the morning.
- I gotta feed them, and make sure they're clean.

These reasons suggest to the worker that the mother knows the basic skills and responsibilities required and simply does not want to carry out these tasks. The worker comments that at this point 'it's like a different [Mom]. She knows what she has to do, but chooses not to do it.' The mother has also told the worker why she is making this choice. She wants the freedom to have sexual relationships with men. This mother has previously been chastised for having gentleman callers and for wearing the evidence of her sexual life on her person, in the form of 'hickeys' on her neck.

However, the resources provided by the agency do not recognize mothers as sexual beings. In fact, embedded in discourse about mothers and mothering is an 'assumed incompatibility between sexuality and motherhood,' including a view that mature women are less sexual than immature women (Chodorow and Contratto, 1982: 66). Certainly, sexuality is often at odds with the requirements of mothering, as this client has decided. She has also realized that she will not get agency resources that help her pursue her sexual interests. It is lack of nurturing in her own childhood that provides the basis of our resource provision, but this mother's account of her situation does not fit that scheme. The worker, in commenting that Mom seems different, that she does in fact appear to understand what is involved in caring for her children, recognizes and acknowledges a discrepancy between the mother's account and her own previous assessment. However, the mother's interpretation of her own needs is not actionable in terms of resource outlay; nor does it provide the worker a viable strategy for her own involvement with the client.

The worker's task is now to recast the mother in terms that the agency provides. The mother's sexual proclivities become her 'inability to put her own needs or wants aside long enough to meet the needs of the kids,' a circumstance explained by emotional deficits in the mother's own childhood. Recast as immature, the teaching resources offered by the agency appear reasonable. The worker is forced to take this position by the professional discourse on the matter, one that allows no other view of neglecting mothers, as well as by resource availability, which does not recognize the sexual needs of mothers as legitimate – in fact, does not recognize this aspect of women at all.

The professionals involved in this case express feelings of regret at the mother's decision. A collateral tells the child welfare worker: 'I just knew if you apprehended those kids she [the mother] would get some freedom, and then she wouldn't want them back.' Both workers see value in the idea of finding a foster home for Mom, 'so she can get the nurturing and the guidance that she hasn't had and be able to pass on to her kids. We'd love to be able to do that but we can't.'

We may notice two things here. First, it is not only the child welfare worker or agency who sees this woman primarily as a mother, but collateral agencies as well. What we see, again, is an absence. When the mother withdraws provision of care, even for relatively short periods of time, there is nothing adequate to replace it. Social service workers know this, and try to marshall whatever resources are available to keep this mother at her work. We fear her taste of freedom, for she might find that life has other opportunities for her. Unlike her husband, who has long since deserted his post, pressure will be brought to bear in hopes of bringing her back to the tasks of caring.

Second, we notice that the mother's needs are invariably welded to those of her children. Although the (non-existent) foster home suggested here by the worker is ostensibly for the mother, a chance to get her own needs met, that outcome is not presented as justifiable or valuable for the sake of the woman but is seen instead to be in the best interests of the children. Furthermore, the sexual needs the mother has presented have disappeared; her needs are now presented as being for 'the mother she never had.'

As we spoke about this mother, both the worker and I hoped for her return. As mothers ourselves, we could imagine the feelings of the abandoned children, and we feared this mother would someday come to regret her decision. From the point of view of the agency, and of child welfare services in general, however, the problem is one of everyday practicalities. The worker herself must constantly attend to the resource issue. Arranging foster care, bringing the case to court, determining the adoptability of the children, anticipating action should the mother return, notifying the father of his rights, arranging visits, and so on, are all resource deployment issues that must receive attention. Our emotional responses are put to use here, directing us towards the issues of the mother's 'defection' and the children's loss. We wish for her to 'return to work,' for this appears as the most viable solution, the one that merges care and love, and thus approximates the ideal of motherhood.

Our emotional reactions, in other words, serve an ideological purpose. They direct us towards two options: producing a better mother, which is the favoured option, or 'firing' her if absolutely necessary. At the same time, our feelings direct our attention away from the mother's expressed needs, from her lived experience, and from the social and economic relations that have produced the context in which her mothering work has become, for her, untenable. They also direct our attention away from the likely outcome if she does return. The care the children have been receiving is documented by child welfare workers themselves as highly questionable over several years. The mother's life has also been documented as harsh, punctuated by frequent bouts of violence. Yet we yearn for her to return and continue on in these circumstances. Child welfare services can offer nothing to change this context. What is offered is to change the mother. Even then, resources likely to be given are very slender in the face of her difficulties. She can be taught to manage better, and she may be offered a chance to become less needy and dependent, a state however, that she must achieve for herself, because resources do not ordinarily provide this. In one sequence, we get a glimpse of the dubious rewards of independence for this mother. The mother has been assigned a homemaker, who is dissatisfied with cat droppings found on the kitchen floor. She undertakes to get the mother to clean this up, a feat which she eventually achieves through repeated directions and demonstrations: 'And that floor was spotless, and [Mom] did it.'

'I LOVE ROSES BUT I CAN'T GROW 'EM'

Love, according to the dictionary, is 'a feeling of warm personal attachment or deep affection.' The idea of motherlove has more connotations. In fact, few emotions have been as often eulogized and idealized as motherlove. As a feature of the relationships between these mothers and their children, signs of and comments on love are strangely missing from file recording and especially from written accounts of family life prepared for court proceedings. While workers spontaneously volunteer their beliefs that many parents accused of neglect love their children deeply, they may well be recommending in court that these same parental relationships be permanently severed. Love, and other emotions, are, of course, problematic to determine, while administrative rationality requires specificity and measurement. The idea of parenting has provided a route through which love appears measurable in terms of adequacy of care provided. Parenting is care of a special administered kind determined in relations outside the mother's experience, but imposed upon her (and all mothers) as a standard to aim for. The technology of modern social science provides the tools for measuring and administering these standards in particular situations. As it applies to mothers accused of neglect, this administration is oriented, as we have seen, towards evidence gathering. Both mothers and their children are subject to intelligence tests, professional assessments of mental health and emotional development, and medical investigations. Child welfare agencies are part of a web of institutions and professionals designed to conduct these tests, the results of which can and often are used in court as evidence of the mother's effectiveness as a parent. Children who are behind in school, whose milestones or growth rates fall too far behind the norm, are at risk of permanent wardship.

Child welfare workers refer parents and children for assessments and tests as part of their routine work, especially if they are making preparations for court. If the experts who conduct tests suggest follow-up treatment and procedures, a mother will be expected to make and keep the recommended appointments; failure to do so will be used as evidence against her in court. The implicit goal to which these tests are aimed is one of helping individuals develop to their full potential, which is both a social goal and a specific objective of social work practice. Connections between individual development and formal test procedures are made through several implicit assumptions. One assumption is that it is possible to reach accurate conclusions about the 'full potential' of children, based on our current knowledge base. A second assumption is that what we measure are the most important things to know about. Measurement of IQ and developmental milestones are, of course, geared to the requirements of an industrial–technological job market, while affect, which does not lend itself to measurement, tends to recede in the test results. This absence allows substitute measures of development to stand in as a representative of affect. Finally, we assume that when a case can be made that children are falling behind, it is mothers who are responsible. Again, the image of an ideal mother emerges, against which the actual mother is found wanting.

This way of assessing children poses individuals, both mothers and children, as floating free of social structure. Features of social organization and relations that work to contain and direct the potential we have measured are not relevant to this assessment procedure. School systems that 'stream' children, a 'dual' job market that directs women into marginal and temporary work; issues of pay inequity that ensure women will receive substantially lower wages for the same work as men are issues that do not enter into the assessment procedure. The image of 'full potential' romanticizes the lives and futures actually faced by both the mothers and their children.

As workers and I spoke about these mothers, we wanted their affection for the children to be expressed as care, a response that actually reflects on the paucity of alternatives. We want mother to do the work partly because there is no one else who will do is so cheaply. We know that personal daily care can be consistently provided to children by skilled workers other than their mothers, for instance, in day care centres and via professional nannies. We also know that the current economics of child care simply do not allow caring work to be purchased in quantity for poor mothers. Because this is not a viable alternative for care under present circumstances, it is screened from our minds as we contemplate particular mothers.

Workers involved with these families do not necessarily merge the concepts of love and care as they speak about them. They are perfectly able to see affectional ties and mutual attachments (and in some cases the limits of those attachments) and to evaluate quality of care separately. What workers do accept, uneasily, is that love is insufficient. One worker expressed the idea with this analogy: 'I love roses, but I can't grow 'em.' Care *is* required.

The relation between poor families and the state recognizes and in a number of ways ensures that the mother is usually the only person clearly available to do this caring work. In this arrangement, the nurturing which she is expected to provide has become associated with functional outcomes. Mothering is the 'means' for producing particular kinds of future adults needed by society's economic arrangements. As we witness lapses in care by mothers, however, our emotional responses direct us away from this administered and functional view of nurturing and towards the idea that her failure to care will result in the children being abandoned and unloved. Attention is diverted from the reality that permanent separation of mothers from children is seldom initiated by the mother herself. Rather it is the socially available alternatives – care by mother *or* wardship – that force a separation, sometimes permanently. Although it is usually our own interventions which actually produce permanent separation, the schema of neglect directs us to blame the mother.

PROBLEMS OF CAREGIVING

The focus of child welfare on performance failures of particular mothers obscures the work involved in providing even sporadic care for children on an ongoing, everyday basis. Also concealed are the social and economic conditions under which this work must be done by many mothers accused of neglect. The category 'neglect,' as defined in discourse, carries instructions to see the problem as one of passivity, as 'omission' of necessary care (Kadushin, 1967, Kadushin and Martin, 1988). Polansky et al. (1972, 1981) solidify this view with their extensive work on the 'apathetic-futile' mother, a concept that conjures up images of children in the care of a lazy, despondent mother. The reality beneath the surface for many of these mothers, however, is that in addition to long-term poverty and resource deprivation, their lives are filled with violence perpetrated by fathers, husbands, and lovers, numerous examples of which can easily be found in the case files of neglect.

Children are also subjected to substantial violence by relatives, boyfriends, or others who have access to their homes. Some children are physically attacked or threatened. Children are present at drunken brawls and sniffing parties that sometimes lead to serious illness or death of people they know. Many of these children live in neighbourhoods where violence is a regular occurrence.

The concept of neglect, however, does not take account of violence as a factor in the lives of children or in the quality of care provided by the mother. Protection of the children is seen as the responsibility of the mother, and the instructions of neglect tell us to perceive violence to the children as a sign of her apathy or incompetence. These incidents appear as background information, as the reason for case opening, or as an occasion for intervention by the worker. They are not usually directly connected to neglect in file material nor are they suggested as causes of neglectful behaviour. Because the mandate does not include violence against the mothers as a reason for ongoing intervention, workers find themselves in a contradictory position when abuse against the mother is uncovered. It may be seen by the worker as 'one more crisis' on a list of many, and therefore not perceived as an issue related to the care of children. In other cases, it may be seen as evidence of the mother's failure as a caregiver. Mothers may be charged and convicted of 'failure to protect' for continuing to live with an abusive partner, even when he is the father of the children. Workers may see male violence as a normal feature of clients' lives, explained as 'the way this family operates.' The mandate provides no instructions for acting on this eventuality, a fact that reminds us of the very different social location of children and mothers vis-à-vis the state. Through child welfare legislation, children are explicitly, if often only theoretically, protected from violence in their homes; women are not. On the contrary, women are responsible for 'the home,' for its atmosphere and for what goes on in it. If violence occurs, the woman is culpable. Workers do have instructions that cultural differences and privacy are to be protected, however. Principles established in legislation are explicit on this point, instructing workers to respect the 'cultural and linguistic' heritage of clients (Manitoba Child and Family Services Act, 1986). Given the vagueness of this directive, workers, even those who may privately see male violence against women as highly undesirable, explain away what they know with 'I'm not saying it's right or it's wrong.' To do otherwise may be perceived even by the woman herself, they fear, as undue interference and/or intrusions by a representative of the dominant culture into class or cultural mores. This is a contradictory position, of course, since child welfare involvement in the case already represents an intrusion by the dominant culture.

This focus on the mother's comprehensive responsibility performs the ideological function of covering over features of social relations originating outside the mother's immediate experience and not subject to her control. Social relations that produce violent 'ghettos' and that allow if not actively condone male violence against women and children operate invisibly to create the conditions of life in which mothers must function. Mothers attempting to manage child caring in these circumstances are repeatedly encouraged to 'do it on their own.' Files are sprinkled with the urgings of workers to women to get out of abusive relationships, advice against allowing their own mothers, brothers, or sisters to stay with them, or to allow particular friends or relatives to care for their children. Workers are usually responding in such instances to repeated episodes of drinking and violence, which appear to be encouraged by problematic family members. This problem definition, however, reflects a profound contradiction between 'the family' idealized in discourse and the reality of family life for many people. The advice offered perpetuates the idealized version. If the mother can 'get out on her own,' it is suggested that she still has a chance to create the ideal family.

Our proposed solutions minimize the problems of doing this, especially if the mother is single. The care of children by single mothers poses potentially serious logistical problems, because there is no automatic or immediate backup should the mother become incapacitated. A specific example, quite common on neglect caseloads, is alcohol addiction. Professional literature on alcoholism usually alludes to this condition as a disease. For child welfare workers, however, an alcoholic mother means poor care for the children. Even if the father is present, the mother is still expected to be the primary caregiver, and the onus for recovery will be on her. She will be expected to choose a recovery program, to follow through, and to maintain sobriety. If her child welfare worker has stipulated that she is to stay away from relatives, she may be entirely on her own in this endeavour.

Workers understandably become frustrated when mothers fail in these attempts. They witness the anguish of children as they are shuttled back and forth from home to foster placements, and they are aware of the risk and harm children sustain as dependents of an addict. As a reader of such files, I also yearn for the mother to right herself, to get back to the business of raising the children. Behind this yearning is again the image of the nuclear family – happy children at home with their mother. In this image, the work of caring merges into affect and disappears. The actual caregiving, and the resources required to produce it, are not part of this vision. Nor is the mother's actual state of health and addiction. Workers often visualize the mother as an individual of free choice, and they express shock and disapproval if she backslides.

Looked at from the perspective of caring work which this mother must provide, we see a different picture. We see the children increasingly upset and perhaps difficult to manage as they move back and forth from home to foster care, each move accompanied by attendant strains of loss of friends, schools, belongings, and so on. To maintain the support services the mother receives through her status as a child welfare client, she has to submit to ongoing scrutiny and criticism when the children are in her care. In fact, the support staff who help her will also act as scrutineers and may testify against her in court. The mother may often be required to make 'contracts' with the worker, imposing conditions on her lifestyle and relationships. If she has relatives with addictions, she may be asked to sever ties with them, which means cutting herself off from the very family we are taught to revere, and she will then be even more reliant on the agency to supply needed supports.

Mother, if single, is dependent on her children for support. They provide the official reason for her welfare benefits, and if they are taken into care, she loses these benefits. She may also lose her housing, because she needs these sources of income to pay her rent. She may lose her belongings as well: 'When the workers come to pick the kids up out of the home, they just pick up the kids. And if the mum is sort of transient and sort of down and out, the belongings get sent to some Salvation Army by the landlord.'

If she is not pursuing the return of her children, the mother may also lose contact with her child welfare worker, and whatever resources that contact has represented to her, because the mandate of the agency is not to offer support to women but to children. If children remain in agency care for any length of time, the mother finds herself in the position of starting over, looking for housing, re-establishing her benefits, and creating a new set of relationships with various workers. In line with the individualist ethic that underlies the ideal of the nuclear family, the onus is on her. Child welfare workers encourage her to recognize that she has to learn to achieve independence if she is to have the children back: 'She's going to have to learn to be very strong for herself, because she is going to have to ask for service. She won't be able to handle all her children herself, so it's a skill that she's going to have to acquire.'

Workers do this because they recognize the social reality that awaits this mother, a reality based on the belief that individuals in our society can and must 'make it on their own.' The proof of self-reliance in the context of child welfare is a mother caring for her own children with minimal or no assistance. Ironically, evidence of self-reliance soon leads to resource withdrawal, because it will be interpreted to mean she is able to manage without help.

The reality for such a mother if she keeps her children with her is a difficult and poverty-stricken life, involving attempts to manage several children
on below poverty-line resources, often living in barren cold quarters, possibly in an unsafe neighbourhood. The children will share this poverty-ridden
existence with her, based on the rationale that she has a right to the 'least
intrusive' alternative. This is considered a successful child welfare outcome,
because the mother is together with her children and is doing it 'on her own.'
Because the child welfare mandate does not 'see' poverty, does not include
protection of children from poverty, and does not warrant helping the
mother enrich her own life, the case will likely be closed at this point. Such
are the rewards of sobriety and hard work.

LIVING POOR

The outcome is that children do 'come to live poorly' (Polansky et al., 1972).
And so do their mothers. Arguments posing the rights of parents to autonomy against the rights of children to safety have concealed this fact. If we
examine the function of 'rights' in child welfare more closely, we see that in
neglect situations, they in fact have the effect of pitting mothers against
their children, while generally eliminating fathers from the picture altogether. As Fraser (1989) argues, the social programs that have men as their
main beneficiaries position recipients as 'rights bearers,' while the programs
serving women position recipients as 'dependent clients.' The argument for
parents' rights, however, welds the interests of both parents together, suggesting that mothers and fathers have access to the same social status and
resources. This issue is explored further in Chapter 8.

Child welfare solutions in the most intractable situations involve removal
of children from their immediate surroundings, producing the appearance of
a resolution. We know that this solution often leads to serious problems for
these children (Hepworth, 1980; Johnston, 1983). Yet when we ourselves
take children into care, it is cast as 'help' or 'rescue.' Mercifully, we usually
do not have to view the outcomes.

As Fraser (1989) suggests, welfare models, growing out of the relations
and requirements of capitalism, are based on the household as a unit of receipt. Mothers who attempt to band together, share responsibilities, swap
and trade, and provide in-kind services to one another must disguise this
from welfare authorities. The example of the mother arranging her lunch
outside the household demonstrates this response. If she does not purchase,
prepare, and serve food strictly within the household unit, she can be cast as
too dependent and risks losing some of the slim resources allocated to her.

Our emotional responses are geared to understanding motherlove as properly expressed in terms of care given within the confines of the private dwelling.

The analysis suggests support for Gordon's contention (1988) that neglect has historically reflected anxiety over women's departure from the private domain. Documents in cases of neglect select information that serves to justify inserting mothers into a particular relation to the state. In this relation, the state continues as enforcer of the work of mothering, supplying the least possible public resources that can be justified in order to ensure that the work is continued. Mothers are produced as far from the ideal – slovenly, dull, and needy; and as caring poorly for children as a result of these characteristics. The contextual information that might help to explain problems in child care is stripped away from the mother, and she is looked at as an 'individual,' a process that warrants the efforts of the state to focus its change efforts on her – in fact, which makes any other effort appear off the point. Poverty, class and race relations, gender issues, and fathers all vanish. Mothers are produced and reproduced as the 'causal variable.'

Specific features of cases serve to warrant prepackaged resources. Presenting mothers as dull or unskilled, for instance, justifies a need for parenting courses. At other times, mothers' behaviour is seen as dependence, which warrants the rationing of resources to her. This way of presenting mothers reproduces the relations of state and family. The family retains its ideological appearance as a unit with rights, only infringed by the state when 'parents' fail to protect children. The state's intrusive and rationing actions appear as justifiable in the circumstances of documented poor care. What completely disappears from the picture are the problems of the mother in the caring work that must be done. Also invisible are the poverty-ridden lives that mother and her children will share if they do escape the notice of child welfare authorities, along with any other life options for her. Thus, mothers must appear incompetent in order to qualify for the resources they need. In appearing incompetent, they bring the supervision and scrutiny of the agency upon themselves.

7

The Colour of Neglect

Since Greek and Roman antiquity, and especially since the Renaissance up until today, European scholars have been engaged in the study of other, non-European peoples. (van Dijk, 1993: 158)

The propensity, which van Dijk observes, for Europeans to examine what he refers to as 'the Other' has important implications for an examination of child neglect. For Europeans and their descendants in North America – 'white society' – have not simply studied Others, but judged them and have tried to change them. A substantial portion of modern social science is in fact occupied with the business of classifying, describing, and especially with trying to explain why groups or individuals behave 'differently.' Why do some people become criminals, why do some have babies out of wedlock, what characteristics are associated with child abuse, why do mothers neglect? Such studies implicitly or explicitly express socially legitimated norms of behaviour and 'hold' hierarchies of value.

Racial and cultural groupings have long been a topic for North American social science. In recent years human rights legislation and antidiscriminatory laws extending to virtually all areas of public life make the straightforward use of racial categories socially and politically unacceptable in many circumstances. Nevertheless, a part of the scientific endeavour is ongoing development of classification schemes that divide people into different groups. Standing in contradiction to this way of thinking about people are the homogenizing processes brought about through the extension of bureaucratic forms and practices into all arenas of life, both public and private. Such processes are built upon a premise of equal treatment and on the possibility of response systems *not* based on categorical differences such as race.

Social workers, along with other human service personnel, are placed at the juncture of these often opposing forces – those that insist on categorical difference and those promising equal, undifferentiated treatment. They are asked to classify people into problem categories in the context of work settings organized by bureaucratic processes guaranteeing similarity of treatment. To function in this contradictory position understandably creates tensions for workers as well as distortions in the way reality is experienced and acted upon.

In this chapter I examine how these opposing forces are played out in a way that presents the category of child neglect as unrelated to race and culture. In this sense, neglect can be seen to operate as part of a secondary level of socially and scientifically supported classification schemes, allowing for and in fact promoting social divisions based on race and/or culture under the rubric of 'equal treatment.' This contradictory effect is often hidden even from those most closely involved in screening people in and out of undesirable categories. This occurs for the very reason that the processes through which people are classified appear to guarantee equal treatment. This categorization process serves an important social purpose, which is to assist in the maintenance of existing power relations between the dominant white society and Others, that is, non-white races. Categories such as neglect help this to happen without an appearance that is explicitly racial. The bureaucratic sameness imposed through child welfare processes helps to hide from the workers themselves – who do the categorizing – the underlying racial and ethnic divisions they are helping to maintain and legitimize.

In this examination, the focus is on Canada's Native people, especially those coming into contact with child welfare authorities off reserve. An important reason for this focus is that it has been Native people who have developed the most trenchant and significant challenge to the Canadian child welfare system, and there is much to learn from this history and analysis. Native Canadians are a unique population within Canada, and I refer to some specific aspects of their history in this discussion. However, the propensity to classify racial and ethnic Others into the category neglect in disproportionate numbers does not apply only to Native people, but to other non-white groups as well (Hutchinson et al., 1992). As Armitage (1993) notes, other minority groups watch anxiously the efforts of Native people to regain control of the care of their own children; it is apparent that a precedent for culturally separate child welfare service is potentially in progress.

As noted in Chapter 2, race and culture are not synonymous terms. For purposes of this discussion, race and culture are viewed as two closely related, often overlapping, and indeed often indistinguishable aspects of minority group status in Canada, as well as in other Western countries. As Pinderhughes (1989) notes, 'race takes on a cultural significance as a result of the social processes that sustain the majority-minority status' (p. 9). Culture, as we shall see, also takes on ideological meanings in the context of a population set apart and discriminated against on the basis of race.

NATIVE PEOPLE AND THE CHILD WELFARE SYSTEM

Canadian social policy towards Native peoples has generally been referred to as one of 'assimilation,' which implies the transformation of a population from its traditional ways of life to the style preferred by the dominant culture. From the perspective of the dominant society, the assimilation of Native people has typically been characterized as a positive transition from wardship to citizenship (Satzewich and Wotherspoon, 1993). However, the term 'assimilation' does not adequately evoke the power relations involved in this transformation, nor does it make explicit the interests of ruling elites in promoting it. Histories of the conquering, colonizing, and subsequent domination of Native people and their resources reveal the depth and complexity of power brought to bear by Europeans not only in extracting wealth from the original inhabitants of Canada, but in transforming Native people and their cultural forms. One important feature of the colonizing process that Europeans have visited upon Native peoples has been the wresting of resources – land, water power, timber – from them. Miles (1989) describes in detail how colonizers frequently move from the claiming of resources to the transformation of indigenous populations into specific types of labour pools required by the new owners of the means of production, a process requiring 're-education' both in terms of skills and in terms of social and personal characteristics required of that labour pool. Miles's concept of racialization, outlined in Chapter 2, helps to reveal how racial characteristics of the conquered population become signifiers both of the presumed inferiority of their traditional characteristics and of the new expectations imposed upon the colonized group.

The role played by child welfare in reproducing relations of colonization of Native people has been explored by many (Hudson and McKenzie, 1981; Satzewich and Wotherspoon, 1993; Armitage, 1993). As Armitage notes, an important aspect of this role has been a consistent and strenuous attempt 'to change the culture and character of [Native] children' (1993: 131). Policies with this intent were carried out from the late nineteenth century through the 1960s largely through the medium of residential schools. The strategies and effects of these schools have been widely documented in recent years (King, 1967; Johnston, 1983; Miller, 1989). Through several decades, a large proportion of Native children were required to attend English-speaking residential schools for many of their formative years. Children were forcibly removed from their families at an early age. They were often forbidden to speak their own languages and were offered instruction in 'agriculture or a trade' (Miller, 1989). Documents of the time attest to the unquestioned superiority of culture assumed by the white colonial officials of the day, as they described the need for 'civilizing' influences on Native people (Armitage, 1993). The assimilation policy adopted by successive federal governments was intended to teach and retrain Native children to fit into the emerging economy of the developing country in these specified ways. However, ambivalence about this goal has regularly been expressed, and some officials clearly were sceptical from the outset that such a goal could be met: 'The Indian,' according to one official, 'has not got the ... moral get-up to enable him to compete' (quoted in Armitage, 1993: 135). As Miles points out, the processes of colonizing and racializing a population are contradictory. Attempts to invest a population with an image of inferiority often clash with efforts to remake them into an appropriately skilled labour force. While the playing out of this contradiction is still in progress, and widely debated, there is no doubt that these attempts have proceeded unevenly, in terms of both geography and gender (Bourgeoult, 1988, 1991).

There is some agreement, however, that the expedient of residential schools did not prove particularly effective in retraining or assimilating most Native pupils. The schools are generally seen, from the vantage point of the 1990s, as the too blunt instruments of cultural disintegration. Loss of language, interference with cultural styles of child-rearing and education, and prohibitions against rituals and traditional spiritual life left many reserves across Canada with 'a broken culture' (York, 1989). Over time, children who spent years at residential schools often became alienated from their own families as well as from life on the reserve. Furthermore, in recent years, allegations of ongoing physical and sexual abuse of many children in these schools have been made. And, as Armitage sums up, 'In the end, the residential schools were no preparation for life in any type of community' (1993: 142).

Until the 1960s, the federal government retained almost complete authority over life on reserves, including the management of child welfare issues. In spite of growing problems of family and cultural disorganization, the federal goverment provided very little in the way of protective services for children. Only in life and death circumstances would authorities intervene to protect children. In the absence of any real services, residential schools were sometimes used for child welfare purposes. Children thought by the Indian agent to be neglected might be sent off to school. However, the same circumstances might be used to justify leaving a child at home, on the theory of providing a 'stabilizing' influence on the family (King, 1967).

In the late 1940s, social workers helped to sway the federal government towards revision of its policy. A report of the Canadian Welfare Council and the Canadian Association of Social Workers to a Joint Committee of the Senate and House of Commons suggested that Native people on reserves were being deprived of the child welfare services available to white children. It was recommended that such services be extended to Native people by provincial governments. Many years passed before these recommendations were implemented. However, in the 1960s, as residential schools were phased out, child welfare services funded by the federal goverment but controlled by the provinces were gradually extended to reserves across Canada.

The idea that 'equal' child welfare service has ever been extended to Native people is questionable. For one thing, services across Canada have been highly variable. Johnston (1983) documented 'unequal treatment' for Native people, depending upon the efforts and policies implemented by different provinces. Nor have precisely the same services been offered to Native families as to others. Hepworth's study (1980) of foster care in Canada revealed a substantially higher proportion of Native children in the care of child welfare authorities than represented by Canadian children overall. According to Hepworth's research, at least 4 per cent of all Native children in the country were in the care of child welfare authorities, compared with about 1.5 per cent of Canadian children overall. Hepworth's research also showed that Native children were much more likely than others to remain in care. A short time later, Johnston (1983) published a book focusing solely on Native children and their historic and current relationship to the child welfare system in Canada. He documented the 'sixties scoop' in which many thousands of Native children had been apprehended from reserves, primarily in western Canada. Some reserves, he poignantly notes, lost virtually a generation of their children, for many of these children never returned home and some have simply disappeared without a trace.

The termination of residential schools, in other words, had not necessarily resulted in 'equal treatment' of Native families by the authorities. Nor had efforts to change Native families and their children ceased; rather, these efforts had merely changed form. Through child welfare practices, family separation via apprehension, foster home placement, and adoption continued to occur. In some ways, child welfare practices in fact represented an even more radical method of forcing cultural change (Armitage, 1993: 146–9). Many Native children were permanently removed not only from their families but from their bands, their culture, and from Canada. Children were sent to the United States or other parts of Canada for adoption, many with white families.

As these practices came to light in the 1970s and 80s, advocacy efforts aimed at legislative and institutional changes grew. As a result, several provinces have now incorporated in legislation clauses designed to discourage these practices, to insist on respect for the cultural background of the child in choosing foster placements, and to involve bands more consistently in decision-making processes. Various protocols have been developed in these provinces to ensure child welfare workers comply with legislation. In addition, a substantial trend towards the transfer of child welfare responsibilities to Indian bands has occurred. Many different kinds of 'tripartite agreements' involving bands and provincial and federal governments have been developed, involving various degrees of devolution of authority from provinces to bands (Timpson, 1990; Satzewich and Wotherspoon, 1993). Although there are problems in these arrangements (Wharf, 1989; Armitage, 1993; Satzewhich and Wotherspoon, 1993), this transfer of authority and decision-making power is a significant achievement, as well as an important step in the direction of self-government by Native people.

In spite of these gains, child welfare practices as developed over the past one hundred years continue to affect many Native families. One reason is that even bands operating under tripartite agreements generally must operate within the basic confines and definitions of provincial legislation (Morrissette, McKenzie, and Morrissette, 1993). Second, an exodus from reserves into cities has occurred over the past several decades. By 1986 nearly one-third of Canada's registered Indians lived off reserve (Satzewich and Wotherspoon, 1993: 95). Those families and children moving to urban areas are subject to child welfare and other forms of dominant society authority, and they have come to constitute a pool of clients dealt with through provincial child welfare authorities. Although Canadian figures are not readily available, it is likely that off-reserve Native families continue to be considerably overrepresented as clients of the child welfare system in urban areas. In my research (1990), for instance, Native families constituted only 4 per cent of the general population of the catchment area studied, but 50 per cent of the agency caseload. In other words, the process of 'decolonization' (Morrissette et al., 1993) is proceeding unevenly, and cultural hegemony continues to be exerted through child welfare in general and through the application of 'neglect' as a specific social category.

A BETTER FUTURE?

According to information reported to Johnston (1983), many child welfare workers have felt that in apprehending Native children from reserves, they were rescuing them from lives of poverty and squalor. They saw the conditions on reserves as extremely neglectful and believed that substitute care by more affluent, stable families could provide decent lives for the children. In spite of significant changes in legislation and decision making processes concerning Native children during the 1980s, such practices of thought and reasoning continue to be expressed by workers employed in urban agencies. In the following example, a worker struggles with a decision concerning permanent wardship for children of an off-reserve Native mother. The mother is single, has several children, and suffers from severe, long-term alcohol addiction. It is a tough decision, this worker says, 'whether the attachment with the natural parent is more significant than *a better future*' (italics mine).

On the surface, these words express a truth about the situation. Documentation of this case reveals many episodes of heavy drinking, resulting in unquestionably dangerous conditions for the children, poor housing, and many temporary foster care placements. The hope of a better future with an intact family follows from a hundred years of child welfare philosophy and belief in the foster care system. The 'better future' also carries with it more modern implications of permanent placement in a home offering high standards of safety, health, and education – the elements of a 'normal' life in Canada. The idea is also predicated on the values of the dominant culture which, as Blanchard and Barsh (1980) argue, pose material abundance as a supreme value while negating the importance of racial and cultural heritage in the development of healthy individuals. The choices available to mainstream professionals are, of course, built in varying degrees upon these cultural values. Thus, it is possible to imagine 'rescue' of these children leading to a better life – children settled in a comfortable home, going to good schools with interested teachers, making new friends, and so on. The children, as I note in my research commentary, are 'cute, adorable.' It is difficult to imagine that such charming children will be denied permanency, a 'real home' in which they can settle and be loved. The dilemma of this kind of decision is not restricted to 'biased' white workers, but rather it is one imposed by requirements of the work. A Native worker faced with a similar decision concerning permanent wardship recognizes the material benefits offered by the child's current foster home. In this case, the mother's drinking problem has led to abandonment of the child on many occasions and eventual foster placement. The worker agonizes over contradictory values, and recognizes she must decide between them: 'It tears me apart when I have to go there [the foster home] and see this little kid. And yet he's got a very good home. He's got his own room, got toys, they're just giving him everything. But that's not good enough. If I take him away from Mum, what the hell am I doing to him? How do I know?'

The evidence, of course, suggests the validity and importance of the concerns expressed by both workers. Bonding theory tells us that a child's continued attachment to the mother is extremely important to healthy development. Furthermore, the realities of placement for many Native children are far different from our imaginings. Many continue 'drifting' through different foster homes (Rosenbluth, 1994), experiencing abuse and racism along the way. Stories of suicide made public, for instance, through the diary and subsequent film concerning Richard Cardinal, who experienced countless placements (National Film Board), make clear that child welfare services do not necessarily provide a better future and in a vast number of cases have been a central factor in the further destruction of individual lives as well as of Native families and culture (Westermeyer, 1979; Armitage, 1993; Johnston, 1983).

It is important to notice the structure of decision making expressed by both workers. Documentation of these cases over many years, and a history involving placement of the children many times, suggests attachment of children to mother as risky and precarious. This attachment cannot, does not compare with the implicit images 'held' in the idea of a better future. For the second worker this comparison is completely explicit: material advantages vs. an unstable mother. Again, this is not idiosyncratic thinking on either worker's part, but a reflection of a widely held comparison structure, one reflecting a dichotomized and unequal choice, and one which has always posed the opportunities offered by the dominant culture – and its underlying economic arrangements – as the better and only rational choice. Both workers ultimately decide to recommend permanent wardship; in so doing they inadvertently help to reproduce the value structure of the dominant society. They really have little choice, given the unequal nature of the two available options.

CHILD NEGLECT AND CULTURAL RELATIVITY

As in Canada, American literature documents overrepresentation of Native children in the care of child welfare authorities (Byler, 1977). An issue of considerable importance emerging from publication of this information in the 1970s was whether child neglect was in reality an ethnocentric concept applied by white social workers to Native children and families. American social workers were subsequently accused of not realizing their own cultural moorings in making judgments about neglect. A child found alone on a reserve, they were told, was not necessarily an abandoned child. Nor were parents who did not issue 'obvious' disciplinary measures necessarily neglectful. Many social workers were 'surprised' to learn their practices were considered discriminatory (Kessel and Robbins, 1984). Similar issues were taken up in Canadian child welfare literature (Johnston, 1983; Falconer and Swift, 1983).

Discussion of the cultural dimensions of neglect was later taken up by Polansky et al., who asked in their research 'Is there such a thing as an American standard of minimal child care?' (1983: 345). This question was raised in the context of cultural challenges to the Childhood Level of Living Index (CLL), developed primarily by Polansky et al. (1972). In response to questions about the applicability of the scale to cultural Others, both black and white mothers of various social and class backgrounds were offered vignettes of child care situations and asked to respond on a Likert-type scale. Polansky et al. do not withhold from readers their starting position: 'Proponents of cultural relativity usually emphasize diversity, the things that divide people,' they comment (Polansky, Amons, and Weathersley, 1983: 341). In reporting the findings, they also instruct readers that 'any experienced social worker is well aware there are vast segments of family living in which the commonalities among people are far more impressive than their minor differences' (p. 345). The findings of this study are summed up in this way: 'Mothers may differ on whether children should be pushed to clean their plates or at what age they should be weaned, but nearly all believe children should be fed regularly and well' (p. 345). In other words, they concludes, there is an American minimal standard of child care which may be 'invoked … for legal and social work purposes' (p. 345). Cultural differences, (and by implication racial differences, because these are treated as identical in the study) become relatively trivial matters, not to be seen by social workers as affecting their judgments concerning neglect. Polansky et al.'s approach sidesteps both the overrepresentation of minority children in care and the vociferous complaints of minority groups about the practices of mainstream social workers. Invoked instead are the arguments in discourse, reviewed in Chapter 4, about whether child welfare should be in the business of encouraging an adequate standard of care or enforcing a minimal standard of care in order to 'ensure equal protection and standards for children and families' (Craft and Staudt, 1991: 368–9).

Others writing from the cultural perspective have tried to explore elements of cultural differences in child care standards and practices. Giovannoni and Becerra (1979), for instance, found cultural differences among blacks,

Hispanics, and whites with respect to the degree of seriousness specific incidents and parental behaviours were considered to pose. Korbin, an anthropologist, concluded in her cultural examination of abuse and neglect that 'there is no universally accepted standard for optimal child rearing or for abusive and neglectful behaviours' (1981: 205). At present, nevertheless, the most prominent recommendations in discourse are the need for 'definitional clarity' (Rose and Meezan, 1993) and standardization of the definition of neglect (Craft and Staudt, 1991). Remaining at issue is the question of whether a clear and standardized definition, even if claimed to articulate only the most minimal of standards, could still be used to impose the values of the dominant culture on minority groups.

In discourse, the question of whether neglect has, or should have, a cultural component has not actually proceeded much further than this. Instead, the site of debate has come to revolve around issues of culturally correct placement of children already apprehended by child welfare workers, possibly a result of the way issues have been framed in legislation over the past two decades. In 1978, the American Indian Child Welfare Act was passed in the United States. This federal legislation concerned itself not so much with definitional problems as with increasing in specified ways Indian control over child welfare decision processes. Sections concerning Native children entered into provincial legislation in Canada also focus on decisions taken after a child is in care.

A debate appearing in the journal *Social Work* concerning the effects of such legislation capsulized some of the issues involved. Fischler (1980), one of the discussants, does not consider the possibility of culturally different ideas of child care. Instead, he sets out to prove that American Indian families are no less likely than other American families to neglect or abuse their children, and they should therefore be subject to the same legislation and practices as others. On the basis of two studies, Fischler finds it 'likely' that 'the personality profile of maltreating parents are similar in all cultures.' He refers to both neglect and abuse as 'family affairs,' and brings in the concept of the generational cycle, familiar from previous chapters, to explain the ongoing nature of neglect and abuse in American Indian families (1980: 343). From Fischler's point of view, special legislation for Native people is not warranted.

A response in the same issue (Blanchard and Barsh, 1980) comments on what they regard as a contradictory position taken by Fischler regarding bonding theory. Fischler uses this concept selectively, they maintain, in the service of arguing against increased Native control in child welfare. As used by Fischler, the effects of severed attachments only emerge *after* the children have been removed from their original parents. His concern is with the attachment between Native children and their (usually white) foster parents, and he argues against legislated Native control which could lead to breaking that attachment in favour of returning children to their parents, bands, and culture. Blanchard and Barsh further comment on the cycle idea from the perspective of American Indian culture. This concept, they say, is especially powerful because 'the propensity [to neglect and abuse children] is seen as 'transmitted by those individuals with whom the child initially bonds' (1980: 352), which in some cultures involves group members in addition to the mother. Although not explicit in the article, the implication is that the cycle idea, applied to caregivers in such cultures, may be used to indict the whole group. Implied are more drastic measures than changing mother, for it is not simply the mother who must be changed but the group. This logic legitimates the necessity of removing children not only from the family but also from *the group* as the only effective method of breaking the cycle. Permanent wardship of Native children is then easily seen as beneficial to future generations, because the cycle of neglect will be broken.

To summarize, the child welfare systems in both Canada and the United States stand indicted as discriminatory to Native people. Certainly, some important legislative, policy, and service changes have grown out of the ongoing debate and the struggle of Native people to care for their own children. However, Native children still come under the authority of mainstream child welfare legislation and services. Various debates in discourse demonstrate continuing and considerable mainstream resistance to developing definitions, legislation, theory, and social work approaches that are specific to the history, culture, and caregiving problems faced by Native families.

Workers in mainstream organizations now have a dual and contradictory mandate. They are to recognize some special issues with respect to Native families and children, and yet they are to assess and intervene in families in terms of concepts – neglect, abuse, the cycle theory – invented, defined, and enforced by the dominant culture. Child neglect has come under the scrutiny of both Native and white critics with respect to its cultural implications, but these remain marginal to understanding and defining neglect. Although some attention has been paid over the past fifteen years to the possibility of neglect 'holding' cultural standards of child caring, this idea has not taken precedence in discourse nor has it affected the way neglect is framed in legislation. Although some authors have suggested that cultural differences in child-caring behaviours and expectations exist, this idea has not widely entered child welfare discourse; it has been refuted by the most prominent scholar of child neglect, Polansky, and is not supported by most scholars trying to define neglect. Concepts related to neglect through the cycle theory may supercede neglect itself in thought processes through which apprehension of Native children is justified. Meanwhile, the processes of colonialization that have so drastically affected Native people move to the background as causal factors in cases of neglect. In the following section I examine the kinds of instructions social workers receive through discourse about 'culturally sensitive' practice.

PROFESSIONAL SOCIAL WORK DISCOURSE

There are two parallel but generally separate streams of professional discourse guiding social workers in the 1980s and 1990s in their work in child welfare. In fact, with respect to issues of race and culture, the discourse could be said to have developed a split personality. The first stream is the traditional social work and child welfare discourse, referred to in previous chapters. This stream of literature is not centrally occupied by issues of culture and race in service delivery, but neither is it completely unresponsive to developments 'in the field.' However, traditional ideas of the nature of social work, its mission, and its clients continue to appear very much as always in texts and articles about social work generally and child welfare in particular, regardless of racial, cultural, and political debates. Of course, many of the texts used to teach and convey social work ideas are American. These standard texts portray social work, by and large, as a culturally and racially neutral profession. Standard topics in general texts include social work values, the problem-solving process, interviewing skills, engagement of clients in the treatment process, termination of the helping relationship with clients, and so on.

Texts written or revised in the 1980s provide at least limited references to cultural issues, reflecting the emergence of these ideas in the larger social context, and in general counselling social workers to work towards cultural sensitivity. A 1984 text by Garvin and Seabury, for example, has a chapter devoted to cultural issues. In another section of that book, a discussion of possible barriers practitioners may face in engaging clients in the treatment process includes a brief mention of 'ethnic, social or racial differences' (1984: 121). Suggestions to social workers faced by such differences include attempts to find a worker or layhelper who is better 'matched' to the client. Another suggestion is creation of a group of clients of similar background. These recommendations are relatively non-controversial but do not match the circumstances in which many social workers find themselves, especially in mandated services such as child welfare where client assignment is usually based on geographical boundaries rather than on worker characteristics.

Hartman and Laird, writing on family-centred practice, suggest workers 'always keep in mind our own ethnocentric view' (1983: 277). They also include brief discussions of cultural variations in family structure, but they do not emphasize race as an issue. Perhaps just as significant, case material used in this and many other social work texts very seldom identifies clients · by race or culture, implying that the same approaches and processes are appropriate for all.

The specific arena of child welfare also reflects this generic approach to professional training. Various editions of Kadushin's standard text, *Child Welfare Services*, show that treatment of race, ethnicity, and culture reflects the changing temper of the times. In the 1967 version, for instance, poverty is a main theme, and issues of race are to some extent put forward. The discussion of child neglect in this volume places it in the context of socioeconomic circumstances of client groups; Kahn is cited as suggesting that 'misfortune' may be a more appropriate designation than neglect. In the edition published in the following decade, a more clinical approach is taken, with the section devoted to minorities considerably shortened and references of poverty and race sinking to the background in the discussion of child neglect (1974; 1980). In the most recent edition (with Martin, 1988), some attention to Hispanics and Native Americans is added as a general topic. However, in the discussion of neglect, Kadushin cites Polansky on the issue of definition, concluding: 'There seems little to suggest differences in the conceptualization of child abuse and neglect despite ethnic differences' (p. 232).

The only topic consistently dealing with race and culture in all four versions of Kadushin is cross-racial adoption. Considerable space is given to this topic and to the cultural implications of such adoptions. While there are brief references made to American and Canadian Indians and to black and other minority populations in various contexts, relatively little space is allotted to special issues faced by these groups; most advice on intervention does not recognize culture or race as issues; and case examples do not identify clients as members of cultural or racial groups (Kadushin, 1967, 1974, 1980; Kadushin and Martin, 1988).

A second, and largely separate, discourse concerned with social work services to culturally and racially diverse groups has made an appearance in the 1980s, both in the United States and Canada. It is usually referred to under such titles as 'multiculturalism,' 'cross cultural service delivery,' and, more recently, 'anti-racism.' In contrast to traditional texts, this literature focuses on race and/or culture as absolutely essential features to consider in planning and delivering human services. This body of discourse is fed by several related streams. Much of it has developed within the specific historical contexts of immigration and race relations in the United States and Canada. Pinderhughes's (1989) discussion of the origins of these new ideas suggests that the idea of 'black pride' that grew out of the American civil rights movement, has had substantial ripple effects for the entire American population. As this idea took hold in the black community, other groups such as Native Americans and Hispanics, groups long subjugated in the United States, began to advocate more actively for their rights and to promote their own culture and identity as valuable. Eventually, according to Pinderhughes, even white ethnic groups who had formerly appeared to accept the WASP (White, Anglo-Saxon, Protestant) values of the dominant society began to reclaim their cultural heritage and to promote the value of cultural identity. The appearance on television of the serialized *Roots* was a seminal cultural event, for both Americans and many Canadians. The idea of recovering one's cultural roots captured the imagination of a population almost all of whom had in some way lost touch. The multicultural model has enjoyed considerable acceptance in Canada. Indeed, the federal government has located multiculturalism in its institutional structure, in legislation, in social policy and funding, and in its public relations campaigns. Canadians are frequently enjoined to 'celebrate diversity,' to be tolerant of newcomers, to see the national identity as inextricably bound up with a racially and culturally diverse population – to take pride in being cosmopolitan (Bissoondath, 1993). All of this stands in considerable contradiction, of course, to century-old policies respecting Native peoples.

In the field of human services, attention to culture-specific service delivery issues appeared in the literature, especially in the fields of education and counselling, beginning in the 1970s and early 1980s (Pedersen, 1976; Sue, 1981). Within a short time other professionals, including social workers, began to pay attention to cross-cultural issues in their work (Green, 1982; Falconer and Swift, 1983; McGoldrick, 1982). In the early 1980s, this discourse dealt with such questions as posed by Jenkins in *The Ethnic Dilemma in Social Services* (1981), asking how, where, and when ethnic factors should be incorporated into service delivery. Green's *Cultural Awareness in the Human Services* (1982) elaborates these issues. Some work takes up specific service arenas, for instance, McGoldrick's text on *Ethnicity and Family Therapy* (1982). Recent work centres more explicitly on race and racism as issues in the social and human services as, for instance, does Davis and Proctor's *Race, Gender, and Class* (1989). Canada has contributed its share of discourse in this arena (Kallen, 1983; McKague, 1991) as has Great Britain (Dominelli, 1988; Miles, 1989). In addition to texts dealing with culture and race, a substantial array of work is becoming available that expresses the experiences, thoughts, feelings, and perspectives of immigrants, refugees, people of colour, and other identified minority group members (e.g., Maracle, 1993). An interesting feature of the literature that has emerged is a splitting off of race and culture. Thus, there is literature focusing on 'ethnicity,' which emphasizes that everyone has culture (McGoldrick, 1982); and literature emphasizing race and racism as underlying issues that are seen as more volatile and intractable (Dominelli, 1988).

DIFFERENT/SAME

This body of literature, in all its variations, has developed around the idea that the existence of racial and/or cultural differences between service providers and consumers has implications not only for service effectiveness but for the very shape and kind of services offered. The central concept of difference, and its obverse, sameness, have perhaps been best explored by Pinderhughes (1989), who reports verbatim the thoughts and feelings of human service workers about their experiences of being the same as or different from other people. Her approach avoids the problems of choosing an emphasis on either race or culture, posing power differentials as a primary feature requiring attention. As van Dijk's analysis (1993) suggests, categories of difference are not value free, nor without social purpose. People are not posed as simply different; they are cast as better or worse, above or below, more or less. Pinderhughes shows how such evaluative procedures occur in everyday thinking about differences from our friends and family, as well as from those we work with. Also examined are typical affective responses that accompany the identification of difference. Far from a 'celebration,' Pinderhughes suggests that most people identify difference with isolation and abandonment, and react with 'negative' emotions like fear and anxiety (pp. 29–30). Various service providers speak more specifically about racial difference: 'I want (people of colour) to stop bringing up [race] all the time because it's like a barrier' (p. 102). Racial differences appear to evoke in white people feelings of fear, guilt, and powerlessness. Suggestions that a different kind of practice ought to be provided to racially and culturally different Others often produce in white professionals, according to Pinderhughes, a sense that their credentials and expertise are being attacked and undermined.

Even as this discourse on difference develops, a contradictory ethic of equal treatment has emerged. For the past several decades, an emerging priority has become the delivery of equal, non-discriminatory services across geographical and demographic lines. The connotations of sameness in this context are quite positive, suggesting efforts of the dominant society, which mounts services, to be fair, to provide the same kind and level of service to all those eligible for it. The social work proposal to extend 'equal' child welfare services to Native people, cited earlier, is an example. Many white human service professionals eagerly express attachment to this value, often finding in the process that diversity is of lesser importance. Both Polansky et al. (1983) and Fischler (1980), cited earlier, show how this value is expressed with relation to child neglect. Green (1982) quotes one professional expressing a common sentiment: 'I try to meet all ethnic groups on an equal basis' (1982: 179). The value placed on sameness in service provision is generally posed as positive. In fact, when the idea of 'equal treatment' comes up, the value of celebrating or even noticing cultural and racial differences moves to the background. Some authors explicitly justify this removal: 'Proponents of cultural relativity usually emphasize diversity, *the things that divide people*' (Polansky, et al., 1983: 341; italics mine). Polansky et al. explicitly state here that a focus on diversity is divisive, which is negative; by implication, attention to similarities then must be inclusive, which is positive.

In summary, there are contradictory messages to workers in discourse about how to do social work in general and how to understand child neglect in particular. Although fraught with many contradictions, both streams, the latter much more than the former, encourage 'cultural sensitivity' in the worker. Although people engaged in human service planning and delivery are exhorted to recognize and become comfortable with difference, workers often harbour negative feelings about difference. They also receive a contradictory message from other sources, a message counseling them to provide the same service to all, to see sameness as good and as inclusive, and, by implication, to see dominant culture values, ideas, and categories as the terrain on which Others should aspire to operate.

STANDARDIZING NEGLECT: PROCEDURES AND EFFECTS

Clearly, today's child welfare worker approaches a minority family accused of neglect with a daunting array of conflicting ideas, ideals, standards, and instructions in mind. Workers no doubt have variable awareness of the instructions provided through discourse, and somewhat different rules to follow depending on their agency setting. However, the predominant instruction, in discourse as in legislation, is 'equal treatment.' In my 1990 study, assessments of neglect by workers were expressed as having nothing to do with race or culture (Swift, 1990) even though 50 per cent of the agency's clientele were Native people. In speaking about Native families, workers virtually always discussed the problems and prospects of those families in exactly the same way as they spoke about other families. Identifiers of clients as Native people all but disappeared in files as well as in most talk about clients, and very few connections were made by workers between the history of Native people in Canada and the current circumstances of the Native families on their caseloads. With a few notable exceptions, this 'silence' about race and culture persisted even when I explicitly raised the issue. This way of 'standardizing' neglect through silence reflects examples and perspectives found in mainstream social work discourse, and certainly fulfils the legislative mandate requiring that definitions apply to all parents alike.

Files from past years show that workers did explicitly identify and speak about Native families as distinct. Many written comments, however, were questionable, insinuating that people with 'decidedly Native features' were somehow naturally connected to histories of alcoholism and violence. In more recent written records, such connections have become rare. Current emphasis on Native rights and culture, coupled with the possibility of records becoming public in court, cause workers to avoid identifying families by race or culture, except by means of the official categories provided on forms. Certainly, workers are aware of current political issues of equity and discrimination. One worker puts the issue this way: 'I've gone through files from the 50s and 60s where people are referring to clients as 'this family of drunken Indians.' If I were to go into court today with that written in the file, the judge would say "obviously you're a bigot ... you're damning not only the family but the Native race." I believe the judge would throw [the case] out.'

Naturally enough, workers do not want to be seen as bigots, nor do they want to risk having their cases thrown out of court, not only because considerable effort goes into preparing cases, but because workers generally see court action as the last resort to protect a child in danger. Because connections between race and problem behaviour presented in the file could appear as the reinforcement of a stereotype, workers now generally leave out these identifiers, except where required to check off specific categories provided on agency forms. This practice might be seen as 'equal treatment' for Native families; the absence of racial identifiers in effect operates as a statement of fairness – assurance that the family is being viewed and judged the same as any other.

A contradiction is embedded in this practice, however, which is that along with the identifiers also disappear connections between current problems and the historical context out of which the present situation has developed. One worker shows how this removal leaves a space for racialized judgments to be inserted. In a previous file recording, this Native mother had been described as 'dull.' The worker explains: 'I can understand what they're saying. Mom will let you do the talking for her. She would wait to hear what you wanted her to say.' Encouraged to elaborate, this worker supplies an alternate explanation, one emphasizing the mother's creativity in managing a problematic social context: 'I don't find that to be dull, I find that to be very intelligent. A group of people that are systematically put down as much as Natives – I find that to be a most intelligent way to survive. And that's what she did.' However, this kind of connection is not made in file recording. Hence, in the records kept for child welfare purposes, 'Mom is dull.'

Native people have written eloquently about the importance of viewing problems within the historical context of attempts to destroy their culture and families: 'We have lost our languages, medicines and religions. We have lost our pride, dignity and confidence. We have lost our family values, social patterns and political structures. We have lost our stewardship over the land. We have lost control of our lives and our destiny. We have lost almost everything a race of people can lose' (Maracle, 1993: 9). This is part of the context from which individual families are extracted in the ordinary course of working up a child welfare dossier. Each family, one by one, is identified, diagnosed, judged, treated, as though the problems, the deficiencies of caring and of living arose within this individual family and must be solved by this particular family, and as though behaviours are unrelated to historic and current power differentials. This process helps to remove the context of colonialism to the far background, both in everyday work with clients and in recording. Meanwhile, the individual family becomes accountable to child welfare authorities for its behaviour. Simultaneously, through attention to protocols within the agency, the appearance of dealing with 'Native issues' is created and maintained.

Treating Native families as any other means not only the disappearance or dilution of history and background; it also means acceptance of knowledge, understandings, and experience taken from the dominant culture and its members as adequate and best for all families. As we have seen, much professional discourse encourages workers in this way of thinking. As seen in previous chapters, workers draw from a store of shared knowledge of the cycle theory to explain neglect. This approach, developed within the dominant culture, is applied to Native parents as to any others: 'It's a generational thing.'

Following from this understanding, a central and socially legitimated focus for workers is to teach and enforce 'what everyone knows' individual mothers should do to break the cycle of poor mothering, instructions referenced in file recording:

'Mom has not learned her lesson'

'These parents need to realize the effects of their own behaviour'

Invoked here is the nuclear family model developed and sustained in modern capitalist society, in which parents have a particular relation to the state, together with implicit and mostly exclusive responsibilities for care of children. To 'realize' carries implications that there is a normal course of events and parenting behaviours, and that parents can exert control, through cognitive processes and force of will, to achieve these certain outcomes. In this model, however, the *common interests* of Native parents and their children · – history, culture, a shared destiny based on both different cultural patterns of child rearing and on processes of colonization and racism in white society – do not make an appearance. Attention is instead directed to assumed contradictory interests of parents and children, an issue further explored in Chapter 8. The ideas, institutions, and rescue operations of the dominant society and their representatives then appear as the only real safety for children whose parents are failing.

In addition to employing standardized definitions and explanatory theories of neglect, workers also apply standardized work procedures and case management approaches to families accused of neglect. These are matters about which they appear to have little choice, because they are expected to follow established protocols and to offer only sanctioned resources to clients. Through these ordinary approaches and procedures, however, Native families continue to be viewed, documented, and managed in ways that help to reproduce relations of subjugation for Native people. An example is case monitoring – common in neglect cases – through which Native families remain subject to very considerable scrutiny and control of dominant culture institutions.

The plethora of related problems appearing in case files tends to confirm many Native families as 'multiproblem.' A review of some stressful issues found in records of several Native families I surveyed includes an overwhelming array of life problems and crises, including substance abuse, serious health problems in parents (including tumours and diabetes), health issues and disabilities in children (including deafness and cardiac arrest), frequent and ongoing domestic violence, sexual abuse of children, unemployment, incarceration of the breadwinner, widespread drug abuse within the extended family, long-term poverty, overcrowded housing, frequent moves, loss of Treaty status and benefits, divorce and violent death of loved ones.

In mainstream society, responses to these issues are divided among many professionals: contributions by public health nurses, doctors, lawyers, welfare workers, housing authorities, psychologists, school and day care personnel, employment counsellors, child guidance clinic staff, among others, appear in these files. Of course, these professionals are not all working simultaneously or necessarily in concert. Newly assigned to a case, one worker describes attendance at a case conference of all involved professionals: 'I learned an important lesson there, that the new social worker on the block shows up and goes to a case conference meeting, they're the ones that walk out doing everything. [The others] had all their reasons ready why child welfare should be involved. And they were also pretty concerned about welfare. I remember driving there with the welfare worker. The guy sort of slapped me on the shoulder and said, "it's you and me, pal.'"

Given the number of involved professionals in many families, considerable information sharing about the family occurs. Ordinarily the family will be asked to sign a 'release of information' to protect agencies from breaching confidentiality. From the family's point of view, these practices mean substantial scrutiny of their private lives by many people, for virtually all involved personnel will have some information and can get access to considerably more. At the same time no one professional is fully accountable; it is a 'team' effort.

In practice, pressure is often exerted on child welfare services to become involved in a central way. This centrality of child welfare in the running of a multiproblem case both ensures that the appropriate personnel will be on hand to enforce legal mandates and that the plethora of problems involved will come to appear primarily as child welfare problems. These practices are perfectly understandable in Foucault's terms. They allow us, as representatives of the dominant culture, 'to know them,' 'to alter them.' The professional team provides the appearance of and structure for a concerted effort of professionals who are helping the family. At the same time, these professionals have the legitimized expertise to name the desired and required changes expected of the family members. The centrality of child welfare provides the categories that allow us to focus on either changing the parent or rescuing the child. The repetition of problems serves to move parents to the unworthy category, while the desperate problems of ill-health, poverty, poor housing, violence, and so on, become not the central issues to be acted upon but simply the attendant issues of the multiproblem family. Each of these is 'just one [problem] on a list of many' for the client, as one worker said. However, repeated instances counted as neglect are more than 'just one problem.' The child welfare mandate makes this issue central for the family; abstract debates about whether the main issue is neglect or poverty or addiction become irrelevant, because repeated neglect incidents mean children will eventually be 'rescued' from their 'multiproblem' families. At best, the family remains subject to the ongoing scrutiny of the agency.

CULTURAL SENSITIVITY 'ON THE GROUND'

In an interaction between a child welfare worker and a minority client, the worker's actions are shaped by and attuned to values and practices developed and promoted by the dominant race and culture. This is so even if the worker is not white, because the individual still brings to the encounter structures and directives shaped within this culture. Clients, by definition, represent a deviation from dominant culture norms, and if the clients are members of a racial and/or cultural minority, they bring a different experience of reality to the encounter. These differences enter into and shape the interaction, even if this is not acknowledged by either.

In reflecting on these differences we can see that it is possible to extract 'culture' itself from the context of its origins and its economic moorings. Bissoondath (1993) refers to social processes through which culture comes to be simplified, made into a relic. The very concept of culture then becomes ideological, hiding from view the original purposes of cultural forms as well as the extent of social destruction that occurs when cultural forms are forcibly altered. An example relevant to Native people might be the kinship group. Satzewich and Wotherspoon (1993) show how this communal form was tied to the productive processes of life for Native people prior to the trade relations established by Europeans. The requirements of capitalism necessitated the reshaping of this form into a nuclear-style family. In this process, as Bourgeault (1991) shows very well, not only the family form changed, but relations between Native men and women were transformed. Native women, like other women in capitalist economies, were reshaped both as workers and as sexual beings, in a way that better fit both the economic needs and the sexual needs of the colonizers.

As later generations of child welfare workers regard Native families, they see the variable results of this process, with remnants of communal and kinship forms remaining, often accompanied by extreme levels of disorganization and violence. Today's child welfare workers are left with highly contradictory instructions to follow. Legislation may suggest that the kinship group and band leaders should be consulted in placement decisions about children. In everyday practice with Native people, however, workers see destructive patterns within extended families and on reserve. Case files show many examples of workers' efforts to 'get Mom away' from various relatives who appear to be interfering with child care. Instructions to mothers to 'throw out' abusive partners; insistence that mothers move out on their own; promises extracted not to invite alcoholic siblings into their homes are common examples. Although the immediate reason for these instructions is to increase safety for children, these directives also continue to operate in the reshaping of Native people into units approximating the nuclear family. This is a form better suited to the norms and requirements of modern capitalism, and one in which mother's job, at whatever cost, is to reproduce members of society.

'Cultural sensitivity,' prescribed as an add-on in so much social work discourse, is an inadequate conceptual tool for understanding the nature and power of the economic forces that create and sustain these contradictions (Morrissette et al., 1993). When clients of the child welfare system are cultural and racial Others, several levels of ideology are operating simultaneously. Individuals and families, removed through everyday work processes from a complex historical context, come to appear to members of the dominant race and culture as 'multiproblem.' Culture appears to white workers as a somewhat anachronistic relic of the past, which we are asked to honour without quite understanding why, given that the 'fit' of this culture with modern economic life is poor. Meanwhile, issues of race are subsumed by talk about culture. Race is simultaneously obvious to white workers, and yet it is made to disappear from talk and writing, and possibly from much conscious thought as workers strive to treat the family as any other. In this process, racism as a social form also disappears as an issue for white workers, while for Native and other non-white clients it remains an everyday experience.

The ordinary processes of work with families in mainstream child welfare then continue the reshaping effort, begun through other institutions, under the contradictory guises of equal treatment and culturally specific service. The efforts of workers to apply equal treatment and standardized definitions amount to denial of the cultural and racial realities of Others. The casting of Native families in the same light as all others denies them both their unique heritage and the specificity of their oppression by the dominant group. The child care issues faced by Native people grow from a particular historical context, one of ongoing colonialization by the dominant society that has condemned Native people to specific kinds of loss and deprivation. The results of this oppressive process have now reemerged as neglect, seen as the fault and responsibility of individual Native parents – again, the surface appearance of neglect. The criterion of chronicity, built into the definition of neglect, ensures years of poor care and suffering as well as innumerable placements for many Native children – such are the effects of a 'least intrusive' policy. Meanwhile, ongoing scrutiny, justified by various neglect incidents, ensures that the behaviour and organization of the family continues under the control of several agencies and organizations. The coercive power of the state can be and is invoked when behaviour slips too far from accepted norms. Consequently, Native children continue to be removed from the care of their families, just as they were before child welfare legislation became 'culturally sensitive.'

Child welfare, in other words, is a system well suited to keeping order, the order required for existing power and economic relations to be maintained, and child neglect is a concept well suited to justifying processes through which order is maintained. Child welfare is not, however, a system well suited to meeting the needs of Native people; surely several decades of destructive outcomes resulting from our efforts provide sufficient evidence of this. Nor is neglect a category that actually serves Native people or saves Native children, although it may appear this way in individual cases. Child welfare work with Native people, in fact, illustrates very well the way Althusser's concepts of repressive and ideological apparatuses operate in concert to produce desired effects, purposes captured in the phrase 'teaching Mom a lesson.' Bureaucratic processes work simultaneously to produce the appearance of equal treatment and 'business as usual' for workers in the system. Workers apply the schema of neglect in more or less the same way to specific families and, most of the time, are unable to see beyond their own fragmented work processes to observe the part this classification process plays in the subjugation and racialization of the whole group.

PART 3: THE RESPONSE SYSTEM

This part explores two responses to the issue of neglect. The first, presented in Chapter 8, is the current mandated approach, characterized by a contradiction between helping involuntary clients and exerting authority over them. In this chapter I explore this fundamental contradiction, show how it is ordinarily resolved by both practitioners and researchers, and comment on the effects of this resolution.

In Chapter 9, the directions suggested by the critical model are examined. Critical knowledge is knowledge for use in social transformation. The focus here is on transformative processes within individuals involved in the social services. This chapter explores different directions for everyday perceiving and thinking, for professional knowledge building, and for working with clients, directions aimed at changing the social realities explored in Part 2.

8

'Good Parents': The Current Approach to Neglect

We are accustomed to thinking of ourselves as living in a 'free society.' State repression is usually far from our thoughts, except as we read about events in far-off regimes. If we think of repression in the terms that Althusser suggests, however, it can be seen as residing in the ordinary affairs of everyday Canadian life. In his terms, repression involves the securing by force, physical or otherwise, of those conditions that ensure the reproduction of the relations of production. An example is the presence of uniformed police officers at the scene of a legal strike action. Their visible presence informs us of the state's unswerving intention to ensure the ongoing relations of production. If striking workers exceed warranted boundaries, these police officers can and will be seen exerting force against them.

In child welfare, the image of the 'baby snatcher' is familiar. The widespread use of this derogatory term reflects a shared, but usually unspoken, social knowledge of the repressive powers of the state that reside in the person of the child welfare worker. Child welfare workers, of course, do not ordinarily engage in violence, but the legally forced and enforced separation of parents from their children is, in Althusser's terms, repressive. As we have seen in previous chapters, workers consciously and often use this power to coerce clients, although expressed intentions of workers relate to what they believe are the client's best interests.

In contrast to this view of child welfare, the literature used for training and education of workers does not usually mention or implicitly refer to the apprehension of children, either as a threat or as an actual occurrence, as repressive. Discussion centres instead on the apparent contradiction in practice between the authority of the mandated child welfare role and the helping role propounded in and through social work. In this chapter, I will examine how this kind of advice functions in relation to the issue of helping clients accused of neglect, and I will also explore in more depth some repressive and ideological functions served by training materials.

THE FAMILY, THE STATE, AND CHILD WELFARE

Workers really feel we're in the helping professions. (Worker)

There's a lot to be said for being the bad guy in social work. (Worker)

Getting evidence and establishing a relationship with the client are not antithetical procedures. (Kadushin and Martin, 1988)

Is the purpose of child welfare to help clients or to exert authority over them? Or is there no real contradiction between these two ideas? In order to understand fully the nature of this problem, it is necessary to place it in the context of family–state relations. Child welfare practice, procedures, and legislation rest upon a relation between the family and the state. From its earliest beginnings, child welfare work has posed the family as a private entity, one responsible for its own destiny and for particular aspects of the care of their children. The state, as 'parent of the nation,' is responsible for enforcing this ideal. This conception of the relation between the family and the state implies the possibility of 'intrusion' by the state into the private family. When children are involved, child welfare workers, as agents of the state, are the 'intruders.' The term 'intrusion' refers implicitly to the various rights of the involved parties. Traditionally, as we have seen in Chapter 3, the balance of rights has been viewed as residing between parents and the state. When parents can demonstrate that they are carrying out their responsibilities, the state has no rights of intrusion. This is expressed in child welfare as the 'least intrusive' principle. However, if evidence suggests parents are not adequately protecting their children, parents' rights to privacy may be abrogated.

The child welfare mandate requires that every complaint concerning the maltreatment of a child be investigated. Thus, any complaint about parents, regardless of the source, constitutes sufficient evidence for a potentially intrusive investigation.[1] This kind of intrusion is socially and legally justified by the vulnerability of children vis-à-vis adults; they are understood to require the protection of the state because they are not fully able to defend themselves. In other words, children are a third party with rights in the child welfare situation, a fact that has only recently become fully explicit.[2] These rights are given moral support through such scholarly works as Lloyd de Mause's research (1974) on the history of childhood, which promotes a view that children have a right to expect a relatively carefree and protected childhood. This sentiment usually goes unquestioned among child welfare workers, and it provides the justification for intruding upon the private family. One worker phrased the connection this way: 'If you didn't neglect your child and breach his or her right to a healthy, happy childhood, then I wouldn't breach your right to privacy.'

Both workers and experts are sensitive to the issue of 'unwarranted intrusion,' meaning interference in the internal workings of a family, when evidence suggests that parents are carrying out their duties towards children. This concern expresses acceptance of an implicit social contract between the family and the state. The 'family' as posed here is a unit. Child welfare legislation typically speaks of the family as society's basic unit: 'The family is the basic unit of society and its well-being should be supported and preserved' (Child and Family Services Act, Manitoba, 1986).

Implied in the term 'unit' is the existence of agreements and common interests among family members; that is, families are thought of not only as units but as unitary in their needs and feelings. Recent feminist analysis suggests this presentation of the family is ideological in nature, covering over the contradictory problems and interests of various family members (Hartmann, 1987). In Hartmann's work, the family is viewed instead as a locus of struggle, based on the different nature of work people do within the family and on different levels of control people have over the products of their labour. By examining the family as a location for production and redistribution, Hartmann exposes the contradictory nature of the family unit. Families do act as unitary agents at times, she argues, setting themselves against other entities such as the state. This occurs because the social relations of production and distribution ensure the mutual dependency of family members. However, those same relations create tensions within the household, because members have different levels and sources of income, different socially allocated tasks and expected responsibilities.

With this framework in mind, even a cursory look at child welfare shows that the special rights we now recognize for children are actually expressive of the particular interests and social location of children within the family. Looked at from this perspective we can see that children stand in yet another relation than either fathers or mothers to both the state and to forces of production. First, through child welfare legislation, the safety of children within the family is theoretically protected. As Eichler (1988: 69) points out, children have ordinarily been viewed as passive family members, available to be acted upon by their parents. The state expresses this view through legislation that differentiates children from other family members for protective purposes. Although this idea is completely obvious, its significance has been covered over in the way we usually think about child welfare. Goldstein, Freud, and Solnit (1979) show how this is done: 'So long as the child is part of a viable family, his own interests are merged with those of the other members. Only after the family fails in its function should the child's interests become a matter for state intrusion' (Introduction).

As these authors pose the issue, the interests of family members ordinarily 'merge,' and a special or different relation of children to the state only exists as the result of family failure. In law, however, this different relation exists at all times, as ordinary families know. Jokes that mothers exchange reflect this 'common knowledge.' A mother whose child has a bruise might joke that she looks like an abused child; messy housekeeping can call forth a joke about child neglect. These remarks remind us that the grounds suggesting family failure may shift, may become more vague or more clear; the theoretical possibility that one's own children could come under scrutiny is ever-present. Periodically, as the 'home alone' case illustrates, a failure will become prominent and will provide all families with a reminder of this relation and the power of the state to invoke it.

Second, children in modern capitalism, unlike their parents, are not expected to be members of the paid workforce. They are potential future workers, or, we might say, in the process of being produced as workers, not yet expected to be productive members of society but with gradually increasing expectations to participate in the appropriate preparatory activities, especially education. The interests of the state and of productive forces are not unrelated. The state, in protecting children, helps to ensure reproduction of the labour force, largely through the medium of 'the family,' but through enforcement procedures as well; the truant officer provides an example. The state also takes responsibility to provide minimal support for children whose parents do not; and in so doing ensures at least the physical reproduction of the future labour force. Because children are not expected to be self-supporting, they are among the 'worthy poor.' The literature of childhood supports the notion that they, unlike their parents, should be relatively free of responsibilities during youth.

Parents stand in a different relation from children to the state and to the forces of production. Adults are expected to be productive members of society. Fathers, of course, traditionally are expected to be breadwinners, whereas mothers are supposed to be engaged in reproductive work, and frequently nowadays in breadwinning as well. Failure to meet these obligations is likely to cast parents as members of the 'unworthy poor.' This idea of the different relations of family members to forces outside the family is important to an understanding of how help and authority are understood and applied in child welfare.

HELP AND AUTHORITY IN CONTEMPORARY CHILD WELFARE

The primary mandate of child welfare is expressed as the protection of children (Kadushin, 1967; Kadushin and Martin, 1988). Activities through which child welfare workers exert authority, including investigation of complaints, insistence upon particular changes in parental behaviour, and removal of children from parents, always have primacy. However, during the course of its one-hundred-year history, child welfare has also introduced an expanded helping role, mandated primarily through the values and knowledge of professional social work. Historians of child welfare see trends over time in the relationship between these two mandates. Alfred Kadushin's text on child welfare suggests the existence of a trend away from punitive child welfare towards a more cooperative model. Formerly, he says, neglecting parents were seen as 'willful criminals,' whereas now they are seen as 'troubled' and 'needing help.' Neglect of children is seen as 'a defect, not a vice,' and the goal is to help children by helping the parent. The recommended focus is on identifying and treating underlying factors that 'motivate neglect' as against a previous focus on 'investigation, adjudication, and punishment.' Thus, Kadushin sees 'increasing recognition' that both neglect and abuse are problems for social work. Whereas legal sanctions at best can restrain the parent, the best protection is an adequately functioning family 'in which parental roles are effectively implemented' (1967: 247; 1988: 322).

This view is borne out by others in the field. As Teram (1988) notes, most Canadian child welfare legislation now endorses the idea of working with children in their own homes. Over the past two decades, the 'supplementary' role of child welfare identified by Kadushin has broadened considerably. A wide array of support services can be made available to clients of child welfare agencies, including homemakers, child care, medical attention, educational resources, parent aides, specialized services for children with health or behaviour problems, and various kinds of counselling. A primary task of contemporary workers is to ration these resources, which are usually scarce, and to account for their allocation to particular clients. Child welfare workers also spend considerable amounts of their time calling on parents and children at home, and providing, as time and circumstances permit, a counselling function.[3] Among the influences encouraging home-based intervention has been John Bowlby's influential work *Attachment and Loss* (1969), suggesting the deleterious effects on children of their sudden and frequent removal from the primary caretaker. Workers are encouraged to avoid apprehension of children if at all possible and to plan carefully for the removal of children when it is considered unavoidable. Child welfare workers are encouraged to develop the skills necessary to help both parents and children in these varying circumstances; keeping the family together is usually seen as a goal of primary importance.

At the same time that in-home service has been increasing, the legal processes involved in the authority function have become more complex. In cases involving temporary or permanent removal of children from their homes, it is common for all involved parties, including the agency, the child or children, and the parents, to be represented in court by different lawyers. The paperwork involved in calling witnesses and preparing to give testimony occupies a considerable amount of time and training for the worker, as well as anxiety, described by one worker as 'sweating bullets.' Recent changes in legislation oblige workers to stay abreast of developments in the field, including the complex implications of legislative changes as they emerge through case precedent and sometimes through political issues or the media. These increasingly complex procedures have resulted in a concomitant increase in attention to evidence-gathering and recording procedures that facilitate the presentation of evidence in court (Barth and Sullivan, 1985). Certainly, both the helping and authority functions, as they have traditionally been conceived, are subject to the increasingly administrative character of modern society, a point made by Kathy Ferguson in her book *The Feminist Case Against Bureaucracy* (1984). Furthermore, the traditional presentation of child welfare work treats these two functions as separate, both conceptually and functionally. In subsequent sections, the direction and character of both help and authority in cases of neglect are examined with the purposes of understanding both their administrative character and their close relationship to one another.

THE DIRECTION OF HELP AND AUTHORITY

According to Pincus and Minahan (1973), the term 'client' in social work has traditionally been used to refer to 'any expected beneficiary of services' (p. 56). The clients in child welfare, then, should be the same as the beneficiaries of service, or, put differently, those we intend to help. In actual practice, and in keeping with the child welfare mandate, help is clearly directed towards and expected to benefit children, as this message from a judge to a mother in one case makes perfectly clear: 'Always remember this: the Court is not concerned so much with your problems ... the Court's paramount concern is with respect to the welfare of the child ... the whole objective of the law [is] to ensure that the child receives a decent upbringing and is looked after carefully ... So if you people don't, somebody else will.'

Here, a contradiction appears. In social work, we are taught to think of clients as the chief beneficiaries of service; in child welfare, children are intended to be those beneficiaries. In ordinary conversation, however, the term 'client' is consistently used to refer to mothers and occasionally both parents if both were living at home, but the term is not used conversationally to refer to the children. This usage also holds true in most child welfare literature.[4] Asked directly whom they consider to be the client in a case, workers might name the child(ren) or both mother and children – sometimes with a visible moment of disjuncture as they consider the question. Here are some exchanges:

I: When you think about the case, who do you think of as your client?
W: The children.
I: Not the Mum?
W: Well, the Mum too, but I guess my stronger feelings will go to the children.

I: Who do you think of as the client in this case?
W: I think it's both, it's both, although my main concern is for the kids.

I: Who do you see as the client in this case?
W: Oh, that's a really good question. Both are the client. Like the mother is my client as well as the children ... but the children in this case are going to have to come first.

In ordinary usage, then, the word 'client' is an understood reference to the one we hope to work with, to change, the one over whom authority is being exerted. This common usage is more in keeping with Ferguson's definition of clients (1984) as those who must interact with bureaucracies over which they have little control. When explicitly brought to consciousness, however, the word 'client' is associated with the feelings and sympathies of the worker. In an interview, a worker explores some of these emotional reactions: 'They [the worker's feelings] run the gamut ... at times I earnestly hated these people with all my being. I loved the kids, hated the parents. The kids are darlings, no question about it, but I just could not handle the parents. There were times that I really related to the parents, I thought they were really good people. There were times I was furious with them, times I was cheering for them.'

This worker presents a common view, a reality for child welfare workers. The children are appealing, and are usually seen as 'innocent victims,' especially when younger. Images of the children draw out protective, warm feelings: they are the worthy poor. The parents draw forth a complex range of feelings, sometimes including sympathy but often frustration and anger. Parents are seen to be behaving in ways that damage children and ruin their chances for a good life.

These subjective reactions are not simply the spontaneous and idiosyncratic responses of individual workers, but are socially structured. They reflect the social and economic expectations we have of different family members in our kind of economy. They reflect the personalized definitions of causation worked up in discourse, which implicate parents, particularly mothers, as the direct cause of their children's suffering. They reflect the individualized patterns through which cases are organized and acted upon, patterns held in place by a complex supporting structure of legal and administrative practices that continually direct our attention to individual 'perpetrators.' They reflect socially constructed images of perpetually scarce resources for the poor, of the experienced problems of rationing resources, and of social definitions of worthiness required of recipients.

Furthermore, we know as we deal with such situations that the parents, in most cases the mothers, of these children are usually all that stand between the child and complete abandonment. The arrangements that idealize and legislate the nuclear family as the only appropriate locus of care and that allocate responsibility for this care to mothers produce this problem. Children can only be both cared for and cared about if mothers are brought into line; otherwise a state-organized substitute must be found. The social worker's helping impulse, directed towards helpless children, accompanied by an authority response, directed at mothers, thus emerges as an appropriate focus for our attention. These subjective reactions are also continually reinforced by work procedures.

WHAT CONSTITUTES HELP IN CASES OF NEGLECT?

Not all child welfare workers are trained social workers, but the principles of service, the values, and the theories that underlie child welfare practice are drawn from social work. Because of this connection, understanding of the nature of help offered in child welfare organizations relies on some knowledge of professional social work concepts of help.

Central to social work, according to England (1986), is the 'helping relationship.' Beginning with Mary Richmond in the early part of this century, near unanimous agreement has existed as to the importance of the helping relationship to foster 'growth, learning, change, and corrective experiences' for clients (Goldstein, 1973: 138). Although there is less agreement on the definition of this relationship or how it works, it is generally acknowledged that such a relationship is achieved through the practitioner's 'use of self.' England (1986: 40) describes the idea of use of self as being centrally important to social work but only marginally explored. It is 'conspicuous,' he contends, but not understood. Nevertheless, this idea is familiar to anyone trained in social work. Social work students are taught that using the 'whole self' in a disciplined way and engaging with the 'whole life' of the client are goals. Many people are in fact drawn to the profession, England believes, because they see it as a way to function in 'real life' rather than from a position once removed from the scene. Social work, according to England, is distinct in this way, and he cites a research project (Prins, 1974) showing that use of self is an important factor in attracting people to social work.

In contrast to, and perhaps because of, this interest in real life, social work practitioners often express suspicion about professional theories and abstractions. Studies cited by England show social workers as having a strong preference for using experience and imagination rather than formal theory or research findings in their efforts to help others. This anti-intellectualism is true not only of social work, but it certainly is a very pronounced view in the profession, to the point that some practitioners appear to reject abstraction out of hand (Carew, 1979). England suggests that 'material derived from the social sciences is too abstract and general' to serve as a prescription for practice. As a result, practitioners are quick to discard theory – it simply does not 'fit' (p. 62).

Much the same idea emerges in interviews with workers, an idea expressed as a progressive experience of disillusionment and fatigue as workers deal with the 'real world':

W: As a new social worker out of the School of Social Work you have all kinds of ideas of how you're going to run a case, how you're going to treat it. I had models of working with this family in my head, of which was most appropriate.
I: Can you remember what some of these models would be?
W: Gee, I'm so jaded now, I'm not sure I can. (Laughter)

In child welfare theories about the helping relationship itself can be experienced as disillusioning. According to experts the problems workers experience may be partly induced by the fact that clients are usually involuntary. The concept of a helping relationship is ordinarily premised on the existence of both a helper and someone who wants to be helped. Child welfare clients, as most of us know, are frequently hostile even to the presence of a worker; building a relationship often seems unrealizable.

Furthermore, according to Kadushin and Martin, the specific kinds of problems presented by a clientele of neglecting mothers create special problems for the building of a relationship and for using the self in a disciplined way. 'Neglecting mothers,' it is stated, 'are generally suspicious and difficult to engage in an effective relationship: 'Depressed, irresponsible and generally slovenly, they make it difficult for the social worker to like them' (1988: 266). These sentiments are central to Polansky et al.'s research findings in the area, and their work is called up to support this view.

Training material, however, is obliged to provide guidance. The problem here is to breach contradictions and still present usable, practical advice. A contradiction exists between the relationship theory and the circumstances of child welfare practice. Another contradiction exists between authority and the helping function proposed by social work. The client is seen as needing help, but she does not accept it. The worker must establish a helping relationship or resort to authority.

To resolve these dilemmas, Kadushin and Martin (1988: 270) recommend the 'good parent' role as the most successful casework approach. The worker should demonstrate a 'willingness to help effect some improvement, however slight, into the client's living situation.' Through this route, the worker has a better chance of protecting the children.[5] 'Like children,' the authors counsel, the clients 'simultaneously welcome and resent being told, in clear unequivocal terms, what to do.' In the 'good parent' model, help and authority are merged; the worker's advice is both helpful and authoritative, in the manner of a good parent. Simultaneously, help, in the form of authority, is provided *to* mothers but is actually *for* children. Disjunctures between relationship theory and practice disappear in the model; a relationship is in fact established, and the worker is able to use the self in a way that preserves the child welfare mandate.

To summarize the direction of the discussion thus far, child welfare is presented in training literature as a blend of authority and help delivered through the front-line child welfare worker to individual families. The general drift of expert advice on the subject attempts to merge these two apparently contradictory functions into an approach approximating good parenting. This advice is premised on a childlike clientele, dependent and difficult to engage in a traditional social work helping relationship. When the idea of help is pursued, it is clear that the mandate of child welfare directs help to children; it requires that any actual help provided to the mother be justified by showing how such help benefits the child or children in the family.

The model cites client characteristics as the problem in relationship building, and overlooks the issue of barriers produced by everyday work processes. One important barrier encountered in cases of neglect is their length of life. Some families have been child welfare clients, both as children and as adults, for virtually their entire lives. Given the bureaucratic nature of the work outlined in Chapter 4, and the issue of high worker turnover, some clients have been assigned dozens of different workers over the years. The establishment of a helping relationship, or any relationship, with many social workers is obviously problematic:

They had gone through it all before. I was just, 'Oh here's the new guy': 'We were tolerated rather than encouraged ... they tried to be cordial, but they weren't really eager to have me visiting ... they basically went about their business, kind of half ignoring me.' Clients employ this experience in their side of the new relationship: 'Sometimes when she's mad at me, she says, "The other worker wouldn't have done that."'

Workers employ a variety of 'styles' to accommodate this circumstance. They may find a mutual interest with a client, take a special interest in a difficult child, take a client to lunch, and so on. However, authority lurks behind all these activities, many of which are quite genuine attempts on the worker's part to relate to the client. At all times, the worker must be alert to danger for the child; if a child meets with harm, the worker must be able to demonstrate that appropriate investigative and preventive measures have been taken at every step. One worker describes how she learned to listen for 'underlying messages' as the result of injuries a child received after being returned to his mother: 'The first time I went out I believed her ... I believed her because she seemed sincere and she was crying. But now if she'd come to me and she'd be crying, I'd say "uh uh," not this time, you're not going to put one over on me.'

Now, this worker doublechecks the mother's story, checks to see that food is in the fridge, follows up to see if the mother has applied for recommended kinds of help. This is what Zimmerman (1969) refers to as the 'investigative stance,' which consists of a 'thoroughgoing skepticism' directed towards the client. This stance is seen as 'good work,' a way of establishing facts as opposed to the client's 'mere claims.' In child welfare, this is the common approach of seasoned workers. The worker in my example has now become experienced; he takes for granted the possibility that mothers will try to fool and manipulate. He has learned the skill of taking the investigative stance towards a client in order to guard against deception. This stance reflects in the worker–client relationship a bureaucratic dichotomy identified by Ferguson (1984), one that poses the organization as objective and scientific (masculine), as evidenced by the consistency of its procedures, while clients are 'feminized' by being posed as subjective beings whose stories must be taken as biased representations of their own interests.

Another approach to the work is to take the stance of 'cop' from the beginning. Sometimes, workers operate in pairs, agreeing beforehand that one will be the 'good cop,' offering sympathy and support to the parents, while the other will be 'bad cop,' reflecting an attitude of disbelief in the client's story. Through this procedure, help and authority are offered simultaneously in the hope that a client will divulge needed information about the care a child is receiving. Again, this approach reflects the knowledge of the seasoned worker, who expects manipulation, deceit, backsliding, and considerable resistance from clients.

These manoeuvres and the counter-moves made by workers may appear as a game the client is playing with the worker, one of feigning compliance while striving to 'get away' with rule-breaking behaviour. The good parent model of help is operative in our understanding of this game, although the worker may not be consciously aware of it. The model not only supplies the worker with an approach to take, but with the explanation for the client's behaviour as well. She is essentially a child herself, engaged in testing rules, testing the 'parent's' authority. Kadushin (1967: 234) instructs us on this point: 'The social worker has to be frank in exercising the authority of his agency affiliation and the authority of his position. This is expected, and abrogation is regarded as a sign of weakness.'

The model simultaneously supplies the causal variable for neglect – a needy mother who has not been adequately parented – and warrants the investigative, authoritative approach.

Standing behind the personal relationship of client and worker are the power relations of the society. In these relations, the worker represents more than herself; she also represents the interests of the dominant class and culture, and she is vested with an authority created and sanctioned by those groups. The client is a member of the underclass, by virtue of status and income, and often by virtue of gender and/or race. The issue of neglect itself grew out of a set of class relations in Canadian society of the past century. These relations allowed the concerns of middle and upper class reformers about proper family life to prevail in the public domain and to enter into legislation. As we saw in Chapter 3, these class-based interests reflected not only sympathy for children of the poor, but fear for the middle and upper classes and a desire to protect their way of life. Much of what has been written since reflects neglect as a concept useful to society's more powerful classes to insist on a certain kind of family organization for poor and marginalized groups (Pelton, 1981; Wald, 1976; Horowitz and Wolock, 1981; Hudson and McKenzie, 1981).

When the worker–client relationship is seen as reflecting these larger social, political, and power relations between dominant and subordinate groups, each in turn affected differently by economic forces, job structures, resource allocation, and so on, a different view of that relationship comes into view, and the 'fooling' behaviour of mothers takes on a different appearance. Members of marginalized groups have little power at their disposal in these relations. They often cannot even sell their labour in the market-place; their living conditions are at subsistence level; and the usual hedges against state intrusion, such as special assistance for children with learning or health problems, licensed child care, or cleaning services, cannot be purchased.

Nevertheless, even the most poverty-stricken clients show little inclination to ease their lot by giving up their children. On the contrary, resistance to the intrusions of child welfare is usually vehement and can last for years. Clients also understand child welfare as a potential provider of needed resources. As Young (1964) noted some years ago, 'They [neglecting parents] understand power.' Although her statement appeared as an indictment of these parents, it might be viewed instead as perfectly appropriate and indeed necessary knowledge of subordinate groups, who must understand the power relations of the society to survive.[6] Subterfuge is one of the few forms of power available to subordinate populations. The case for or against clients relies on documentation of behaviour witnessed by workers. Through subterfuge and deceit, there is some hope of concealing a documentable instance of damaging behaviour or of appearing to qualify for a needed resource. Ferguson (1984: 128) refers to this behaviour as 'impression management': 'Like the administrators who staff bureaucracies, clients who receive the goods and services issuing from bureaucracies are required to attend constantly to the image which they present to the organization, to engage in successful impression management, to anticipate the demands that the organization or its representatives will make, and to modify their own behaviour accordingly, or be denied crucial services.'

Some workers are acutely aware of the relations of dominance and subordination. In the work setting, however, the worker's attention has to focus on the protection concern. As illustrated in Chapter 5, the individualized structure of 'cases' quickly narrows issues to the personal relations involved in each case, and the worker must necessarily be concerned to accomplish her part in the protection process efficiently and in a way that provides her with an appearance of having competence in her role.

Furthermore, workers confront on a daily basis contradictory demands that must be resolved through action. To do this, the status and power of the role can be brought into play, which then becomes an inadvertent act of re-producing relations of dominance and subordination. Consider this example: As a court date for permanent wardship of children approaches, a worker discovers the existence of a natural father who has rights to be notified of the court case. The worker does not have even a name or address, but she must, by law, go through a series of attempts to find him in order to satisfy the court that his rights have been honoured. This process, as workers know from experience, can delay a court case indefinitely. Such a delay means that an already agonizingly lengthy process to determine guardianship of the children, currently in temporary foster care, will be postponed indefinitely. This eventuality conflicts with the social work belief in finding permanent homes for children at the earliest opportunity, a solution grounded in the findings of respected experts in the field (Goldstein, Solnit, and Freud, 1973, 1979). To avoid this delay, the worker approaches the mother for identifying information: 'She wasn't too cooperative ... so I made a deal with her. "If you make it rough for me, I can make it just as rough for you visiting the children."'

The worker does this in the interests of finding permanent homes for the children in the short run. To accomplish this, he appeals to the repressive power of the state, and in so doing reproduces the social relations of domi-nance and submission, via the children. As clients recognize, placement of the children in care further reduces their power; the children become a weapon in the hands of the dominant group. In this case, the mother pro-vided the information – she had already played her last card.

What the analysis suggests is that workers relay to clients, through the 'helping relationship,' the structures that the dominant group wish to repro-duce. The 'self' that workers present to clients is not simply the sum of one's individual life experience and personality organization, as much discourse would have us believe. This 'self' is necessarily attuned to the tasks at hand (Schutz, 1962) and reflects the structures of the dominant society. The jobs we pursue, our work practices, and sanctioned ways of thinking about this work, are organized and structured prior to our own entry onto the scene. Our usual concept of 'use of self' hides rather than exposes the way this work organization operates through us. In our individualistic society, the self is thought of as unique. We learn to speak of being true to ourselves, of finding ourselves. We are taught to think of individuals as able to float free of social structure. In this context, the idea of 'use of self' inserts the worker's personal traits such as humour, generosity, empathy, as the crucial ones in our work with clients, screening out the way our work practices enter into and structure relationships with clients in the bureaucratic context (Ferguson, 1984; Fraser, 1989).

DOCUMENTS AND THE HELPING PROCESS

Social workers are taught to use documentation and recording as an integral part of the helping process. As we saw in Chapters 4 and 5, documentation is generally shaped by work relevancies and contingencies. Thus, examination of the way cases are documented reveals how help is structured in cases of neglect. Aspects of help and documentation in child welfare are examined here, using two examples for the analysis: contracts and resources.

Contracts

In the early 1980s, social work literature appeared on the benefits of contracting with clients. Garvin and Seabury (1984) trace the idea of contracts back to the writings of Freud. They take note of concerns raised by social workers about the use of the term 'contract' because of its legal usage and connotations. They counter these concerns by contrasting legal contracts, which they say are 'static, binding, promissory agreements,' not easily renegotiated or changed, with the social work contract, which is supposed to be a dynamic and flexible arrangement between parties. In law, they note, remedies for failing to follow through on contracts are usually spelled out, but in social work such consequences are 'rarely discussed' and may not exist at all.

Transposed to the child welfare setting, both the legal connotations of the term and the hidden nature of consequences do become concerns as we consider issues of help and authority. Literature on contracts does readily recognize the special circumstances of involuntary clients, a situation that renders true mutuality impossible. However, this problem can be circumvented or minimized, Garvin and Seabury suggest, through such devices as a 'dual' approach that clearly separates court-ordered issues from others. The presentation of the contracting process can offer comfort to the harried worker, whose clients are often beset with an overwhelming number of major life problems. Contracting procedures provide a way of partializing and prioritizing problems, suggest ways of determining a definite sequence of tasks, and establish methods of goal-setting that allow both client and practitioner to identify progress. Another advantage, authors say, is that workers also become accountable to clients for their part of the bargain.

Following is an example of a child welfare contract:

Mother agrees to	Worker agrees to
• No extended family staying at home	• Provide a teaching homemaker
• Provide safe living environment	for 4 months
• Provide appropriate babysitters	
• Have weekly contact with counsellor	• Meet bi-weekly with client
• Have bi-weekly contact with worker	

The child welfare contract is virtually always geared to the problem of children's safety. This sample refers to issues seen by the worker as contributing to neglect of the children, including the presence of relatives with drinking problems, hazardous living quarters, and the mother's resort to unreliable babysitters. Behind these specific issues is a larger issue for the worker, namely the mother's failure to take charge of her own living situation. We see in the first instance that in establishing a contract, the mother is obliged to accept the worker's idea of the problem and its causal factors. These factors are nearly always perceived to be in the immediate life situation of the mother – unreliable relatives, poor housing, and so on.

These factors refer us back to images of the private family, which supply us with knowledge of the proper allocation of responsibility for child-caring activities. The contract takes account of the mother's needs and problems as they become obstacles to providing this care, placing this mother in somewhat the same relation to the state as an employee. Her job functions are based on the unwritten, implicit contract between parents and the state. As in a job evaluation, the personal and socially situated problems of the client disappear, except as they create difficulties in job performance. The mother's experiences as a woman with a long history of alcohol abuse, as a woman of intelligence but little education, as a person who has lived in poverty all her life, as the daughter and sister of people with severe alcohol problems, as a woman with sexual needs and relationships, as a person who has experienced discrimination and racism – all of this vanishes. These unmentioned problems render some contracts untenable at the outset. In the example cited above, for instance, the mother soon broke the contract by inviting a destitute relative to stay with her. In the file, the worker comments that Mom is 'unable to turn them away,' but she is 'turning her children away instead, without realizing.' In this note, the worker gives us a glimpse of contradictions the mother faces in her own life. The worker notes the contradiction and resolves it in the contract in accordance with the protection mandate. Consequently, the contract, and the worker's attentiveness to the implicit and unquestioned child-caring responsibilities upon which it is based, screen out the mother's problems. The mother has chosen to resolve the contradiction in another way, a way in keeping with the unseen context of her own life. The underlying social forces through which this contradictory experience have been structured in the first place are completely missing from the picture.

The contract, as a document entered into the file, then takes on a second life as an administrative tool that can be used to exert authority over the mother. The contract can be presented in court, for instance, as evidence that the mother has not kept her side of the agreement. The contract can also be used to justify apprehending the children, if the mother breaks her side of it. In this sense, the contract in its document form serves to mediate and reproduce the social relations of dominant and subordinate groups. The surface appearance of this situation, meanwhile, remains straightforward and unproblematic: A contract has been made and broken.

Resources Offered in Cases of Neglect

The offer of resources to clients is often seen as the purest form of help that can be provided in the child welfare setting. Resources are concrete and presumably designed to support parents in specific ways. An array of resources is available under the general rubric of 'supplementary care.' For mothers categorized as neglecting, a few of these are staples: Parenting classes; homemakers, and parent aides are commonly mentioned in files. The use of homemakers shows the contradictory effects of provision of resources.

On the surface, it appears that homemakers are a logical, useful response of the agency to a mother attending to the ongoing needs of several children. This could clearly be seen as 'help' offered the mother on behalf of the children. Indeed, some mothers request or even insist that a homemaker be supplied. However, like the contract, homemakers also have another life. As for any agency resource, the homemaker's time and work must be accounted for in terms of the agency's mandate. Furthermore, even though the homemaker may be seen as a supplementary service, the original protection issue remains paramount – after all, if a protection concern is not identified, the cost of the homemaker is much harder to justify, given the scarce resources of child welfare agencies. Because she is on the scene, and because the protection mandate remains operative, the homemaker becomes a kind of 'supervisor' of the mother,[7] with the responsibility to report on her progress and 'mistakes.' In fact, she may be assigned to the mother primarily for that purpose, although the mother would not ordinarily be told this. This is referred to as 'monitoring' the home, and it is one of the chief ways workers use to justify leaving children in a dubious situation.

The homemaker then has reporting responsibilities, as do workers, to make black-book notes on lapses from acceptable practices personally witnessed by her. Homemakers may be called to testify in court, and their records can and are used as evidence against the mother. If the mother does not accept the offer of a homemaker, this fact can also be used in court to show her as uncooperative and suspicious.

In the example of the homemaker, what appears on the surface as help for the mother can be seen underneath the surface as fitting into a course of action oriented towards the authority function. The legal processes that are the basic source of child welfare authority provide, in other words, a course of action to which all elements of help must be oriented. Their character as 'help' is entered in document form, usually as a notation that particular resources were offered or allocated. In files, the quality and effectiveness of resources is virtually never evaluated. One worker complained, 'I can't tell from these records what worked. Did she ever get help? I can't tell.' What is retained in files is an accumulating list of resources allocated, a list that can eventually be entered against an evaluation of the parents' improvement vis-à-vis identified problems in child-caring practices. In one very long-running case, a supervisor recommended that the only way to gather sufficient evidence to apprehend the child was to 'keep putting in resources until they break down.' If problems cited in child care have improved, then resources have been justified. If not, the list of efforts can become part of the case against the parent in court. One worker writes in the file a list of apparently appropriate services given and concludes that despite many attempts to 'assist and support' the family, 'they refuse to change.' Refusal to change, in the face of substantial documented evidence of 'help' is damning in court.

The work procedures involved in this process closely resemble those of a modern performance evaluation. In modern personnel practice, the performance of an employee one thinks of firing must be constantly documented against the contract, or job description, to which the employee originally agreed. Certain details are selected to be shown, others omitted; whatever is entered into this record must be re-interpreted to fit existing categories and organizational purposes. Child welfare documentation is essentially for the same purposes: to provide a record of evidence demonstrating the individual's poor performance, as against documented efforts of the employer to provide needed assistance. This evidence, in documentary form, will be needed if the employee decides to appeal the decision. And so it is in the case of parents who are being 'fired.'

CASE CLOSED: PROBLEM SOLVED?

In child welfare, the final method of 'solving' the problem of neglect is permanent wardship of the children by the state. Ordinarily, this means permanent separation from the parent(s).[8] This is the ultimate 'help' which the agency has to offer the child.

In files, a wardship decision may appear as a flat statement of fact: 'Case closed, guardianship settled.' Such unemotional notes, of course, cover over a world of pain for all concerned. Most of us can easily imagine feelings of desperation and despair that might be experienced by parents confronting the permanent loss of their children and the grief of the child losing contact with her or his natural parents.

The decision, flatly stated, also suggests unambiguous agreement by decision-makers in the case. For workers, however, bringing a case to court for permanent wardship appears as one of the greatest areas of authority remaining to them, and the exercise of this authority can fill the worker with ambivalence. In the following passage are the painful reflections of a worker as she recalls the problem of reaching a decision. 'I had a good cry with my supervisor about this. [The child] and her mother were very close, because wherever she went [the mother] took her. [The child] was very withdrawn in the foster home. She would just lay there. It's like she gave up on life ... she'd cry, just for no reason at all. I went to [my supervisor] and told her, 'I feel like I'm torn apart. I know if I place these kids back with Mum, they're going to be neglected. She's not keeping up with her contract and she's not seeing public health. And yet, if I pull her away from Mum, how much damage am I doing to this little kid?'''

Behind this anguish are social processes that have generated only two solutions to the apparent problem. Either this mother must provide the care or she will lose her children – and they will lose her; there are no authentic alternatives. The legally mandated course of action produces a win–lose situation for the parents, and for the agency. However, at this point the worker in fact has little choice. Evidence collected by the worker herself documents an ongoing series of episodes involving violence, hunger, illness, and abandonment. As readers, we do not doubt the misery that the child has endured. To ignore such evidence would itself be neglectful.

That help has failed to change the child's situation does not mean that the worker has not tried or that she has failed to recognize the mother's problems. Workers often recognize parents as victims themselves and make efforts to help. But the protection mandate from which child welfare helping processes ensue makes actionable only certain forms of helping. These are directed primarily towards children, whereas we are instructed to regard parents as ineligible to receive help on their own account. Even workers' feelings come to reflect the social structure standing behind child welfare processes. The disappearance of parents' lived experience in the helping and recording processes, the absence of knowing in present, immediate ways, what parents have experienced and are currently living through, and the screening out of social relations standing behind visible behaviours of parents, operate to direct our sympathetic feelings towards the children, whose immediate suffering is apparent. Help for parents is only justified if they use it to benefit the children directly; feelings of sympathy, accompanied by frustration with parents' backsliding, help the worker to accept responsibility for what is in fact a brutal decision. This structure of 'knowing' screens from attention the paucity of real alternatives that could allow support and help to both parents and children. In Chapter 9, I discuss an emerging discourse that suggests different ways of conceptualizing such alternatives.

That the agency exists to help children is not a secret. It is completely obvious. However, the idea of Kadushin (and many others) that the help we offer parents through child welfare can 'save' their children represents the ideological character of much social work training and wisdom. The analysis shows that help offered through child welfare agencies departs in almost every way from our usual professional ideas of what constitutes real help. Procedures through which this help is offered conceal or distort the very serious problems many of these parents face, and they conceal as well the class-based nature of the concept neglect itself. These outcomes are facilitated by our work practices that are oriented at every step to the agency's mandate of authority.

CONCLUSION

The analysis suggests that we have been asking the wrong questions about help and authority in child welfare. In beginning to untangle these concepts as they appear in actual work settings, the issue of whether they are contradictory loses its force, as the predominance of the authority function becomes apparent. The image of 'help' offered to families through child welfare now appears as ideology, serving at least two purposes. One is that the image of help distorts and partially conceals a highly repressive state apparatus at work. The second is the presentation of 'family' as a unit in receipt of help through child welfare. Analysis shows that traditional arguments about the proper balance of rights between the family and the state obscure important differences in the social locations of family members. Through everyday work practices, these different social locations are concealed.

The 'good parent' model, through which help and authority are apparently merged, continually produces the mothers as unworthy of help. Their own lived experience disappears through procedures designed to examine their present suitability for the job of parenting. The same procedures produce children as actually being helped through the exertion of state authority over their parents. We may notice that most of the help that in fact is provided children is theoretical. They are rescued from dangerous situations to be sure, but their futures are far from ensured through these repeated rescue operations.

9

Transformations

It can make a difference to clients whether they are dealing with someone committed to change or someone committed to the status quo. (Moreau, 1989: 278)

If you're not part of the solution, you're part of the problem.

The arena of neglect has been the point of entry through which the reproduction of relations of class, gender, and race has been explored. In this
book I have examined several aspects of the way neglect comes to appear as
it does. 'Hidden realities' and the appearances they produce vis-à-vis child
neglect can be summarized as follows. On the surface we see a picture of
child neglect characterized by repeated episodes of 'poor care,' that is, care
authorized as unacceptable by personnel mandated to act by sets of sanctioned social processes. Once intervention has occurred, the families are
subject to two sets of visible processes, help and authority. Helping processes involve resource outlay, which must be justified through documentation showing potential recipients as appropriately qualified. Workers act to
effect this 'fit'; in so doing mothers are continually produced as faulty or
damaged individuals requiring ongoing supervision and authority. At the
same time, this view of mothers justifies our continued failure to solve the
problem: Damaged individuals reproduce themselves in their children; it is
a rising tide that our helping efforts can barely stem. Although mothers may
insist on 'minor' child-rearing differences owing to race, racism, or cultural
background, the basic standards and causal explanations apply to all. Repeated episodes of poor care act to produce evidence requiring interventions of authority. The surface picture of neglect fits these pieces logically
and coherently together, so that both the helping procedures and the authoritative interventions appear as entirely warranted and necessary.

Outside of this visible reality are converging processes that operate to reproduce this ongoing picture. The fragmentation of the work process requires a simplified version of 'facts' to which each new worker can quickly and unequivocally attend. The procedures of thought involved in doing this are entirely hidden from view in records and in fact are not an obvious feature of the work to those performing it, because their vista is limited by the rigour and busy-ness of the positions they occupy. The discourse concerned with neglect provides a generalized picture of families likely to fit the category, suggesting the nature and reasons for their problems. The worker can and does invoke this picture in the interpretation of facts already recorded in the file and as a guide to the selection and shaping of new facts and events that she will document.

The resources that the worker has at her command to offer must be warranted by features of the client. She must be 'in need' in particular ways, as we have seen, and the discourse provides us with the theoretical underpinnings that allow specific facts of the client's life to be understood primarily in these terms. As individual clients are worked up to mesh with this understanding, current budgets and service structures appear as the 'right ones,' if rather too sparse. For the mother, becoming a client of a child welfare agency is often the only route to needed resources, such as a homemaker or day care. To achieve access to resources, however, the client must become categorized in some understandable way. Complaints of wife abuse do not produce resources, nor do single episodes of abandonment of the children. The case must go on long enough and must feature characteristics understandable as child neglect in order to warrant resource outlay: A bad mother is manufactured. Clients need help, in some cases enough to create or at least allow incidents to occur. As these incidents recur, the documentary process ensures that the multiproblematic nature of these families will be reproduced.

The documentary practices of child welfare are geared to the requirements of the legal process as well as to resource outlay. Operating under the surface, then, are procedures through which this mother will either be produced as 'unable to care' or will not remain as a client. For those who remain as clients, the discourse of parenting is also operative. The gendered, administered, and culturally neutral character of 'parenting' is a taken-for-granted feature of child welfare work. It is the care, or parenting, that comes to be adjudicated, while love, affectional ties, and 'roots' move to the background in court cases concerning neglect.

The personal and individualized nature of child welfare work functions to separate mothering work from its context. As Griffith and Smith (1987) note, the 'categorical character of the standards' take no account of practicalities and conditions. The work processes of child welfare systems take little account of social, contextual information. Both legal and helping processes are at work in producing clients as individuals with problems. When the situation is notably bad, for instance, involving domestic violence, comparison structures, as described in Chapter 6, are brought into play to show the mother how other women in even worse situations are able to provide needed care. These socially organized processes and practices of thought, which are widespread and taken for granted, operate as hidden realities that help to produce the appearance of neglect.

Race and culture have in some respects been noticed and entered into both discourse and legislation. However, as we have seen, changes in legislation and in some organizational arrangements must not be mistaken for a reordering of power relations. Such changes can in fact hide more durable processes that sustain relations of domination. Silence, and the continual reproduction of silences, help to achieve this effect. Standardized definitions of child neglect impose meanings and regimentation of behaviour on minority groups, while the insistence in discourse on equality and equal treatment justify and remove these concerns to the background.

EFFECTS OF NEGLECT: SOCIAL REPRODUCTION

Keeping in mind that we speak of neglect not as a set of parenting practices nor as a standard of care but as a socially produced category, the reproductive effects of its maintenance are explored. While research into specific treatment approaches may help us to refine and improve some techniques, the fact remains that reportable problems like neglect and child abuse, which are central to social work practice, are not seen to diminish. Many argue, in fact, that these are problems that have escalated to record numbers over the first century of our existence as a profession (Nagi, 1977; Rose and Meezan, 1993). Nevertheless, the 'treatment' approach continues to be seen as credible, and serious challenges to the child welfare system as the best and only way to address the issues have not been mounted. The category neglect itself remains generally unexamined and unquestioned, and research dollars flow in much the same direction as they have done for several decades. Both the category itself and our responses to it have become durable features of social structure. Each creates and sustains the other; the central outlines and organization of each justify the existence of the other: Neglect arises and is sustained through child welfare practice, and child welfare practice is justified because of the continued and growing existence of neglect. This is one aspect of the reproductive process.

A second aspect of the reproductive process is the way neglect and the work processes that sustain it help to hide social divisions of class, gender, and race. The appearance of neglect as a social entity – a 'thing' – requiring study distorts and covers over the lived experiences of families slotted into it. Even the fact that these 'parents' are mothers is glossed over by the seemingly genderless category. This is significant, for as Fraser (1989), Gordon (1989), and other feminists are now demonstrating, the omission of gender from analysis distorts our understanding of the welfare state on many levels. Gordon cites gendered meanings of dependency, sources of stigma, sexual standards, sources of poverty, and even gendered 'work expectations' associated with collecting benefits as previously unexplored issues. But neglect, like welfare, implicates mothers, and screens out fathers. Although many of the fathers of children in neglect cases have completely abandoned caring work, financial support, and even occasional contact with their children, the category neglect directs us not to perceive these omissions as 'child neglect'; the category asks us instead to direct attention to the quality and consistency of the mother's contribution, attention that helps to reproduce gendered social divisions.

The instructions of the category 'neglect' also direct us to perceive the issue as one of passivity or omission in the tasks of caregiving. Problems in the household are separated from their social base and come to be viewed as a dynamic between mothers and children. The historical violence involved in colonial relations, wife battering, and poverty all disappear and consequently cannot be used to help us understand the lived experience of the mother and her children. Removed from their social roots, and placed outside the bounds of our category, the poverty, violence, and discrimination to which both mothers and children are regularly subjected can remain either as a background issue or can perform the ideological service of indicting the mother's care; she is charged with 'failing to protect.' Thus, the category operates not only to exclude social context but can be deployed to redistribute responsibility from fathers to mothers, from colonizers to the colonized, from the well-to-do to the have-nots.

The legalization of child welfare continually reinforces the idea of neglect as a personal problem rather than as the visible appearance of underlying social relations. Workers with thirty or forty cases requiring investigation go through the work day prioritizing cases and attempting to ensure that the most dangerous situations do not result in actual injury to a child. Whereas workers may and often do theorize in their 'off time' about what is needed in the child welfare system, the organization of their daily work does not ask for or usually allow their perceptions or information to enter the arena of policy discussion. Work practices engaged in by individual workers, as they try to attune themselves to the needs of the organization, continually reproduce the appearance of personal problems. Because work processes direct attention of workers to the here-and-now needs and problems of individual clients, workers are not placed to grasp either the generalizing processes at work in a case or the part they themselves inadvertently play in reproducing these processes. While the appearance of neglect is worked up through the convergence of many social forces and socially organized processes, it emerges whole in itself, detached from these processes.

As Keller (1985) points out, similar processes occur in widely disparate fields, in physics, to use her example. Through work and social processes a 'central dogma' is created and handed down through discourse. The prevailing view appears as formal knowledge, and it is revalidated and fed constantly by new research. The 'central dogma' validates not only the current resource outlay – always with the proviso that more money is needed – but also the traditional and accepted discourse and forms of research. The construction of 'central dogma' works also to reproduce the existing power relations of the society, providing implicit instructions concerning the identification of wrongdoing and wrongdoers, and posing elite groups as the ones best able to understand and solve problems.

Furthermore, 'central' dogma works to close off competing ideas. One very important idea closed off by 'child neglect' is that of caring for children as labour. Caregiving work, the tasks and resources required, the skills and efforts involved, costs to the caregiver, variations in work practices, and the benefits to society of having this work done have remained hidden realities of social reproduction. Caring work, in both its public and private forms, is done almost exclusively by women, and material remuneration for this work is invariably low, often altogether unpaid (Baines et al., 1991). Women who do this labour constitute a pool of invisible, unpaid, or marginally paid labour whose service is bent to the purpose of reproducing members of the future labour force. Two major concepts through which ideology is brought to bear in keeping these women at their work are 'motherhood' and 'parenting.' The idea of motherhood conveys powerful ideals of selflessness. Through this concept, the work of caring and the resources required to accomplish this work disappear. The notion of mothering as an emotional relation, through which labour is welded to love and thus willingly provided, allows the caring work required of these mothers to go largely unnoticed and unrecorded. Motherhood as an idea provides the ground for the many mechanisms of this 'forgetting' to occur. At the same time, the welding together of love and labour allows emotional attachments to be measured in terms of labour.

The concept of parenting serves a more complex function in this respect. In appearing genderless, it obscures the fact that the work implied by proper parenting is virtually all done by women. Second, it sets standards that appear classless and culture-free, thus obscuring the very different conditions in which the work is done. Third, parenting takes account of the entry of women into the labour force during the past generation. In moving somewhat away from the more simple and clearly gendered idea of motherhood, it allows the mother who is not devoting herself full time to her children to be a 'proper' parent, through the hiring out, with proper supervision, of parenting tasks. The administrative character implied by this concept moves the tasks of caring for children to the position of job outcomes. This form of parenting is geared to the requirements of the labour force, focused as it is on skill development, independence, and the creation of social habits such as punctuality and task completion. Culturally different attributes enter this scheme only peripherally, and race and racializing processes are entirely absent from view. The time, effort, and resources needed to accomplish tasks of parenting are obscured, culturally different objectives of child rearing are eliminated, and the goals of 'good parenting' enter and exert their effects on every Canadian home.

We do not expect perfectly identical outcomes through this application, however. The standards derived through this approach are applied differentially to different groups of mothers, depending on their relation to productive and reproductive forces. The social objective is not, after all, to produce an entire population harbouring the same middle class skills and expectations. The task of marginalized women is to provide sufficient caring and reproductive labour to fill particular social needs. In this endeavour, both ideological and repressive measures are brought to bear. These particular mothers are not fully amenable to the effects of ideology, because the limits of their lives and their children's lives are visible to them. However, their underresourced and apparently deviant social position renders them especially vulnerable to state repression through the apparatus of which child welfare is a part. Workers, meanwhile, are more amenable to ideology because it assists them in resolving contradictory aspects of their work. By substituting 'imaginary' positive outcomes for the more common realities of broken attachments and severed roots, many workers are able to face the coercive nature of their work. Fragmented work processes also assist in this outcome, screening as they do actual outcomes from the worker's view.

The repressive measures to which mothers are subject serve two important social purposes. One is to provide a model of submissiveness to both the mothers and their children, and by example to other mothers and children. The position of these particular mothers vis-à-vis mainstream society continues as one of submission. The second purpose is to ensure that mothers continue in their unpaid labour, at least at a minimal level, through the constant and real threat of having their children taken from them. As a judge reminded one lax mother, 'If you people don't [take care of your children], someone else will.'

It is important to notice that the system that takes over in the event of the mother's failure is also organized around divisions of class, gender, and race. A 'substitute' mother is provided with slightly more resources than the original mother. She is subject to the same performance appraisal, and much the same authority as the original. She too is part of a pool of caregivers, a hidden labour force that is poorly paid, rewarded primarily through ideological mechanisms that withhold punishment rather than provide material rewards for work well done (Smith and Smith, 1990). If she is a foster mother, she may well be of the same class and race as the original mother, because modern ideas encourage racial and cultural similarity in placement. It is perhaps not a coincidence that this 'progressive' step is being taken just as white working and middle class women, who used to form the main pool of foster mothers, are entering the paid work force en masse. Whatever the intent, the effect is that this inexpensive form of caring is now being allocated to a new labour pool, minority women. Those in the system receiving higher status and rewards are still white women and men. Adopting parents, who get full rights to raise a child, have traditionally been white and middle class; hence, the large literature on cross-racial adoption. The majority of professional workers in the system will have come from white, middle class origins. In this arrangement, men supersede women in terms of authority, position, and material rewards (Baines et al., 1991; Swift, 1995b). The clientele remains, as in the original days of child welfare, the poor, the dispossessed, the immigrants – the Others.

Child welfare workers occupy an important position in maintaining these sets of relations. It is workers who actually do the work of screening people in and out of social categories like neglect. Workers may be unaware of the full extent of their contribution, because bureaucratic work organization fragments the work to such an extent that individuals cannot easily see and evaluate the outcomes of their own labour. Workers, of course, are only a part of the picture. The complexity of social organization requires many individuals, distributed throughout the social structure, to complete successfully reproductive processes. However, because child welfare workers are so visible, they are commonly held responsible for all that is wrong with child welfare, for callous brutality in 'babysnatching' activities, for racism in file recording and placement procedures, and so on. Following from this analysis, we might see the term 'front-line worker' as having more and somewhat different meanings than we usually imagine. It is the front line, after all, that serves as cannon fodder.

Workers at the front line are primarily women (Miller, 1991; Callahan, 1993). Like mothers, they provide caring labour, and they have been given responsibilities that they do not really have the power to carry out. The options from which they can choose are firmly in place, the resource base is well known to be inadequate and the class, race, and gender nature of child welfare is thoroughly established before individual workers come on the scene. Furthermore, much of the knowledge they are taught is highly ideological in nature, predisposing them to see social work issues as personal, teaching them that ideological forms of practice are professional – and therefore desirable. These ideological practices, as we have seen, are everywhere present in the daily world of work. Workers experience their work as interpersonal, as larely contained within itself and the organization, and these perceptions are reinforced at every turn. The available resources and alternatives allow a very narrow range of (usually) undesirable choices for them to make, and they require them to work up clients to fit this resource availability.

We must constantly remind ourselves in looking at this work organization that if the object of this work were really to 'rescue' children, we could do so. We are a rich country; the resources are there. Baths and clothing could be given, housing provided, education ensured, treatment programs funded. It is not workers, after all, who object to help being provided; ordinarily workers act to provide what little help there is. However, in the contradictory fashion that characterizes child welfare, workers themselves are presented in the prevailing debates as central to the problem. This fact itself becomes a further identifiable mechanism of social reproduction, one which obscures highly complex and deeply rooted relations of class, gender, and race at work beneath the surface.

In the course of examining processes of social reproduction, we can begin to see why so few middle class families are caught in acts of child neglect; why so few on the caseloads are two-parent, white, and middle class – why 'home alone' families are a rarity. It is not because this group of parents never neglects or because they all invariably do an outstanding job of caring for children. It is because the category itself holds instructions that do not include these parents except in very unusual cirucumstances. It is also because the scrutiny and coercion imposed on neglecting families works to reproduce relations of subservience for both mothers and children. Some clients are being prepared as future workers, mostly in low-paid jobs; some have already had their wealth and resources extracted from them, and the goal is to make them less dependent on social resources; some are to be created and maintained as a reserve labour pool; some are providers of children for the childless; some are to do the free caring work necessary for the reproduction of labour; some will become 'sex workers.' In Althusser's terms these are the groups of people being prepared for subservience in the relations of production. The middle class does not often have to be scrutinized in the same way because its members are being prepared for mastery (or at least a reasonable facsimile) in the productive process. This goal is a desirable one, and so coercion is seldom required. When the goal is subservience, coercion is required.

FROM SOCIAL REPRODUCTION TO SOCIAL CHANGE

The fundamental tasks suggested by this analysis are those of learning to see, hear, and perceive differently, to come awake, to regain consciousness, to become aware of contradictions and how we resolve them, and to take in and acknowledge hidden realities and their relation to appearances. For concerted change to occur in the child welfare system, these tasks need to be addressed not just by child welfare workers but by others positioned in various locations in the system – academics, managers, supervisors, clients, volunteers, activists.

How might we begin to use critical analysis in everyday working life?

Represented in various chapters of the book are many contradictory views of everyday reality:

- Father has abandoned family. It is mother who neglects.
- Client has no resources. Client needs to be out on her own.
- Care of children is parental responsibility. Caring is women's work.
- People of all cultures have similar propensity to neglect and abuse children. Native families are greatly overrepresented in the child welfare system.
- Mother is overwhelmed with responsibility. How can Mother think of leaving her children?
- Difference is divisive. Let's celebrate diversity.
- Diversity is celebrated. We treat everyone alike.
- Threats and coercion represent help for poor mothers.
- Start where client is. The good parent model is best for neglecting mothers.

Recognition of such contradictions provides a moment of 'disjuncture' as two realities are suddenly experienced as conflicting: What has been hidden in our usual perceptions of reality becomes momentarily visible. Our habits of thought, however, teach us that it is safer and less frustrating not to dwell on these contradictions. We have learned 'tricks' to 'get us back on track.' Typically, we accomplish the disappearance of the contradiction by rearranging pieces of visible reality or by adding or eliminating a piece. We remove fathers from our thoughts. We bring in idealistic notions of motherhood to explain to ourselves why mothers should do the caring work no matter how difficult. We tell ourselves that culture has no place in the assessment of neglect.

A primary method of erasing contradictions is silence. The analysis shows how we 'forget' poverty in our zeal to explain neglect as a personal issue. The vast silence surrounding issues of race and culture allows us to avoid discomfort and guilt. Caring labour goes unnoticed because it does not fit the schema of neglect. The actualities of mothers' daily lives and caring labour are not appropriate topics of 'treatment' or recording. In fact, the social roots and lived experience of families charged with neglect are strangely absent from our thoughts, our explanations, our writing, and our scientific studies.

Erasing or avoiding contradiction in conscious thought results in the reproduction of the status quo. We briefly wonder how a mother can manage in such poverty, but record her behaviour as representing neediness. We mention dad, but turn our thoughts to mother's deficiencies. We check off 'Status Indian' on the intake form, but prescribe the standard 'parenting' class to address the issues. We reproduce what is, in other words, through practices meant to avoid disjuncture and contradictions. We continue to see and reproduce surface realities, and allow hidden realities to remain hidden.

What the analysis suggests is that if we want social change, we must first learn to perceive hidden realities – to 'hear' silences, to 'see' the invisible. It asks us to actively attend to moments of disjuncture; to interrogate the contradiction; to challenge our own habits of thought and action; to identify and include as many pieces of reality as we can locate to enhance our understandings of clients; to develop, as Leonard says, a 'critical consciousness' (1984). This is at once an obvious and a complex suggestion. The background, that which is silent or hidden or contradictory, does not easily present itself as closely connected to 'objective reality.' Work processes, ideology and the scrutiny of supervisors encourage us to 'forget,' ignore, live in the moment, handle the crisis, record the 'fact.' Priorities in research funding encourage us to proceed in tried and true directions rather than risk new terrain. Student demands for social work 'technique' push us towards the standard texts and sets of instructions.

Examination of neglect 'from the inside out' shows us the work of mothering, identifies connections between social context and instances of poor care, and reveals obstacles to good care that lie outside the control of the mother. Viewing poor caregiving as one feature of life, connected to other contextual features, suggests holistic solutions, those that tie caregiving not only to personality features of the mother but to her material and social circumstances. A different style of resource deployment is also suggested. With the personal approach, as we have seen, goes considerable blame – 'unworthiness' still adheres to clients of the child welfare system. A perception of mothers labouring in a specific historical and social context suggests an entirely different ethic of help, one which confirms rather than denies the self-worth of the one being helped (Noddings, 1984). Along these lines, Dalley (1988) proposes collective rather than individualized forms of care, involving group interaction which allows both the helpers and those being helped to know each other personally and to develop concern for each other. Through this approach, a person who is helped may move eventually into a role of helper, rather than being consigned forever to a position of moral inferiority. Some Native communities are engaging in 'community healing,' a process that distributes responsibility for help and self-help throughout the community. Neysmith (1991) has proposed a model of social care, one in which caring responsibilities are shared by communities rather than confined to the family, presently idealized as the only and most appropriate locus of care provision. These ideas, of course, run counter to our belief in privacy and individualism, yet they hold possibilities for much more effective kinds of care for children currently at risk.

As we become more conscious of the labour and responsibility involved in caring work, different ideas of care provision come into view. A small but interesting literature dealing with this issue has emerged. Caroline New and Miriam David (1985), for instance, challenge the mystique of mothering, citing a wide variety of collective forms of child care that exist in the present as well as in the past. Along with Gillian Dalley (1988) they argue that collective forms of care can not only free mothers from the exclusively held responsibilities that now exist, but can also help to shield children from unnecessary threat owing to a mother's lapses in caring. Collective forms can produce high quality care for the many children who are not living in the ideal nuclear family. Kinship systems that are the heritage of Native people and other cultural groups, for instance, help to free mothers from exclusive labour of caring, as well as to provide children with affectional bonds and ties to a variety of adults. This is a protective device that allows children to thrive even when mothers cannot do the work of caring. Rather than inducing mothers to cut ties with kin, healing and strengthening of the kinship group is called for.

Of course, these understandings are not completely new and different. The point is that understandings and perceptions available to our reflective selves are frequently lost in the course of everyday work practices. During interviews held with child wefare workers, both they and I frequently 'lost consciousness' in speaking of clients. Unspoken, shared assumptions about clients and their motivations crept into the discussion, while the social context and lived experiences of clients remained outside the main framework of our talk. Analysis of this occurrence required several steps on my part of locating hidden realities, followed by examination of the relationships of these realities to the specific case. Griffith and Smith (1987) note that 'confinement of the everyday world is a severe limitation on what we can offer ...' It is the 'sociological discourse' that makes possible the investigation and analysis of 'how the everyday, the personal, the level of feeling are embedded in larger social, economic and political relations' (1987: 89). In order to see reality more completely, then, requires reflexivity, a stepping back from one's everyday practice, a reflective stance that allows us to examine the particular in its dialectical relation to larger social forces. The 'immature' mother may then be seen *at all times* in relation to her context: as an individual carrying a large social burden; as a person shouldering a share of labour out of keeping with available resources; as a woman struggling to fit fragments of traditional culture into an isolating urban environment; as someone facing racial discrimination on a daily basis; as a victim of violence herself; as a person whose problems and resource deficits are shared by many others.

This is a proposal implying a radical reorganization of child welfare work. Although such an endeavour may seem at first impossible, a Canadian dialogue on the topic of 'rethinking child welfare' has already begun (Wharf, 1993) and there is, as Mullaly and Keating (1991) have suggested, a rich store of alternate approaches and a genuine tradition of 'radical' social work to guide our efforts.

WORKING DIFFERENTLY WITH CLIENTS

In social work, we are taught to think of the helping relationship as one in which the worker employs the 'self' to assist the client in determining and managing his or her own life. If we think of the helping relationship as one 'moment' or act in a larger course of social action, however, this relationship takes on a completely different character. The worker in fact occupies a pivotal position in mediating many contradictions between social structure and the client. Through workers in an organizational setting, features of social structure are selected and conveyed, both to the client, and to the file, which preserves them. We might see this as sort of a 'laundering' process, one which operates, via rules of objectivity, to hide the way social structure operates to organize the work, the worker–client relationship, and the possible outcomes. These hidden realities are, in fact, obscured by the individualistic ethic that permeates society in general and social work in particular. As a profession, we have paid relatively little attention to the field within which individuality and self-determination are to unfold. The focus has remained on the concept of choice, while the trickier problem of how choices come to be organized and distributed is largely unexamined.

In Chapter 8, for instance, we saw how mothers accused of neglect may choose between remaining with their children in circumstances of poverty or losing them. This is the choice provided by social structure, and thus it is the one to which workers in the child welfare setting attune their efforts. The substructures of class, race, and gender that confine this mother to welfare-recipient status, low educational attainment, a dead-end job should she rejoin the job market, poor housing, the absence of ongoing assistance with childcare, and below-poverty-line resources if she remains with her children are known to workers but sink to the background in the face of socially organized alternatives that provide only 'yes' and 'no' as choices.

Power relations in the society are also a feature of this working relationship, although somewhat glossed over by the notion of the helping relationship. At all points in the relationship, both client and worker are aware of the repressive power of the state that can be brought to bear on the client. The power imported into the relationship, in other words, is frequently seen by both client and worker as coercive power used by the worker against the expressed interests of the client. Moreau (1989), in identifying five kinds of power available to professional personnel, makes explicit that other forms of power could be used by workers. The first kind of power he identifies is expert power, including access to information. The second is referent power, meaning the ability to attract others to a cause. Third is the power of numbers. Fourth is legitimate power, which child welfare workers hold through their legal mandate. Fifth is coercive power, that is, the power to reward or punish. In the helping relationships formed in child welfare, these last two forms of power have been overused, whereas the first three remain underused, a pattern certainly encouraged by supervisors, managers, and funders, as well as in child welfare discourse.

The analysis developed in previous chapters suggests how the organization of work processes and information gathering discourage and often seem to preclude bringing these other forms of power into the relationship. As case examples show, workers frequently limit the use of their personal influence and power to the coersion of clients into minimally acceptable parenting practices and to the arena of legitimizing dichotomized, painful choices. In expending efforts on the case-by-case approach, the power of numbers cannot be marshalled, and even the formulation of a cause is made difficult. The characterization of neglect brings workers to wonder if a legitimate cause exists: Whom can they influence to the cause of supporting 'bad mothers'? Existing recording practices deny workers access to a useful social database, so that the wielding of informational power in the service of their clientele is impossible.

These features of the work appear insurmountable to workers, and indeed the pressure on them to conform, to stop questioning, is considerable. That the child welfare system itself needs a radical overhaul is common knowledge among workers, but this task appears too large for most individuals to contemplate. The critical model, however, proposes that social forms and systems are created by the concerted actions of individuals and can only be changed by them. One worker cannot overhaul the system, but concerted efforts by many individuals occupying different locations within and adjacent to the child welfare system, each consciously doing their work differently, can and will make a difference. We ourselves have much to gain in this endeavour. Our own subjectivities are shaped, after all, by our practice. In changing our practice, we resist the penetration of existing power relations 'into the very core' of our own personalities; and as we alter our practice, new capacities become available to us (Leonard, 1984: 214–17).

Working differently means recognizing and using different kinds of power in the service of the client. It means recognizing how social meanings and choices are imported into the helping relationship and consciously bringing to that relationship alternative explanations and choices. Rather than importing unexamined theories and concepts from the dominant culture into the assessment process, for instance, workers and supervisors, as well as advocates, can help to generate alternate hypotheses that explain issues and problems. Assumptions of passivity or character defects as the cause of neglect can be added to or replaced by explorations of the way caring capacity has been affected by experiences in the mother's life, including violence, poverty, addiction, and poor housing. Mothers now characterized as 'needy,' could be helped to explore their own understandings and behaviour in relation to experiences of oppression. Survival strategies employed by clients could be reflected back to them as empowering and sometimes 'heroic' and could be regularly captured in file recording. Homogenized instruction in methods of 'parenting' could be replaced with programs designed to address cultural and social issues important to the clientele. Data could be collected on shared problems faced by clients. Community, social action, and client advocacy could become commonplace features of child welfare work. Research could focus on evaluation of services rather than solely on client deficiencies. Healing could supplant control as a major service goal. Unlike the 'good parent' model, these forms of practice require a leveling of power relations between helper and helped, the creation of relationships between 'struggling human beings who share work and responsibility for social change' (Moreau, 1989: 229). In such relations, neither workers nor clients – including children – can be seen as passive victims whose life circumstances are beyond their own control.

Although the job of child welfare appears fixed, this is, in fact, a surface appearance; there is always some room to manoeuvre. Working differently depends on perceiving differently, on tapping into hidden realities, learning to understand their connections to surface appearances, and on sharing and using this understanding together with and in the service of clients. It suggests a different positioning of the self of the worker viv-à-vis the client: reframing the relationship from that of dominance–subservience, as represented in the good parent model, to one of fellow human beings struggling together. It is partly through this process that different choices can be envisioned and that sufficient numbers of people can be brought together to help operationalize a different set of choices for mothers charged with neglect.

KNOWING DIFFERENTLY

Social workers have a dual commitment to 'the welfare and self-realization of human beings' and to 'the achievement of social justice for all' (CASW Code of Ethics, 1983). In practice this dual commitment has often found expression in two 'streams' of social work practice and discourse, which can loosely be categorized as personal services and policy development. The goals (and databases) of most agencies and organizations are geared to the personal, as in child welfare. Those who work in policy fields do not as a matter of course enter the homes or come in contact with the lived experience of those affected by social welfare policies. Social work education often makes a conceptual distinction between the two as well, offering 'clinical' and 'policy' specializations. We come to think of these as separate spheres, as the two solitudes of social work.

This does not mean that the connection between these two spheres has been ignored. On the contrary, an important social work concept linking the personal with the social is the idea that social work deals with the 'person in the environment.' Unlike psychology or psychiatry, social work has a long tradition of valuing context as an important feature of individual life. Social workers delivering personal services are encouraged to take account of environmental factors in developing plans for and with the client. Several theoretical approaches, especially systems theory and more recently the 'ecological' approach have been promoted as ways of bringing these two spheres into a conceptual relationship that practitioners can use in their everyday work. The distaste that social workers so often display for theory (Carew, 1979) suggests that these attempts have met with limited success. Certainly, workers I have worked with, interviewed, and taught often fail to see helpful connections between social theory and the reality of child welfare practice. This appears as a contradiction, which they likely resolve in the everyday world of work by deciding that most theory is not useful. Theories most frequently retained and used for child welfare purposes have to do with 'the family,' and especially with explanations of repeated family problems as cyclical. This theoretical approach is understood, accepted, and reinforced by other professionals both within and outside of social work. Other social theories and explanations they may have been taught at school simply do not appear as relevant to their work with clients.

The ecological theory, often taught in schools of social work as a conceptual framework for understanding relations between the personal and the social, is easily reducible to the cycle theory. In texts developed from the ecological perspective (O'Neil, 1984; Germain, 1979), 'the family' all too often becomes the primary contextual issue that is considered. Personal services, which constitute the overwhelming majority of social work settings, develop information from the perspective of the person in the family.

Both critical and interpretive social science have significant power to help us overcome these limitations. The tradition of social work, after all, is not to treat the personal and the social separately but as a dialectic. In fact, a good deal of social work actually takes place at the intersection of policy and practice, and the critical paradigm provides a way to examine this relationship. Social workers are positioned in their everyday practice to witness effects of social structure, including specific policies, on individuals in their daily lives, and, furthermore, to see how individuals receive, struggle against, use, support, and act upon elements of socially organized forces. Separating these spheres conceptually, as we do in both practice and in academic life, is confounding, for it does not reflect the real life experience we later encounter. Nor does this conceptual separation make good use of our informational resources. Social workers in all their various locations and employment arrangements have access to massive amounts of data about this dialectical relationship, and they are thus well placed to apply a critical analysis in concrete and useful ways. Social work educators have a responsibility for help-ing future workers see and use this information in the service of clients, but the favoured paradigm does not provide the conceptual tools to do this. A critical approach, however, can help us begin to investigate how seemingly good policies get subverted in the process of implementing them, how the good intentions and ideas of workers lead to frustration, and how the very database practitioners help to develop supports policies we are perhaps, in another arena, fighting against.

By including discourse and work organization in our analysis, a better picture of how the activities of individuals become part of a larger course of action can be developed. The analysis of how 'help' becomes subsumed by authority (Chapter 8) provides one example. Another is the analysis (Chapter 5) of how one discourse comes to dominate a field and crowd out a compet-ing discourse. Through careful attention to the ideological procedures of practice lodged in the everyday work world, social workers can begin to develop a much more sophisticated and useful body of knowledge for under-standing how practice contributes to social reproduction.

Positivist science, as Heineman (1981, 1989) comments, does not provide adequate strategies for the examination of feelings; in fact, it makes an issue of their exclusion. On the face of it, it is odd that a profession so steeped in the importance of feelings as is social work would so wholeheartedly accept a tradition of knowledge requiring its separation from feeling. As James (1989) shows, however, this exclusion is not unique to social work; feelings have been widely ignored in academic discourse more generally. The exclu-sion of feelings, or rather the appearance of exclusion, provides a space for 'needs interpretation' to enter; the use of an increasingly administrative ap-proach to service delivery, one which values 'parenting' at the expense of love and attachment, for instance, provides a clear example. In fact, the feelings of workers (and researchers) are important in accomplishing the everyday tasks of social work, but workers are taught to expunge feelings from the record. This is 'professional'; but in so doing, they fail to explore the ante-cedents and social uses of their own feelings and those of their clients. Forms of knowledge that respect and reveal this aspect of our work are not only appropriate but essential to understanding the character of human service delivery.

While valuing Heineman's suggested research focus on feelings, I believe this issue needs to be placed in a much larger field. The issue is not only that feelings are ignored, but the way that rationality and objectivity are valued and structured into all aspects of the social fabric. Bureaucracy, legal man-dates, professionalism, documentary practices, and knowledge itself are all characterized by and evaluated from the perspective of their adherence to the tenets of objectivity. In this scheme, subjectivity is always perceived as separate, as personal, as biased, and, therefore, as discreditable. In the practice of social work, this division discredits the emotions of both social workers and clients as too soft and too biased to be 'data.' Simultaneously, hard data are credited as the important, objective information needed for decision making in the 'real world.' As we have seen, many contradictions are concealed through these procedures. Workers are to bring their subjectivities into work with clients, but leave them out of documentation. Clients are required to conceal and distort subjectivity if they expect to benefit from agency resources. Simultaneously, workers are expected to enter into relationships of help and trust with these same clients. Workers experience anguish when forced to separate families, but present these decisions as objective and rational. All of these stances reveal ways in which actual lived experiences of both clients and workers come to be deleted, distorted, and discredited in much formal knowledge. Many people, having been convinced that formal knowledge is real and true, whereas their own experience is subjective and false, fail to credit their own experience as actual knowledge. Paradigms of knowledge are needed that value, credit, and make use of knowledge derived through experience.

Social work has always been a value-based profession. Positivist knowledge does not fit all that comfortably with our value orientation. In fact, it could be argued that values are discredited and distorted through the kind of knowledge currently espoused by the profession. Values become easily confused with subjectivity, which we take to be entirely personal, and consequently become cast as mere 'bias.' Critical social science develops knowledge explicitly for the purposes of social critique and change. It insists on values, on a standpoint, and aims to provide knowledge through which social structures that limit consciousness and thus reproduce themselves can be changed. In encouraging the examination of practice as a mechanism of social reproduction and social change, it is an empowering approach, pointing to specific activities that are within the control of individuals to execute and alter.

Attention to individuals and their personal difficulties is, of course, part of the social work mandate. The profession has another mission, which is 'the achievement of social justice for all' (CASW Code of Ethics, 1983). The kinds of knowledge needed to pursue this goal cannot be developed through the positivist paradigm, which denies that knowledge could and should begin from this aim. Through critical social science, knowledge previously relegated to obscurity is 'united by its exclusion,' and, thus, it can come to constitute 'a collective voice against that exclusion' (Ferguson, 1984: 158). Discourse analysis is essential to this task, as the issue of 'neediness' (Chapter 6) demonstrates. Taking as its source unexamined assumptions about maturity, independence, and appropriate adult expectations of women, the discourse brought to bear in understanding the 'causes of neglect' is in fact limited and out of date. A considerable body of literature re-examining differential development in boys and girls (Keller, 1985), critically examining established ideals of maturity as developed from an almost totally male point of view (Gilligan, 1982); examining the mythology of motherhood (Chodorow and Contratto, 1982); and proposing psychological development as circular and heroic rather than linear and stunted (Pearson, 1989) suggest that the underpinnings of the 'cycle of neglect' theory are seriously oversimplified and that they rest on unexamined assumptions about human development as well as gendered work allocation in modern society. This growing literature could provide a way into understanding how a mother would want to resign, could push us to enquire into her experience of mothering and of life, as these are contextually situated. The effective 'sidelining' of discourses concerned with poverty, race, and culture provide other examples of the need for discourse analysis and its effects on the knowledge base actually employed in practice.

Much of what we teach in social work operates not to illuminate reality for workers but to *hide* its character. Documentary practices in the workplace contribute to this effect. The surface appearance of case records is that they are objective records about individual families. However, files about clients, as shown in Chapters 4 and 5, are not simply jottings about individual behaviour. Their content and organization both reflect and help to substantiate the personal service discourse as the most relevant one and 'objectivity' as the goal to reach for. Workers carefully include information that has an appearance of objectivity, which they know to be highly valued in bureaucracies and in the world at large, and exclude what they believe to be subjective. For the worker who sees herself as recording 'just the facts' (as most do), the notion that straightforward objectivity is possible is reinforced daily. For this worker, however, a consciousness splitting process occurs. The helping process recommended by professional social work relies on 'feeling with the client,' awareness of self, recognition and use of one's own subjectivity in working with clients. The recording process requires this subjectivity to be intentionally stripped away. When we think of subjectivity not as idiosyncratic but as organized by and directed towards features of social structure and organization, however, an otherwise hidden effect of this dichotomization appears. The removal of subjectivity from written material strips hidden realities from the file; it is in fact this process that allows files to appear as a collection of unambiguous facts about clients. Social work discourse encourages us to see this procedure as 'professionalism,' as evidenced by its 'objectivity.' The 'subjective' is equated with 'self,' perceived as a collection of characteristics and individual experiences unique to the individual. Because we continue to accept this view and the practices which flow from it, the factual world continues to be seen as 'real,' while our own knowledge and the knowledge we have of clients is fundamentally discredited.

If we examine files not as a personal record of misbehaviour but as a feature of larger social relations, a perspective of individuals and families as the locus of the ongoing attention of a multitude of interrelated organizations is revealed; this is the juridical–administrative–therapeutic (JAT) state apparatus at work (Fraser, 1989). Public health, schools, special facilities and institutions, hospitals and clinics, prisons, police forces, and welfare departments are some of the organizational components of this apparatus. Each organization has a mandate focused at least in part on the 'needs' of these families, who are therefore being 'worked up' somewhat differently in each setting. Although friction between organizations occurs at points, institutions in general work in tandem, a relation mediated through documents. Thus, workers in each setting, although appearing to attend to the needs of the client, constantly but invisibly attend to the larger purposes of the JAT in their work with clients and in the way clients are worked up in documents. In turn, analysis of files shows that they contribute to the construction and maintenance of social categories, which become durable features of surface reality.

Social work discourse allocates very little space at present to recording practices, and no space at all to the organizational and social purposes that records serve. The attention that has been paid to records is dominated by discussion of computerization. Social work educators could begin to draw on poststructuralist theory to help students examine how meanings are constructed and conveyed (Macdonell, 1986). This body of theory adds an important dimension to our understandings of social reproduction and to the roles we may unwittingly play in reproducing an ideology that works against the interests of our clients. When we make explicit and explore more fully the hidden realities organizing documents, the appearances that are produced through them can be understood differently. The 'neglectful mother' who previously appeared as a damaged and damaging person may then come to be seen also as a client unable to command needed resources, one whose case has been repeatedly closed, one who has managed reasonably well for long periods of time, one who loves her children, one who has tried through 'impression management' to gain necessary resources. In addition, the social context, including the organizational context, within which assistance is offered or denied becomes visible. In the aggregate, such records provide a form of social data that can be employed in advocacy efforts.

This way of looking at knowledge production poses front-line personnel and clients themselves as potential *producers* of information and discourse, rather than simply consumers. Discourse, it will be remembered, is a site of struggle, the location of competing ideas. Both social workers and clients, armed with their own experiences and information they find useful, can enter this arena of struggle. Park et al. (1993) comment that 'significant segments of society all over the globe are institutionally excluded from participating in the creation of their own world as thinking, feeling, and acting subjects.' Knowledge, according to Park, becomes a 'crucial element in enabling people once more to have a say in how they would like to see their world put together and run' (p. 1). His work on participatory research draws from both the interpretive and critical schools to examine in a practical way activities leading to transformations of current social reality.

What we take as necessary and sufficient knowledge about the social world has been contained by the limits of our social categories and legitimated knowledge paradigms. Foucault's phrase, 'an insurrection of subjugated knowledges' (1972a: 81) suggests that different kinds of knowing and knowledge are there to be discovered and used. Such knowledge often derives from the experience of exclusion and from resistance to that exclusion. This resistance may be 'improbable, spontaneous, solitary, and savage,' to use Foucault's words. Examples are instances of clients' attempts to fool and manipulate workers; a worker's brief written reference to 'inappropriate resources'; the 'torn apart' feeling of a worker facing two unacceptable alternatives; a mother's attempt to 'resign.' Within the administrative apparatus of child welfare, and assisted by the discourse, these moments of resistance are effectively muted, silenced, discredited, or transformed into 'facts' in better keeping with the prevailing forms of knowledge. Different forms of knowing require and make use of the subjugated knowledge represented in these acts of resistance as part of a process of ongoing discovery and transformation.

Why bother, we may ask. What difference can it really make if some educators teach differently, if more paradigms are used in knowledge development, if some social workers come to perceive reality differently, if some clients become involved in knowledge development about their own problems, if some child welfare workers come to view neglect differently? What effect can it have on social reality, the philosopher Minnich asks, if we change our minds? It will have an effect, she says, *not to* (1990).

REVISITING CHILD NEGLECT

'Child welfare' itself holds competing meanings, as I realized when I recently attended an international conference on child welfare. I came equipped with my knowledge of child protection and its problems. For many Europeans, 'child welfare' actually refers to quality of life for children. A simple change in thinking can open new vistas for us.

Examination and critique of the ways mothers are dealt with in Canadian child welfare are not intended to suggest that mothers are always adequate, that they are always being unfairly judged by workers, or that families would be better off if child welfare workers were to leave them alone. And certainly it is not suggested that the children involved in neglect cases are not really in need of help. As we have seen, the children of mothers classified as neglecting often do have terrible experiences. Poverty, alcohol abuse, violence, and unmet emotional and physical needs are serious problems for both parents and children.

Our rights-based methods of 'helping' as they now stand, however, are often damaging to the children as well as to the mothers, consigning both to ongoing resource deficits as the legal processes move slowly to document and process the innumerable incidents of 'neglect' required to justify resource deployment or change in the situation. The rights approach pits mothers and children against each other in a scramble for scarce resources, and the ultimate effect is the destruction of many families. The answers do not lie in calls for larger budgets to do more of the same. After a century of failure, it is clear that the kinds of resources typically deployed through child welfare systems must be questioned.

To fully recognize and implement a program through which child welfare could become its name, that is, could become concerned with the welfare of children rather than with protective practices, many shifts in funding, organization and orientation of 'the system' are required. Some experts are currently renewing their interest in the topic of child neglect, suggesting revitalization of the definitional debates (Rose and Meezan, 1993). Apparently many people are undaunted by a hundred years of failure to either save children or change mothers. My own view is that these proposals represent hegemony in a new and modern form. Callahan's (1993) recent – and courageous – suggestion that neglect be eliminated as a child welfare category holds more promise. The ideological baggage neglect carries with it, the overly legalized system developed to make determinations of neglect, the paltry resources associated with it, and the abject failure of its use in improving life for clients – children and parents alike – all argue for a radical change in direction. Workers who now spend much of their time policing families might actually be able to provide service, were resources to be diverted, as Callahan suggests, into a system designed explicitly to improve the welfare of Canadian children. Efforts of workers to perceive, work, and know differently could be carried out in a supportive rather than in a hostile environment. In Canada, we are accustomed to incremental change. But perhaps in some cases, we should simply admit failure and begin again. Neglect, for me, is one such case.

Notes

CHAPTER 2

1 The term 'lived experience' refers here especially to the work of D. E. Smith (1980, 1987; Griffith and Smith, 1987), who explicates disjunctures between actual life experience and textual representations of life experience. The term thus infers not only what actually happens in people's lives, but the way experience becomes distorted, 'eclipsed' (1987: 17–43), or made 'social' (1983) through documentary processes. This term, it should be noted, has its roots in phenomenology. Husserl explored the way lived experience is retained in consciousness for later reflection (Husserl, 1913, trans. 1969; Lyotard, 1986, trans. 1991).

2 Most authors concerned with race and culture also deal in some way with the concept of ethnicity. Often, ethnic groups are seen as more or less synonymous with cultural groups. Li (1990), however, calls this equation into question, pointing out that conquest and migration over several centuries have diluted the relationship between ethnicity and culture. Some groups with a common origin, he notes, have not even shared common experiences, let alone a common cultural field. In the interests of maintaining a clear focus, I have confined my analysis to race and culture in the body of the chapter.

CHAPTER 3

1 As Nutter, Hudson, Galaway, and Hill (1994) point out in their recent research, even the literature of foster care has often focused on such issues as cost effectiveness rather than on the needs and experiences of children in care.

2 The word 'Aboriginal' is now often used because it includes all legal classes of Canada's First Nations Peoples. In this book, the term 'Native,' common in everyday conversation, will be used.

3 There have been attempts in some jurisdictions to speed up the judicial process when permanent or long-term planning for children is at issue. In Manitoba, for instance, limits on the amount of time children may be kept in care have been set in legislation in order to force final decisions on placement. This plan has been somewhat subverted, however, by the fact that children are often placed many times for short periods.

4 Fraser (1989) herself makes a connection with Althusser, suggesting that her concept of the JAT 'echoes' Althusser's idea of an 'ideological state apparatus.' Fraser notes that the idea of the JAT is essentially a subclass of an ISA (p. 160).

CHAPTER 4

1 See also Mason and Gambrill, 1994, especially Section II, in which various arguments concerning the relationships between definitions and interventions are presented.

CHAPTER 5

1 See, for example, Mouzakitis and Goldstein, 1985.
2 See Swift, 1988 and 1990, for further discussions of this issue.
3 Information for this case study is documented in Swift, 1990.

CHAPTER 6

1 Portions of this chapter appear in 'Contradictions in Child Welfare: Neglect and Reponsibility.' A chapter in Baines et al., 1991.

CHAPTER 8

1 In practice workers exercise discretion, based on their assessment of the caller and the nature of the complaint; they do not necessarily visit each family about whom a complaint is lodged.
2 In recent years specific legal rights of children have been recognized and entered into legislation and court proceedings.
3 Child welfare workers do not usually think of themselves as providing therapy to clients, but 'counselling,' which refers to goal-oriented activity, is common.
4 Kadushin (1967) uses the term 'client' throughout the section on child neglect to mean the mother or parents. At the very end of the chapter, however, he identifies the child as the client, and the mother as the focus of service. Workers in my interviews echoed this usage exactly.

5 This idea is also reflected in research and evaluation literature. See Hall et al. (1982) for an example.
6 See Hegel's analysis of master–servant relations in *The Phenomenology of Mind* for an account of this socially located knowledge (1807, trans. 1977).
7 Although homemakers are sometimes assigned to two-parent homes, their focus is primarily on the 'mothering' function.
8 There are some exceptions. Sometimes, especially if children are in long-term foster care rather than in adoptive homes, visiting rights are maintained.

References

Althusser, Louis. 1971. *Essays on Ideology*. London: Verso.

American Humane Association. 1966. *In the Interest of Children: A Century of Progress*. Denver, Colo.: Children's Division American Humane Association.

Armitage, Andrew. 1993. 'Family and Child Welfare in First Nation Communities.' In Brian Wharf, ed. *Rethinking Child Welfare in Canada*. Toronto: McClelland and Stewart.

Baines, C., P. Evans, and S. Neysmith. 1991. *Women's Caring: A Feminist Perspective on Social Welfare*. Toronto: McClelland and Stewart.

Barrett, Michele, and Mary McIntosh. 1982. *The Anti-Social Family*. London: Verso.

Barth, R., and R. Sullivan. 1985. 'Collecting Competent Evidence in Behalf of Children.' *Social Work* 30: 130–6.

Beechey, Veronica, and James Donald. 1985. *Subjectivity and Social Relations*. Milton Keynes: Open University Press.

Behlmer, G.K. 1982. *Child Abuse and Moral Reform in England, 1870–1908*. Stanford, Cali.: Stanford University Press.

Benjamin, Michael. 1981. *FBA Mothers and Employment Expectations: The Best Interests of the Child*. Toronto: Ontario Ministry of Community and Social Services Division.

Berger, Peter L., and Thomas Luckmann. 1967. *The Social Construction of Reality*. London: Allen Lane.

Bissoondath, Neil. 1993. 'A Question of Belonging: Multiculturalism and Citizenship.' In William Kaplan, ed., *Belonging*. Montreal: McGill-Queen's University Press, 368–87.

Blanchard, E.L., and R.L. Barsh. 1980. 'What is Best for Tribal Children? A Response to Fischler.' *Social Work* 25: 350–7.

Bolaria, B. Singh, and Peter S. Li, eds. 1988. *Racial Oppression in Canada*, 2nd ed. Toronto: Garamond Press.

Bologh, R. 1979. *Dialectical Phenomenology*. London: Routledge and Kegan Paul.

Bourdieu, P., and Jean-Claude Passeron. 1977. *Reproduction in Education, Society, and Culture*. London: Sage.

Bourgeault, Ron G. 1988. 'Race and Class Under Mercantilism: Indigenous People in Nineteenth-Century Canada.' In B. Singh Bolaria, and Peter S. Li, eds., *Racial Oppression in Canada*, 2 ed. Toronto: Garamond Press.

– 1991. 'Race, Class, and Gender: Colonial Domination of Indian Women.' In Ormond McKague, ed., *Racism in Canada*. Saskatoon: Fifth House Publishers.

Bowlby, John. 1969. *Attachment and Loss*, vol. 1 and 2. New York: Basic Books.

Bradbury, B. 1982. 'The Fragmented Family: Family Strategies in the Face of Death, Illness, and Poverty, Montreal 1860–1885.' In Joy Parr ed., *Childhood and Family in Canadian History*. Toronto: McClelland and Stewart.

Braverman, Harry. 1974. *Labor and Monopoly Capital*. New York: Monthly Review Press.

Breines, W., and L. Gordon. 1983. 'The New Scholarship on Family Violence.' *Signs* 8: 491–531.

Byler, William. 1977. 'The Destruction of American Indian Families.' In Steven Unger, ed., *The Destruction of American Indian Families*. New York: Association on American Indian Affairs.

Callahan, Marilyn. 1993. 'Feminist Approaches: Women Recreate Child Welfare.' In Brian Wharf, ed., *Rethinking Child Welfare in Canada*. Toronto: McClelland and Stewart.

Carew, Robert. 1979. 'The Place of Knowledge in Social Work Activity.' *British Journal of Social Work* 9: 349–64.

CASW Code of Ethics. 1983. In J. Turner and F. Turner, eds., 1986. *Canadian Social Welfare*. Toronto: Collier Macmillan, 451–62.

Child and Family Services Act. 1986. Manitoba.

Chodorow, N., and S. Contratto, 1982. 'The Fantasy of the Perfect Mother.' In B. Thorne and M. Yalom, eds., *Rethinking the Family: Some Feminist Questions*. New York: Longman.

Cicourel, A.V. 1976. *The Social Organization of Juvenile Justice*. London: Heineman Educational.

Cohen, M.B., and D. Wagner, 1982. 'Social Work Professionalism: Reality and Illusion.' In Charles Derber, ed., *Professionals as Workers: Mental Labour in Advanced Capitalism*. Boston: G.K. Hall.

Cohen, Neil A., ed. 1992. *Child Welfare: A Multicultural Focus*. Boston: Allyn and Bacon.

Cohen-Schalnger, M., Ann Fitzpatrick, J. David Hulchanski, and D. Raphael. 1992. 'Housing as a Factor in Child Admission to Temporary Care.' Toronto:

Joint research report of the Faculty of Social Work, University of Toronto, and the Children's Aid Society of Metropolitan Toronto.

Compton, B., and B. Galaway. 1984. *Social Work Processes*. Homewood, Ill.: Darsey Press.

Craft, John, and Marlys Staudt. 1991. 'Reporting and Founding of Child Neglect in Urban and Rural Communities.' *Child Welfare* 359–70.

Custer, L.B. 1978. 'The Origins of the Doctrine of Parens Patriae.' *Emory Law Journal* 27: 195–208.

Dalley, Gillian. 1988. *Ideologies of Caring*. London: Macmillan.

Daniels, A. 1987. 'Invisible Work.' *Social Problems* 34: 403–15.

Davis, Larry, and E.D. Proctor, 1989. *Race, Gender, and Class*. Englewood Cliffs, NJ: Prentice-Hall.

de Mause, Lloyd, ed., 1974. *The History of Childhood*. New York: Harper and Row.

Derber, Charles. 1982. *Professionals as Workers: Mental Labour in Advanced Capitalism*. Boston: G.K. Hall.

Devore, W., and E. Schlesinger, 1991. *Ethnic-Sensitive Social Work Practice*, 3rd ed. New York: Merrill, Macmillan.

Dominelli, L. 1988. *Anti-Racist Social Work*. London: Macmillan.

Downey, Dan. 1986. 'Organizational Change: A Participatory Model.' *Journal (OACAS)* 30: 1–3.

Durkeim, Emile. 1938, trans. 1966. *The Rules of Sociological Method*. New York: Free Press.

Eichler, M. 1988. *Families in Canada Today*. Toronto: Gage.

Engels, Frederick. 1878, trans. 1939. *Anti-Dühring*. New York: International Publishers.

England, Hugh. 1986. *Social Work as Art*. London: Allen and Unwin.

Erikson, Erik. 1950. *Childhood and Society*. New York: W.W. Norton.

Evans, Patricia. 1991. 'The Sexual Division of Poverty: The Consequences of Gendered Caring.' In C. Baines, P. Evans, and S. Neysmith, eds., *Women's Caring: A Feminist Perspective on Social Welfare*. Toronto: McClelland and Stewart: 169–203.

Falconer, Nancy, and Karen Swift, 1983. *Preparing for Practice*. Toronto: Children's Aid Society of Metropolitan Toronto.

Farina, Margaret. 1982. *The Relationship of the State to the Family in Ontario: State Intervention in the Family on Behalf of Children*. Published Ph.D. thesis. Toronto, Ontario Institute for Studies in Education.

Federal–Provincial Working Group on Child and Family Service Information. 1994. *Child Welfare in Canada*. National Clearinghouse on Family Violence. Ottawa: Health Canada.

Ferguson, Kathy. 1984. *The Feminist Case against Bureaucracy*. Philadelphia: Temple University Press.

Fischler, Ronald. 1980. 'Protecting American Indian Children.' *Social Work* 25: 341–9.

Foucault, Michel. 1972a. *The Archeology of Knowledge*. New York: Pantheon.

– 1972b. *Power/Knowledge: Selected Interviews and Other Writings*. New York: Pantheon Books.

– 1977. *Discipline and Punish*. Toronto: Random House.

Frances, R.C. and R.C. Stone. 1956. *Service Procedure in Bureaucracy*. Minneapolis: University of Minnesota Press.

Fraser, Nancy. 1989. 'Women, Welfare, and the Politics of Need Interpretation.' In P. Lassman, ed., *Politics and Social Theory*. London and New York: Routledge and Kegan Paul.

Gandy, John, and Lorne Teperman. 1990. *False Alarm: The Computerization of Eight Social Welfare Organizations*. Waterloo, Ont.: Wilfrid Laurier University Press.

Garbarino, James. 1978. 'Defining the Community Context for Parent–Child Relations: The Correlates of Child Maltreatment.' *Child Development* 49: 604.

Garfinkel, Harold. 1967. *Studies in Ethnomethodology*. Englewood Cliffs, NJ: Prentice-Hall.

Garvin, Charles, and Brett Seabury. 1984. *Interpersonal Practice in Social Work*. Englewood Cliffs, NJ: Prentice-Hall.

Gerth, H.H., and C. Wright Mills. 1946. *Essays in Sociology*. New York: Oxford University Press.

Gilligan, Carol. 1982. *In a Different Voice*. Cambridge, Mass.: Harvard University Press.

Giovannoni, Jeanne. 1982. 'Prevention of Child Abuse and Neglect Research and Policy Issues.' *Social Work Research and Abstracts* 3: 23.

Giovannoni, Jeanne, and R. Becerra. 1979. *Defining Child Abuse*. New York: Free Press.

Germain, Carol, ed. 1979. *People and Environments: An Ecological Perspective*. New York: Columbia University Press.

Gil, D.G. 1970. *Violence against Children*. Cambridge: Harvard University Press.

– 1981. 'The United States versus Child Abuse.' In L. Pelton, ed., *The Social Context of Child Abuse and Neglect*. New York: Human Sciences Press.

Goldstein, Howard. 1973. *Social Work Practice*. Columbia: University of South Carolina Press.

Goldstein, J., A. Freud, and A. Solnit. 1973. *Beyond the Best Interests of the Child*. New York: Free Press.

– 1979. *Before the Best Interests of the Child*. New York: Free Press.

Gordon, Linda. 1988. *Heroes in Their Own Lives*. New York: Penguin.

– 1989. *The New Feminist Scholarship on the Welfare State.* IRP Discussion Papers. Madison: University of Wisconsin.

Graham, H. 1983. 'Caring: A Labour of Love.' In J. Finch and D. Groves. eds., *A Labour of Love: Women, Work, and Caring.* London: Routledge and Kegan Paul.

Gramsci, A. 1971. *Prison Notebooks.* New York: International Publishers.

Grayson, J. Paul. 1980. *Class, State, Ideology and Change: Marxist Perspectives on Canada.* Toronto: Holt, Rinehart, and Winston.

Green, James. 1982. *Cultural Awareness in the Human Services.* Englewood Cliffs, NJ: Prentice-Hall.

Griffith, A., and D.E. Smith, 1987. 'Constructing Cultural Knowledge: Mothering as Discourse.' In J. Gaskell and A. McLaren, *Women and Education.* Calgary: Detselig Enterprises.

Guest, Dennis. 1980. *The Emergence of Social Security in Canada.* Vancouver: University of British Columbia Press.

Habermas, Jurgen. 1968, trans. 1971. *Knowledge and Human Interests.* Boston: Beacon Press.

– 1970. *Toward a Rational Society.* Boston: Beacon Press.

Hall, M., et al. 1982. 'Working with Neglecting Families.' *Children Today* 11: 6–9, 36.

Harris, J. and J. Melichercik, 1986. 'Age and Stage-Related Programs.' In J. Turner and R. Turner, eds., *Canadian Social Welfare*, 2nd ed. Don Mills, Ont.: Collier Macmillan: 154–81.

Hartman, Ann, and Joan Laird. 1983. *Family Centered Social Work Practice.* New York: Free Press.

Hartmann, Heidi. 1987. 'The Family as the Locus of Gender, Class, and Political Struggle: The Example of Housework.' In S. Harding, ed., *Feminism and Methodology.* Bloomington: Indiana University Press.

Harvey, Lee. 1990. *Critical Social Research.* London: Unwin Hyman.

Hegel, G.W.F. 1807, trans. 1977. *The Phenomenology of Mind.* Oxford: Oxford University Press.

– 1812–16, trans. 1966. *Science of Logic.* Woking and London: Unwin Brothers.

Heineman, Martha. 1981. 'The Obsolete Scientific Imperative in Social Work Research.' *Social Service Review* 55: 371–97.

Heineman Piper, Martha. 1982. 'Author's Reply.' *Social Service Review* 56 (June).

– 1989. 'The Heuristic Paradigm: A Unifying and Comprehensive Approach to Social Work Research.' *Smith College Studies in Social Work* 60: 8–34.

Hepworth, Philip. 1980. *Foster Care and Adoption in Canada.* Ottawa: Canadian Council on Social Development.

Horowitz, B., and I. Wolock, 1981. 'Material Deprivation, Child Maltreatment and Agency Interventions among Poor Families.' In L. Pelton, ed., *The Social Context of Child Abuse and Neglect*. New York: Human Sciences Press.

Hudson, Pete, and Brad McKenzie. 1981. 'Child Welfare and Native People: The Extension of Colonialism.' *The Social Worker* 49: 63–6, 87–8.

Hudson, Walter. 1983. 'Author's Reply.' *Social Service Review* 57 (June): 340–1.

Husserl, Edmund. 1913, trans. 1969. *Ideas*. Norich: Jarrold and Sons.

– 1950, trans. 1964. *The Idea of Phenomenology*. The Hague: Martinius Nijhoff.

Hutchinson, S. 1990. 'Child Maltreatment: Can It Be Defined?' *Social Service Review* 64: 60–78.

Hutchinson, Y., et al. 1992. *Profile of Clients in the Anglophone Youth Network: Examining the Situation of the Black Child*. Montreal: Joint report of Ville Marie Social Service Centre and McGill University School of Social Work.

Irving, Allan. 1992. 'The Scientific Imperative in Social Welfare Research in Canada, 1897–1945.' *Canadian Social Work Review* 9: 9–27.

James, Nicky. 1989. 'Emotional Labour: Skill and Work in the Social Regulation of Feelings.' *Sociological Review* 37: 15–42.

Jaynes, G.D., and R.M. Williams Jr., 1989. *A Common Destiny: Blacks and American Society*. Washington, DC: National Academy Press.

Jenkins, Shirley. 1981. *The Ethnic Dilemma in Social Services*. New York: The Free Press.

Johnston, Patrick. 1983. *Native Children and the Child Welfare System*. Toronto: Canadian Council on Social Development, in association with James Lorimer Publishers.

Jones, Andrew, and Leonard Rutman. 1981. *In the Children's Aid*. Toronto: University of Toronto Press.

Jones, Chris. 1979. 'Social Work Education, 1900–1977.' In Noel Parry, et al., eds., *Social Work, Welfare, and the State*. London: Edward Arnold, 72–88.

Jones, J.M., and R.L. McNeely, 1980. 'Mothers Who Neglect and Those Who Do Not: A Comparative Study.' *Social Casework* 61: 559–67.

Kadushin, Alfred. 1967, 1974, 1980. *Child Welfare Services*. New York: Macmillan.

Kadushin, Alfred, and Judith Martin, 1988. *Child Welfare Services*, 4th Ed. New York: Macmillan.

Kallen, Evelyn. 1982. *Ethnicity and Human Rights in Canada*. Toronto: Gage.

Kaplan, William. 1993. *Belonging*. Montreal: McGill-Queen's University Press.

Karger, H.J. 1983. 'Science Research and Social Work: Who Controls the Profession?' *Social Work* 28: 200–05.

Katz, Sanford. 1971. *When Parents Fail*. Boston: Beacon Press.

Keller, Evelyn. 1985. *Reflections on Gender and Science*. New Haven: Yale University Press.

Kempe, C.H., and Ray Helfer. 1968. *The Battered Child*. Chicago: University of Chicago Press.

Kempe, C.H., F.N. Silverman, I.S. Brandt, W. Droegemueller, and H.K. Silver, 1962. 'The Battered Child Syndrome.' *Journal of the American Medical Association* 181 (July): 17–24.

Kessel, Jo Ann, and Susan P. Robins. 1984. 'The Indian Child Welfare Act: Dilemmas and Needs.' *Child Welfare* 63: 225–32.

King, Richard. 1967. *The School at Mopass*. Stanford: Holt, Rinehart, and Winston.

Korbin, Jill. 1981. *Child Abuse and Neglect: Cross Cultural Perspectives*. Berkeley: University of California Press.

Larrain, Jorge. 1979. *The Concept of Ideology*. London: Hutchinson.

Leonard, Peter. 1984. *Personality and Ideology: Towards a Materialist Understanding of the Individual*. Atlantic Highlands, NJ: Humanities Press.

Li, Peter. 1990. *Race and Ethnic Relations in Canada*. Toronto: Oxford University Press.

Lubove, Roy. 1965. *The Professional Altruist*. Cambridge: Harvard University Press.

Lukacs, George. 1971. *History and Class Consciousness*. Cambridge: MIT Press.

Lyotard, Jean-Francois. 1986, trans 1991. *Phenomenology*. Albany: State University of New York Press.

Macdonell, Diane. 1986. *Theories of Discourse*. Oxford and New York: Blackwell.

Macintyre, Ewan. 1993. 'The Historical Context of Child Welfare in Canada.' In Brian Wharf, ed., *Rethinking Child Welfare in Canada*. Toronto: McClelland and Stewart.

McGoldrick, Monica. 1982. *Ethnicity and Family Therapy*. New York: Guilford Press.

Manuel, G., and M. Posluns, 1974. *The Fourth World: An Indian Reality*. Toronto: Collier-McMillan.

Maracle, Brian. 1993. *Crazywater*. Toronto: Viking.

Maslow, A.H. 1954. *Motivation and Personality*. New York: Harper.

Mason, M.A., and Eileen Gambrill, 1994. *Debating Children's Lives: Current Controversies on Children and Adolescents*. Thousand Oaks: Sage.

Marx, Karl. *Capital I: Capitalistic Production*. 1886, trans. 1906. London: Swan Sonnenschein.

Marx, Karl, and Friedrich Engels. 1846, trans. 1947. *The German Ideology*, parts 1 and 3. New York: International Publishers.

McKague, Ormond, ed. 1991. *Racism in Canada*. Saskatoon: Fifth House Publishers.

Metropolitan Toronto Children's Aid Society Archives. Toronto: City Hall Archives.

Miles, Robert. 1989. *Racism*. London and New York: Routledge.

Miller, Jaclyn. 1991. 'Child Welfare and the Role of Women: A Feminist Perspective.' *American Journal of Orthopsychiatry* 61: 592–8.

Miller, J.R. 1989. *Skyscrapers Hide the Heavens*. Toronto: University of Toronto Press.

Minnich, Elizabeth. 1990. *Transforming Knowledge*. Philadelphia: Temple University Press.

Mnookin, Robert. 1973. 'Foster Care – In Whose Best Interests?' *Harvard Educational Review* 43: 599–638.

Moreau, Maurice. 1989. *Empowerment through a Structural Approach to Social Work*. Ottawa: Carleton University School of Social Work.

Morrissette, Vern, Brad McKenzie, and Larry Morrissette. 1993. 'Towards an Aboriginal Model of Social Work Practice.' *Canadian Social Work Review* 10: 91–108.

Morrow, R. 1985. 'Critical Theory and Critical Sociology.' *Canadian Review of Sociology and Anthropology* (December): 710–47.

Mouzakitis, C.M., and S.C. Goldstein, 1985. 'A Multi-Disciplinary Approach to Treating Child Neglect.' *Social Casework* 66: 218–24.

Mullaly, Robert. P., and Eric F. Keating, 1991. 'Similarities, Differences, and Dialectics of Radical Social Work.' *Journal of Progressive Human Services* 2: 49–78.

Nagi, Saad. 1977. *Child Maltreatment in the United States*. New York: Columbia University Press.

Natanson, Maurice. 1970. 'Alfred Schutz on Social Reality and Social Science.' In M. Natanson, ed., *Phenomenology and Social Reality*. The Hague: Martinius Nijhoff.

Neuman, W. Lawrence. 1991. *Social Research Methods*. Boston: Allyn and Bacon.

New, Caroline, and Miriam David. 1985. *For the Children's Sake*. Harmondsworth, Middlesex: Penguin.

Neysmith, S. 1991. 'From Community Care to a Social Model of Care.' In C. Baines, P. Evans, and S. Neysmith, eds., *Women's Caring: Feminist Perspective on Social Welfare*. Toronto: McClelland and Stewart, 272–99.

Noddings, Nell. 1984. *Caring: A Feminist Approach to Ethics and Moral Education*. Berkeley, Calif.: University of California Press.

Nutter, R., J. Hudson, B. Galaway, and M. Hill 1994. 'Specialist Foster Care Program Standards in Relation to Costs, Client Characteristics, and Outcomes.' Paper presented at the National Research and Policy Symposium on Child Welfare. Kananaskis, Alberta.

O'Hagan, K. 1993. *Emotional and Psychological Abuse of Children.* Toronto: University of Toronto Press.

Ohlsson, A. 1979. 'Non-organic Failure-to-Thrive.' *Child Abuse and Neglect* 3: 449–59.

O'Neil, M.J. 1984. *The General Method of Social Work Practice.* Englewood Cliffs, NJ: Prentice-Hall.

Park, Peter, et al., eds., 1993. *Voices of Change: Participatory Research in the United States and Canada.* Toronto: Ontario Institute for Studies in Education Press.

Pearson, Carol. 1989. *The Hero Within.* San Francisco: Harper and Row.

Pecheux, Michel. 1975, trans. 1982. *Language, Semantics and Ideology: Stating the Obvious.* London: Macmillan.

Pedersen, Paul, ed., 1976. *Counseling across Cultures.* Honolulu: University of Hawaii Press.

Pelton, Leroy. 1981. *The Social Context of Child Abuse and Neglect.* New York: Human Sciences Press.

Piele, Colin. 1988. 'Research Paradigms in Social Work: From Stalemate to Creative Synthesis.' *Social Service Review* (March): 1–15.

Pincus, Allen, and Anne Minahan. 1973. *Social Work Practice: Model and Method.* Itasca, Ill.: F.E. Peacock.

Pinderhughes, Elaine. 1989. *Understanding Race, Ethnicity and Power: The Key to Efficacy in Clinical Practice.* New York: Free Press.

Piven, Frances, and R. Cloward. 1982. *The New Class War.* New York: Pantheon.

Polansky, Norman, and Nancy Polansky. 1975. *Profile of Neglect: A Survey of the State of Knowledge of Child Neglect.* Washington, DC: United States Department of Health, Education, and Welfare.

Polansky, Norman, P. Amons, and B. Weathersley, 1983. 'Is There an American Standard of Child Care?' *Social Work* 28: 341–6.

Polansky, Norman, R.D. Bergman, and C. De Saix, 1972. *Roots of Futility.* San Francisco: Jossey-Bass.

Polansky, Norman, M.A. Chalmers, E. Buttenweiser, and D. Williams. 1981. *Damaged Parents: An Anatomy of Child Neglect.* Chicago: University of Chicago Press.

Prins. H. 1974. 'Motivation in Social Work.' *Social Work Today* 5: 40–3.

Proceedings of the Social Service Congress. Ottawa, 3–5 March, 1914.

Red Horse, J.G. 1980. 'Family Structure and Value Orientation in American Indians.' *Social Casework* 61: 462–7.

Red Horse, J.G., et al. 1978. 'Family Behaviour of Urban American Indians.' *Social Casework* 59: 67–72.

Reitsma-Street, Marge. 1991. 'Girls Learn to Care; Girls Policed to Care.' In C. Baines, P. Evans, and S. Neysmith, eds. *Women's Caring: Feminist Perspectives on Social Welfare*. Toronto: McClelland and Stewart, 106–37.

Richey, Betty. 1977. 'The Computer in a Child Care Agency.' *Child Welfare* 56: 259–70.

Rose, Sue, and William Meezan. 1993. 'Defining Child Neglect: Evolution, Influences, and Issues.' *Social Service Review* 67: 279–93.

Rosenbluth, David. 1994. 'Foster Care in Saskatchewan: Drift or Revolving Door?' Paper presented at the National Research and Policy Symposium on Child Welfare. Kananaskis, Alberta.

Satzewich, Vic, and Terry Wotherspoon. 1993. *First Nations: Race, Class, and Gender Relations*. Toronto: Nelson Canada.

Sayer, Derek. 1983. *Marx's Method*. Sussex: Harvester Press.

Schutz, Alfred. 1962. 'On Multiple Realities.' In Alfred Schutz, *Collected Papers*, vol. 1. The Hague: Martinius Nijhoff.

Siporin, Max. 1975. *Introduction to Social Work Practice*. New York: Macmillan.

Smith, B., and T. Smith 1990. 'For Love and Money: Women as Foster Mothers.' *Affilia* 5: 66–80.

Smith, D.E. 1973. 'The Social Construction of Documentary Reality.' *Sociological Inquiry* 44: 257–68.

– 1977. 'The Intersubjective Structuring of Time.' *Analytic Sociology* 1.

– 1980. 'An Analysis of Ideological Structures and How Women Are Excluded.' In J. Paul Grayson, ed., *Class, State, Ideology, and Change: Marxist Perspectives on Canada*. Toronto: Holt, Rinehart, and Winston, 252–67.

– 1983. 'No One Commits Suicide: Textual Analysis of Ideological Practices.' *Human Studies* 6: 309–59.

– 1987. *The Everyday World as Problematic*. Toronto: University of Toronto Press.

Stack, Carol. 1974. *All Our Kin: Strategies for Survival in a Black Community*. New York: Harper and Row.

Stokes, Brenda. 1985. 'Physical Neglect.' In Douglas Besharov, ed., *Child Abuse and Neglect Law: A Canadian Perspective*. New York: Child Welfare League of America.

Streat, Y.Y. 1987. 'Case Recording in Children's Protective Services.' *Social Casework: The Journal of Contemporary Social Work* 68: 553–60.

Sue, Derald. 1981. *Counseling the Culturally Different*. New York: Wiley.

Sutherland, Neil. 1976. *Children in English Canadian Society*. Toronto: University of Toronto Press.

Swift, Karen. 1988. *Knowledge about Neglect: A Critical Review of the Literature*. Working Papers in Social Welfare in Canada, no. 23. Faculty of Social Work, University of Toronto.

– 1990. 'Creating Knowledge: A Study of the Production of Knowledge about Neglect.' PhD dissertation, Faculty of Social Work, University of Toronto.

– 1991. 'Contradictions in Child Welfare: Neglect and Responsibility.' In C. Baines, P. Evans, and S. Neysmith, eds., *Women's Caring: A Feminist Perspective on Social Welfare*. Toronto: McClelland and Stewart: 234–71.

– 1995a. '"An Outrage to Common Decency": Historical Perspectives on Child Neglect.' *Child Welfare*, history edition (in press).

– 1995b. 'Missing Persons: Women in Child Welfare.' *Child Welfare*, Canadian edition. (in press).

Teram, Eli. 1988. 'From Self-Managed Hearts to Collective Action: Dealing with Incompatible Demands in the Child Welfare System.' *Children and Youth Services Review* 10: 305–15.

Thomas, E.J., et al. 1974. 'Computer-assisted Assessment and Modification: Possibilities and Illustrative Data.' *Social Service Review* 48: 170–82.

Thomas, Jim. 1993. *Doing Critical Ethnography*. Newbury Park: Sage.

Timpson, Joyce. 1990. 'Indian and Native Special Status in Ontario's Child Welfare Legislation.' *Canadian Social Work Review* 7: 49–68.

Treudley, Mary B. 1980. 'The "Benevolent Fair": A Study of Charitable Organizations among American Women in the First Third of the Nineteenth Century.' In F.R. Breul and S.J. Diner, eds., *Compassion and Responsibility*. Chicago: University of Chicago Press.

Trocme, Nico, and Kwok Kwan Tam, 1994. 'Correlates of Substantiation of Maltreatment in Child Welfare Investigations.' Paper presented at the National Research and Policy Symposium on Child Welfare. Kananaskis, Alberta.

Turner, Francis. 1986a. 'Social Welfare in Canada.' In Joanne C. Turner and Francis J. Turner, eds., *Canadian Social Welfare*. Toronto: Collier Macmillan, 1–6.

– 1986b. 'The Philosophical Base.' In Joanne C. Turner and Francis J. Turner, eds., *Canadian Social Welfare*. Toronto: Collier Macmillian, 9–16.

Turner, Joanne. 1986. 'The Historical Base.' In Joanne C. Turner and Francis J. Turner, eds., *Canadian Social Welfare*. Toronto: Collier Macmillan, 51–9.

Turner, Joanne C., and Francis J. Turner. 1986. *Canadian Social Welfare*. Toronto: Collier Macmillan.

van Dijk, Teun. 1993. *Elite Discourse and Racism*. London: Sage.

Waerness, Kari. 1984. 'Caring as Women's Work.' In H. Holter, ed., *Patriarchy in a Welfare Society*. Oslo: Universitetsforlaget.

Waitzkin, Howard. 1989. 'A Critical Theory of Medical Discourse: Ideology, Social Control, and the Processing of Social Context in Medical Encounters.' *Journal of Health and Social Behavior* 30 (June): 220–39.

Wald, Michael. 1976. 'State Intervention on Behalf of "Neglected" Children: A Search for Realistic Answers.' In M.K. Rosenheim, ed., *Pursuing Justice for the Child*. Chicago: University of Chicago Press: 246–78.

Weber, Max. 1922, trans. 1968. *Economy and Society*, 4th ed. New York: Bedminster Press.

Weedon, C. 1987. *Feminist Practice and Poststructuralist Theory*. Oxford: Blackwell.

Wellman, David. 1977. *Portraits of White Racism*. London: Cambridge University Press.

Westermeyer, Joseph. 1979. 'The Apple Syndrome in Minnesota: A Complication of Racial-Ethnic Discontinuity.' *Journal of Operational Psychiatry* 10: 2.

Weston, J., and M. Collaton. 1993. 'A Legacy of Violence in Nonorganic Failure to Thrive.' *Child Abuse and Neglect* 17: 709–14.

Wharf, Brian. 1989. *Toward First Nation Control of Child Welfare: A Review of Emerging Developments in B.C.* Victoria: University of Victoria.

– ed., 1993. *Rethinking Child Welfare in Canada*. Toronto: McClelland and Stewart.

Whiting, Leila. 1976. 'Defining Emotional Neglect.' *Children Today*. (Jan.–Feb.): 2–5.

Wickham, Edcel. 1986. 'The Knowledge Base.' In Joanne Turner and Francis J. Turner, eds., *Canadian Social Welfare*. Toronto: Collier Macmillan.

Wolock, I. 1982. 'Community Characteristics and Staff Judgments in Child Abuse and Neglect Cases.' *Social Work Research and Abstracts* 18: 9–15.

Wolock, I., and B. Horowitz, 1984. 'Child Maltreatment as a Social Problem: The Neglect of Neglect.' *Journal of Orthopsychiatry* 54: 595–602.

York, Geoffrey. 1989. *The Dispossessed*. Toronto: Little Brown.

Young, L. 1964. *Wednesday's Children*. New York: McGraw-Hill.

Zimmerman, Don. 1969. 'Record-Keeping and the Intake Process in a Public Welfare Agency.' In Stanton Wheeler, ed., *On Record*. New York: Sage, 319–54.

– 1971. 'The Practicalities of Rule Use.' In J. Douglas, ed., *Understanding Everyday Life*. London: Routledge and Kegan Paul.

– 1974. 'Fact as a Practical Accomplishment.' In Roy Turner, ed., *Ethnomethodology*. Harmondsworth, Middlesex: Penguin.

Index